Education in Exile

SOMAFCO, the African National Congress school in Tanzania, 1978 to 1992

Seán Morrow, Brown Maaba & Loyiso Pulumani

HSRC PRESS

Published by HSRC Press
Private Bag X9182, Cape Town, 8000, South Africa
www.hsrcpublishers.ac.za

First published 2004

ISBN 0 7969 2051 6

Cover photographs and artefacts from ANC Archives,
University of Fort Hare
Cover artwork by Ros Stockhall
Cover and text design by Christabel Hardacre
Production by comPress

Distributed in Africa by Blue Weaver Marketing and Distribution,
PO Box 30370, Tokai, Cape Town, 7966, South Africa
Tel: +27 +21-701-4477
Fax: +27 +21-701-7302
email: booksales@hsrc.ac.za

Distributed worldwide, except Africa, by Independent Publishers Group,
814 North Franklin Street, Chicago, IL 60610, USA
www.ipgbook.com
To order, call toll-free: 1-800-888-4741
All other inquiries, Tel: +1 +312-337-0747
Fax: +1 +312-337-5985
email: Frontdesk@ipgbook.com

Contents

List of figures and photographs

Figures

Photographs

Foreword

I spent more than 30 years in Ireland, a country where for centuries the idea of exile has echoed through its historical, political and imaginative literature. As a political exile myself, that may be a reason, paradoxically, why I felt so at home there.

In some ways, South Africans did not have the same cultural props as the Irish when many found themselves, in the second half of the last century, having to flee their country in the face of oppression and injustice. Each had to come to terms with his or her own displacement, their inner eye fixed on a receding South Africa while engaging with new people and cultures.

Because they are resilient and often assertive, South Africans responded creatively to this challenge. One of the most remarkable instances of this is the Solomon Mahlangu Freedom College, the subject of this book. At SOMAFCO were gathered young people and their teachers, who had been obliged to flee a country whose regime had attempted to miseducate its youth and then turned viciously on them when they resisted. By contrast, in the difficult conditions of exile this remarkable school sustained and developed an education based on principles of equal opportunity, non-discrimination and the dignity and unity of mental and manual labour.

SOMAFCO was a beacon of hope. South Africans from all backgrounds, and solidarity workers from many parts of the world, showed at Mazimbu and Dakawa what a new educational system might be and what new ways of thinking about teaching and learning could achieve. With others I was involved in the ANC's international network of reflection and support that went to make SOMAFCO what it was. My wife, Louise, who visited the school, gave me vivid first-hand accounts of the institution.

Though the scale and context are different, we need to think carefully about how the lessons of this brave and exciting experiment could be utilised in the context of educational planning and change in contemporary South Africa. A book like this enables us to draw the results of this reflection into the debates that are determining our educational future.

I am delighted therefore to welcome this book on SOMAFCO. It describes the school clearly and readably, outlining its many achievements without ignoring the numerous difficulties and challenges of education in exile. I hope it will be widely read by students, teachers, and all those concerned with the future, as well as the past, of South African education.

We showed the world how a liberation movement could reflect in its practices the values that had bound us together.

Professor Kader Asmal, MP
Minister of Education

Preface

This book, commissioned by the Batlagae Trust, re-lives the exile experience of many South Africans from 1978 to 1992 at the Solomon Mahlangu Freedom College.

Much is known about the youth who fled South Africa to join Umkhonto we Sizwe. Less is known about the many who left the country to receive education and vocational training and to be part of a unique, self-reliant community at the ANC (African National Congress) settlements of Mazimbu and Dakawa, near Morogoro in Tanzania. This latter group of mainly young people were equally freedom fighters, dedicated to preparing themselves for service to the struggle and for reconstruction and development in a free nation. Indeed, many are now highly skilled professionals, contributing significantly to the growth and well-being of the new South Africa.

The Batlagae Trust was set up by the National Co-ordinating Committee for the Return of Exiles and the liberation movements in 1991. Its purpose was, through a bursary programme, to integrate repatriated learners from nursery to tertiary levels, many from SOMAFCO, into the education system in South Africa. As part of the integration process, the Batlagae Trust established the Yeoville Community School in Johannesburg for returnee primary pupils and deprived inner-city children, and the Yeoville Educational Polyclinic to provide them with remedial and psychological support. The Yeoville Community School was integrated into the Gauteng Department of Education in 1995, and the Yeoville Educational Polyclinic closed in 2000.

Early in 1992, the Batlagae Trust facilitated the return of SOMAFCO documentation and artefacts to the University of Fort Hare, where the ANC's archives are lodged. This book is part of the rich harvest of articles and papers emanating from research conducted by scholars and others wishing to gain a better understanding of SOMAFCO. It is a critical study of SOMAFCO that will hopefully fill a gap in the history of the struggle against apartheid.

This book is dedicated to former SOMAFCO students, teachers and other workers. Most were aligned to the ANC, but others were politically non-aligned, in accordance with ANC policy to set up an institution for *all* South Africans, regardless of political affiliation. It is also dedicated to the Tanzanian workers who helped build SOMAFCO; to the Tanzanian people for their solidarity and hospitality; to the international workers who helped develop SOMAFCO, and to the fraternal countries, non-governmental organisations and individuals all over the world without whose support SOMAFCO would not have flourished as it did. Finally, and above all, it is dedicated to the memory of Oliver Reginald Tambo, the former President of the ANC, whose vision and love for the young sustained SOMAFCO.

Special thanks go to the Swedish International Development Agency, the Norwegian Agency for Development Co-operation, the Danish International Development Agency and the Finnish International Development Agency for the joint grant for this book.

Barbara Watson
Chairperson of the Batlagae Trust

Mohammed Tikly
Former Executive-Director, Batlagae Trust
Former Director of SOMAFCO

Acknowledgements

We would like to thank the Batlagae Trust, which funded the research for this book, and especially its former Executive Director, Mohammed Tikly. The Trust was supported by the Swedish International Development Agency. The Advisory Committee, comprising John Carneson, Thembi Cele, Mzwandile Kibi, Thami Mali, Alpheus Mangezi, John Pampallis and Mohammed Tikly, provided essential information and courteous critique while at all times respecting our academic independence: we appreciate this greatly. The research was commenced while Seán Morrow was Director of the Govan Mbeki Research Resource Centre at the University of Fort Hare, and Brown Maaba and Loyiso Pulumani were postgraduate students of history and junior fellows of the Govan Mbeki Research Resource Centre: we would like to thank the University for its support, and especially the then Vice-Chancellor, Professor Mbulelo Mzamane, and the subsequent and current Vice-Chancellor, Professor Derrick Swartz, and the then and subsequent Registrars, Dr Isaac Mabindisa and Mr Alan Shaw. Professor Tim Stapleton, now of Trent University, Canada, and Professor John Hendricks, now Dean of African and Democracy Studies at Fort Hare, supported the research in its early stages. In particular, we would like to thank Yolisa Kambule-Soul, the Fort Hare Librarian, Mosoabuli Maamoe, Archivist at the African National Congress (ANC) Archives at Fort Hare, and Sadie Forman and Mark Snyders, also of the Fort Hare Library, for their invaluable guidance in the use of the SOMAFCO and Dakawa documents. All three authors are now working elsewhere, and we would like, respectively, to thank the Democracy and Governance Programme of the Human Sciences Research Council, the Steve Biko Foundation and the ANC Archives Unit for providing us with the intellectual and physical space to complete this book. Seán Morrow benefited from a research fellowship for some months at the Centre for African Studies at the University of Cape Town, during which he worked on this book. Aspects of our work have been usefully discussed at various academic fora: Professor Peter Kallaway has been a presence throughout, and we appreciate his critical and constructive comments.

We would particularly like to thank the numerous interviewees, South Africans and Tanzanians, mentioned in the sources. We did not expect, when we began our work, that they would play quite such a crucial role: it will be clear from the text, however, that their testimonies have powerfully influenced this book. The archives of the Robben Island Mayibuye Centre were important to this research, and we thank the Centre for its assistance, as we do the *Daily News* in Dar es Salaam. We are grateful for access to papers kept by Terry and Barbara Bell.

We have changed or omitted names in a few passages where we have touched on matters that could be considered personal.

Some material in Chapter 11 has appeared previously in Seán Morrow, 'Dakawa Development Centre: An African National Congress settlement in Tanzania, 1982–1992', *African Affairs*, 97 (1998): 497–521. We are grateful to Oxford University Press and the Royal African Society for permission to use this material. We also gratefully acknowledge the ANC Archives Committee for permission to use photographs 2, 3, 7 and 9 to 18, the Centre for Democratic Communication for photographs 4 to 6 and 19, and Marjatta Lahti for photograph 8.

In our travels, many people assisted us. We would in particular like to thank the then South African High Commissioner in Dar es Salaam, Thandi Lujabe-Rankoe, and her staff, who smoothed our way in Tanzania. The authorities at Sokoine Agricultural University allowed us to use their excellent guesthouse in Morogoro. In Johannesburg, we were fortunate to be given access to the ANC guesthouse in Yeoville. More recently, we have benefited from the assistance of Wandile Zulu.

Lastly, we would like to thank our respective families for their support, and in particular our partners, Barbara, Bulelwa and Vuyelwa.

Seán Morrow has worked in History and Education departments in universities in several African countries and is now a Chief Research Specialist in the Human Sciences Research Council's Democracy and Governance Programme. Brown Maaba is Research Manager at the Steve Biko Foundation and a Research Associate of the University of Fort Hare. Loyiso Pulumani is Oral History Co-ordinator at the ANC Archives Unit.

Abbreviations

ANC	African National Congress
BCM	Black Consciousness Movement
CDP	Curriculum Development and Planning Unit
Cosas	Congress of South African Students
CIES	Centre for Information and Education for Development (Italy)
Danida	Danish International Development Agency
EOC	Education Orientation Centre
FEP	Foundation for Education with Production
Finnida	Finnish International Development Agency
FAO	Food and Agriculture Organization
GDR	German Democratic Republic
GCE	General Certificate of Education
ILO	International Labor Organization
ISF	International Solidarity Foundation (Finland)
MK	Umkhonto we Sizwe
NYC	National Youth Committee
Neduc	National Education Council
NGO	Non-governmental organisation
Norad	Norwegian Agency for Development Cooperation
NP	National Party
NSC	National Scholarship Committee
NYC	National Youth Committee
OBS	Otto Beneke Stiftung (German Federal Republic)
OAU	Organization of African Unity
PAC	Pan Africanist Congress
PMD	Project Management Department
RWC	Regional Women's Committee
RYC	Regional Youth Committee
Sached	South African Committee for Higher Education

SANNC	South African Native National Congress
Saso	South African Students' Organisation
Sida	Swedish International Development Agency
SOC	Social Order Committee
SOMAFCO	Solomon Mahlangu Freedom College
Swapo	South West African People's Organisation
TDF	Tanzanian Defense Force
Unesco	United Nations Educational Scientific and Cultural Organization
UNDP	United Nations Development Programme
UNHCR	United Nations High Commission for Refugees
UN(O)	United Nations (Organization)
VTC	Vocational Training Centre
WHO	World Health Organization
WS	Women's Section
Zanu-PF	Zimbabwe African National Union-Patriotic Front
Zapu	Zimbabwe African People's Union
Zimfep	Zimbabwe Foundation for Education with Production
ZPC	Zonal Political Committee
ZYC	Zonal Youth Committee

Figure 1 The regional context: map of Tanzania showing ANC centres in the country

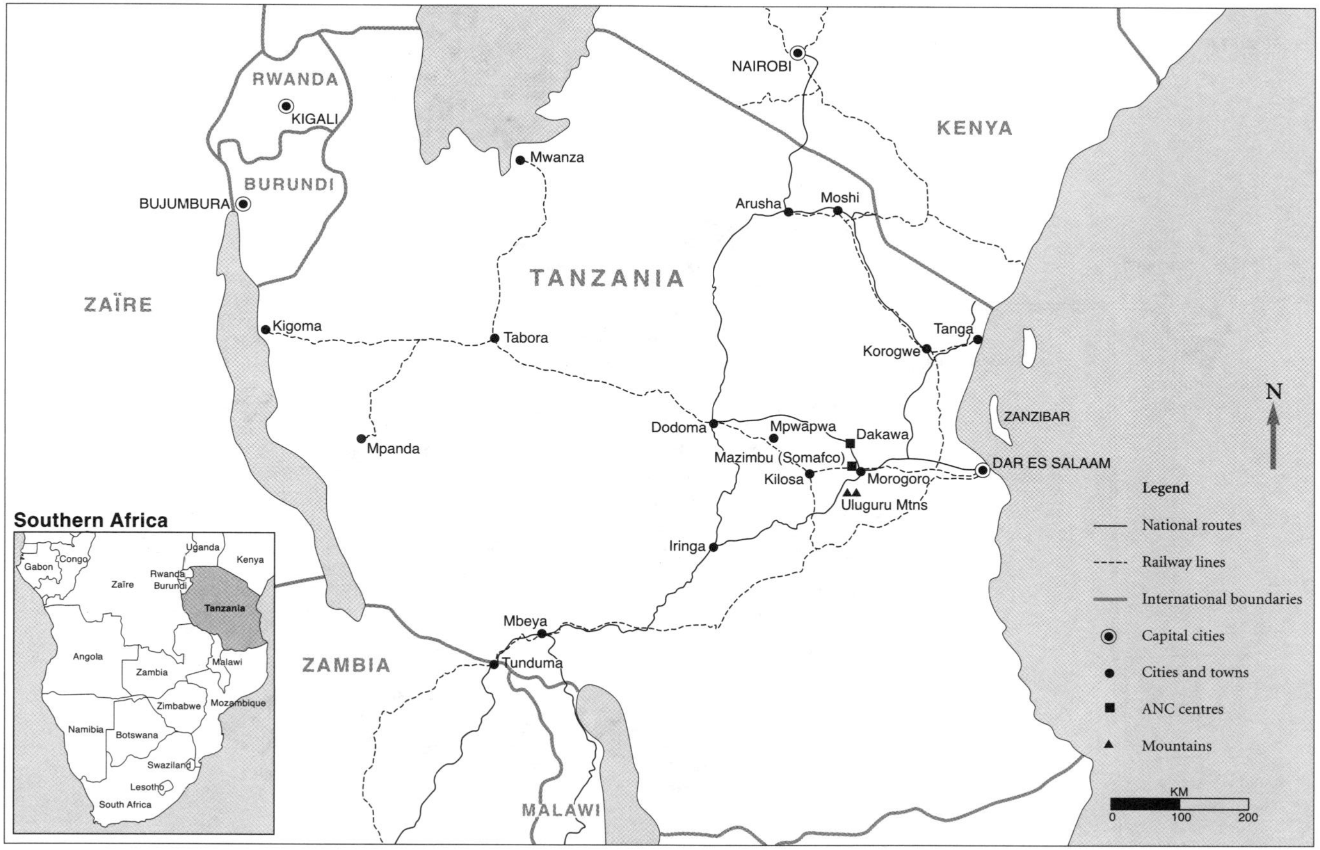

Figure 2 The SOMAFCO campus at Mazimbu in 1992

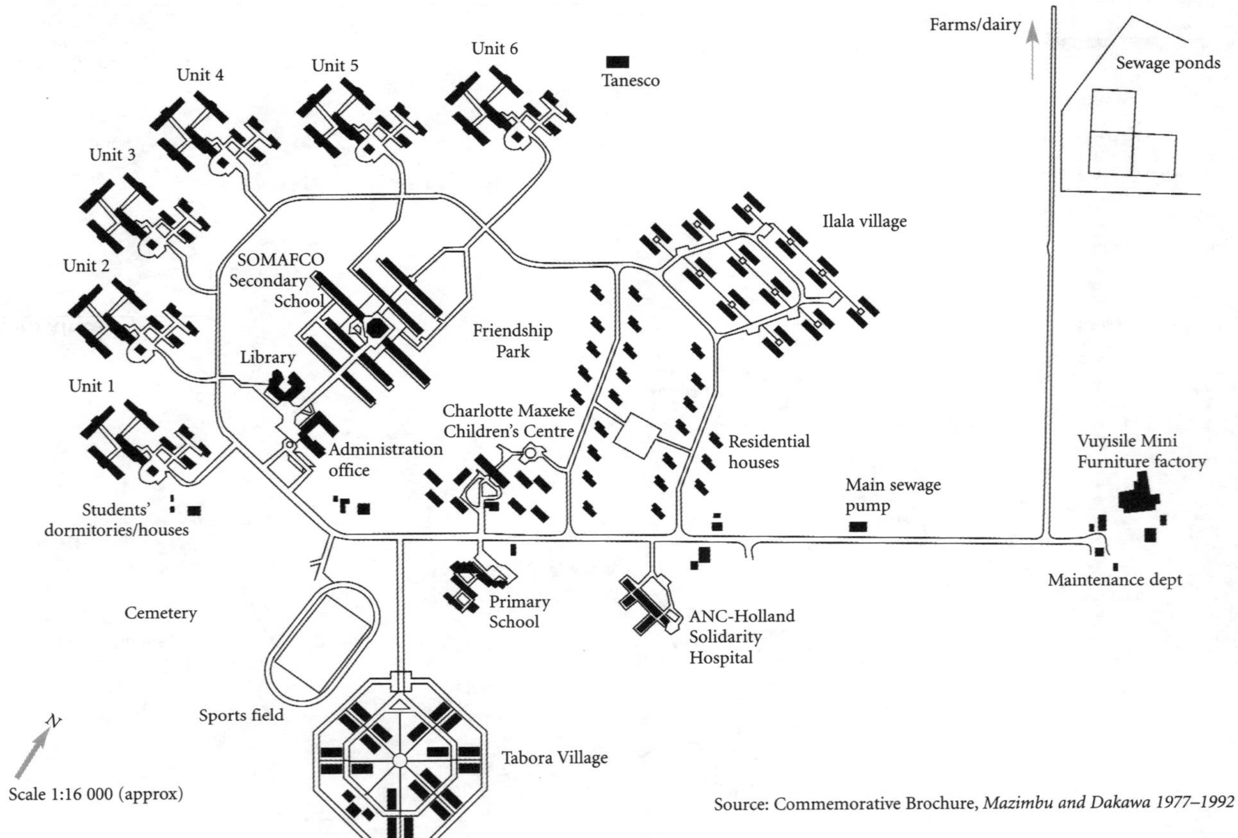

Source: Commemorative Brochure, *Mazimbu and Dakawa 1977–1992*

Introduction

The journey inland from Dar es Salaam, in Tanzania, takes you through the crowded suburbs of the city, past the busy markets and the banana groves and cassava patches alternating with dilapidated dwellings, with occasional high modern buildings perched incongruously amongst them. As you go you will need to avoid the buses weaving around the potholes, and the luxurious four-by-fours, often bearing the names of international organisations, cruising over them. As the city peters out, the agricultural plots, *shambas*, of Tanzania, so unlike the extensive white farms or the congested black homesteads of South Africa, predominate. Further still and the traveler may begin to notice tall men, wearing ornaments made of beads, leather and metal, herding their flocks. These are Maasai, ranging in search of grazing from their established pasturelands to the northwest. In years when the rains are satisfactory, there is enough land in this part of Tanzania to satisfy the needs of the pastoralists with their herds and the farmers on their *shambas.*

The first substantial settlement west from Dar es Salaam is Morogoro, an attractive provincial town whose lack of maintenance, however, indicates Tanzania's poverty, with roads so rutted and pitted that driving requires extreme caution. The shops sell a variety of goods, including the colourful lengths of cloth worn by the women of the country. However, Morogoro, though 200 kilometres inland, is within the orbit of the Indian Ocean bazaar culture. The goods in the shops show Asian and Arabic influences, and the business of the town is done in the vibrant markets and stalls that line the streets and crowd onto open spaces.

There is another Morogoro, that of the *boma,* government offices, typically built in a hollow square with an internal verandah, with messengers, dressed in uniforms much as in colonial times, awaiting tasks outside. Associated is the Morogoro of education, not that of the *madrasahs* attached to the mosques, but rather of the schools and colleges which, like the *boma* and Christian churches, owe more to Western influence than to the Islamic trading culture that the town so visibly reflects. The largest of the educational institutions is the Sokoine University of Agriculture, standing slightly apart from the town at the base of the spectacular mountain that dominates the whole area.

Across town, in an area called Mazimbu, Sokoine Agricultural University has a second campus, where many students live in residence. At the entrance

1. Entrance to Solomon Mahlangu Freedom College, now the Mazimbu campus of Sokoine University

beside the bridge over the Ngerengere River, is a wall with a picture of the head of a young man, and the words 'Welcome – Karibu. Solomon Mahlangu Mazimbu Campus', and, 'Tell my people that I love them and that they must continue the struggle. My blood will nourish the tree that will bear the fruits of freedom. A luta continua!'

Until 1992 instead of 'Solomon Mahlangu Mazimbu Campus' the sign read 'Solomon Mahlangu Freedom College'. It is still maintained as a gesture of remembrance towards the South Africans who once lived here. This was where the Solomon Mahlangu Freedom College (SOMAFCO), the African National Congress (ANC) school in exile, flourished from 1978 to 1992. The secondary school was at the core of the settlement, and around it grew a crèche, infant school, primary school, a productive modern farm, a small but well-equipped hospital, workshops and factories making furniture and other goods, and other divisions. There was extensive boarding accommodation and housing for teachers and workers. There were sports facilities, an excel-

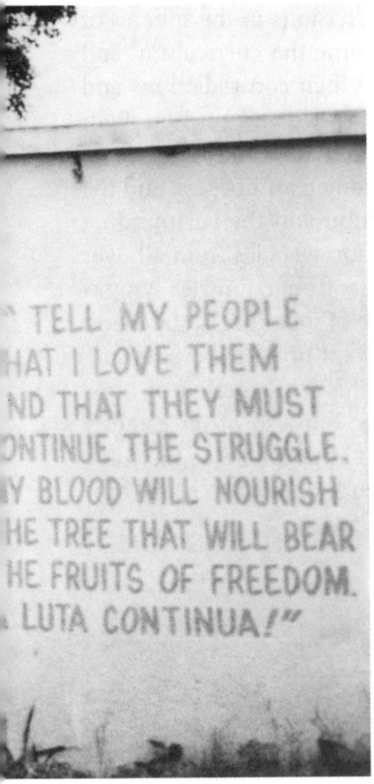

lent library, a large meeting hall, a network of roads and other infrastructure. The complex was constructed and maintained by a skilled and effective Building Department. Every day, large numbers of Tanzanians came to work on the compound in trucks provided by the ANC. Visitors from other ANC settlements, Tanzanian officials, and ANC supporters and sympathisers from all over Africa and the world came and went. Mazimbu was a showpiece of the liberation struggle and a symbol of what could be aspired to in a free South Africa.

Today, however, the South Africans are gone. The Tanzanian government has put large parts of the infrastructure to educational and other uses, with divisions such as the hospital, primary school and farm still operating, and Sokoine University utilising much of the core of the school. The South African High Commission in Dar es Salaam ensures that the graves on the site are maintained in a fitting way. Once, this was the focus of the ANC's remarkable experiment in education, with a population of up to 5 000 South Africans and many hundreds of Tanzanian workers. Now, rather than abandon this inheritance, uses must be found for a site that is inconveniently situated from a Tanzanian point of view.

Though the ANC's aspiration to create a school in exile had existed for some time, it was the student demonstrations of June 1976 in Soweto and elsewhere, and the subsequent suppression, that precipitated its foundation. Thousands of young people fled South Africa to neighboring states, eager to strike back at the regime, but vulnerable and sometimes politically naïve. However, political movements struggling to survive in exile, above all the ANC, were able to harness the energies and idealism of these young people, and were themselves revived and invigorated by this infusion of new recruits. SOMAFCO, mainly educating the young (though also older people deprived of educational opportunities in South Africa), was an important element in this process.

This book charts the debates surrounding the foundation of the school. We describe the challenges of creating a school in difficult tropical conditions in Tanzania, and show how the original conception of a secondary school expanded until SOMAFCO encompassed numerous divisions in the spheres of education, social service and production. We examine the curriculum, and the methods and philosophies of teaching, with all their contradictions and paradoxes. We describe the students of SOMAFCO, a varied and cosmopolitan group, with their campus organisations, political activities and relaxations. We examine the school's relationship with the Tanzanian authorities, and the interactions between the South Africans of Mazimbu and the surrounding population. The school relied on a network of donor agencies from all over the world, and to some extent on teachers and others from countries sympathetic to the ANC, and we describe this complex web of individuals, states and organisations. In the early 1990s, the school was swept up in the events surrounding the profound changes in South Africa. This was a period of hope and anticipation for the school and its inhabitants, but also of uncertainty and anxiety, and we attempt to recreate the fevered atmosphere of the time. Finally, we ask what can we learn from the experience of SOMAFCO, and how relevant this is to contemporary South African education.

CHAPTER 1

Education and the struggle for freedom

The struggle for political freedom in South Africa has always been closely linked to struggles for and around formal education. This has been a complex and ambiguous relationship: education has been the prize of democratic victory and the badge of privilege; the educated have been the leaders of African liberation movements and the sometimes grateful, sometimes resentful recipients of an education seen, for good or ill, as embodying a Western culture that could offer knowledge and power but which also gnawed at the roots of African identity.

As African people were incorporated into the different states that went to make up what is now South Africa, from the mid-nineteenth century Christian missionaries, often British, developed schools that served a minority of the indigenous population. The missionaries brought with them a heritage composed of elements such as loyalty to the imperial power, an unquestioning confidence in the superiority of their own culture, and a patronising approach to the African societies amongst which they worked. However, over time, familiarity with, and greater understanding of, African societies sometimes modified these attitudes. Ideas such as a romantic attachment to a supposedly simple rural society, suspicion of the secularism of colonial governments, belief in the dignity of labour, and, occasionally, a radical commitment – spiritually-based but political in effect – to the people among whom they worked, make it impossible to completely identify missions and mission education with colonial power. At their best, as generally at the great mission schools of the Eastern Cape such as Lovedale, Healdton and St Matthew's, they treated African pupils as capable of absorbing contemporary Western knowledge as understood by the European teachers. At worst, Africans were provided with fragmentary instruction, which was then arrested by the 'relevant education' designed to fit Africans, much as the lower orders in Europe itself, for the sort of life that had been mapped out for them. Though mission schools had many achievements, it was an imperfect system, and they have often been romanticised in retrospect. Throughout, there was never enough mission education; it was heavily weighted towards the early primary years – in the secondary years it was predominantly concentrated in rural areas; and it was chronically under-funded.

All societies possess ways of educating the young, not necessarily associated with formal schooling. In Africa, however, and particularly in South Africa where major industrial development grew rapidly in the midst of predominantly pastoral and agricultural societies, the role of formal education or schooling was particularly crucial, and became increasingly so from (approximately) the 1860s. The scramble for the resources and labour that generate wealth was paralleled by the scramble for control of the mind – though Africans were not just the passive recipients of what others chose to give them. Jostling for a place on the ladder in this new, dynamic, racist and often-ruthless society, Africans found that education was almost the only rung available. However, much of white society, which appeared to promise so much – including freedom for those of any race to rise unhindered in the social scale as far as their talents would take them – turned on those who listened perhaps too trustingly to the messages of equality and snatched from the incipient African elite the prizes which appeared to be on offer.

These messages came in different guises, from that of political liberalism to that of the universal brotherhood of man under God. Indeed, the Christian message as it was preached in Africa was paradoxical, often promoting the supremacy of Western culture while providing a quarry of powerful metaphors and symbols that Africans did not fail to utilise in the interests of their own visions of liberation. For instance, the Africanist, Robert Sobukwe, in solitary confinement at Robben Island, reading deeply in the literature of the West and wrestling with his Christian beliefs, is only at first sight a contradictory figure. The often deep-rooted loyalty of his and earlier generations of educated Africans to aspects of Western culture was cast in their faces by the politicians and functionaries of a society that claimed to adhere to this very culture, and drove them to seek sustenance in the vision of more humane and tolerant African societies. Struggles over education took place not only on the political and social levels, but also within the consciousness of individuals.

The products of mission schools were in an ambiguous situation. They were formed by a Western educational system, yet with their wider vision, and partly because of the intricate inheritance from their education and from the African societies of which they were a part, they were in a position to interrogate and challenge the system that oppressed all Africans. Over the years this educated elite struggled in different arenas such as labour unions, journalism, education, agricultural associations and cultural groups, to establish an authentic African voice in the country of their birth, and eventually to assert the right of the majority, rather than a racially-defined minority, to have the determining voice in the future of South Africa. At the forefront in this diverse and many-faceted movement was the ANC, founded in 1912 as the South African Native National Congress (SANNC), which evolved from a body representing a small, educated elite to a movement containing many different strands of South African progressive thinking.

As Jonathan Hyslop has shown, in the later years of mission education there was much student discontent within the secondary schools catering for older pupils. In the 1940s and early 1950s complaints and sometimes strikes and riots, particularly over food, were widespread, and no doubt, though it is difficult to demonstrate specifically, this merged with wider socio-political disaffection. The mission schools were in financial crisis, and, especially with the increase in demand for education, could no longer maintain their previous level of provision. Though the loyalty that the mission schools generated was often remarkable, this crisis was a reality, and it is impossible to believe, even leaving aside the hostile policies of the National Party (NP) government, that they could have continued much longer as the main focus of black education.

The terms on which education entered the political debate in South Africa altered over time. For many years, the state took very little overt interest in African education. However, the level of state involvement increased in the course of the twentieth century, culminating in the actions of the NP government, representing the most conservative elements in the white population. After it came to power in 1948, this government took the decision, as part of a broad movement to establish its hegemony, to destroy the educational system that had produced the elite of educated Africans so important in the development of a political voice for the majority of the population. At the same time, an educational infrastructure was to be built that would provide, it was hoped, a population sufficiently educated to labour effectively in the mines, factories and farms of increasingly industrialised South Africa. The *Bantu Education Act* of 1953 was the key instrument in this policy.

The implementation of Bantu Education added new problems and intensified old ones. This policy was intended to end the semi-autonomy of the mission schools; implement a system of school boards and committees that would, it was hoped, include conservative elements in the black community; orient education towards the rural areas, in spite, or because of, increasing urbanisation; control black teachers and pupils more completely; and implement a curriculum that was 'appropriate' for Africans. While in some other respects it did not remain precisely the same from 1953 to 1994, the policy was based throughout on the conception that education should be racially divided.

Bantu Education met vigorous opposition in 1955 and 1956, especially from the still-legal ANC. There was a partially successful attempt to boycott schools, and to set up alternative institutions called 'cultural clubs'. However, the resources simply were not available to conduct an alternative system of education, and the cultural clubs touched only a very small proportion of African youth, for a limited period. It was urban parents and teachers, organised mainly by the ANC, who were responsible for the boycott of 1955 to 1956; the bulk of African pupils in towns were young, in junior primary schools, and not of an age to take independent political stands. Secondary pupils were generally at school in the rural areas, and though they had their own traditions of militancy, these tended to find expression in the idiom of food riots and the like. They were far from the urban areas where the ANC was influential and did not link up with the boycott campaign.

In 1956, this campaign faltered and ultimately ceased. With the Sharpeville massacre and the banning of the ANC and Pan Africanist Congress (PAC) in 1960, there was a qualitative change in political conditions, and it became impossible for these organisations to embark on peaceful political protest. Through the late 1950s and 1960s the black population appeared to settle down to a grudging acceptance of the reality of Bantu Education. The banning of the liberation movements thus led to a period of apparent quiescence in education, as in other spheres. In time, however, overt opposition revived. The ANC in exile was far away, and, because of censorship and repression, was nearly inaudible in black townships. Indeed, the emerging student-based Black Consciousness Movement (BCM), with its forerunner, the South African Students' Organisation (Saso), seemed to be eroding its support base. With hindsight, however, student radicalism can be seen to have provided opportunities upon which the ANC later built.

One of the aims of Bantu Education, in line with apartheid ideology, was to concentrate black education as far as possible in the African reserves, renamed 'homelands', though no longer in mission schools. This involved stifling educational expansion in the working-class black townships, especially at secondary level. However, there was a conflict within the NP between the ideologues of racial separation and those who represented a more economically-driven approach. To the latter, it appeared necessary to provide secondary and technical education in the townships so as to supply the economy with the literate, technically competent black workers that were increasingly required. As the economy evolved towards a more skills-based form of industrialisation it became increasingly apparent that the white population could not provide the necessary man- and womanpower on its own. From this internal conflict within the NP a policy change emerged in the early 1970s that involved the rapid expansion of secondary schooling in the black townships.

This expansion, however, took place in the context of an economy that, while changing in structure, was no longer expanding as rapidly as it had done in the 1960s. Also, and above all, the structures of black education were embedded in the conservatism and racism which suffused the NP, and which was particularly strongly entrenched in the Department of Bantu Education. The rapid expansion of the population of pupils of an age to articulate and act upon their grievances effectively, in a context where they were increasingly alienated from the authorities, proved explosive. This was the setting for the

Soweto uprising of June 1976, which led, among other consequences, to the foundation of SOMAFCO.

The precise reasons for the Soweto student uprising have been the subject of discussion again recently. While it is well known that the imposition of Afrikaans as a medium of instruction for black schools in some subjects was the immediate cause of the revolt, there has been disagreement as to the level of formal political involvement, whether by the BCM or by the ANC. Francis Meli, for example, argues that, 'the South African Students' Movement, which represented high school students … played a central role in the whole conflict.' Sifiso Ndlovu, however, argues that political involvement was negligible and that subsequent claims to such involvement are tendentious. 'Liberation movements,' he says, 'and student organisations like Saso and the South African Students' Movement, played no significant role either in the day-to-day major debates in the classrooms or in planning the actual day of protest that involved most of the schools in Soweto.' For Ndlovu, the immediate origins of the revolt are to be found in the specific grievances of the younger secondary students who were to have been the first to be directly affected by the imposition of Afrikaans.

Whether the stress is placed on local agency or on political involvement, there is no doubt that the student revolt marked a qualitatively new stage in South African resistance politics. There was elemental anger, but if it was to have precise effects, some political form was required. In the aftermath of the revolt, thousands of young people made their way across the borders and came into contact with the liberation movements that were already in exile, and, since Black Consciousness had little or no organised representation outside the country, this contact tended to be with the ANC and the PAC. Though the ANC was ill prepared to receive this unexpected influx, its level of organisation was superior to that of the rival PAC. Thus, though at first sight, ideologically speaking, the PAC might seem a more natural home for young people influenced by Black Consciousness, it was the ANC that seized the initiative, proving itself more capable of organising the newcomers.

Organisation was certainly needed. Some young people came under the care of agencies of the United Nations (UN) and other organisations, and were allocated to schools in countries like Nigeria and Zambia. Those who came into the care of the ANC in Tanzania, the future home of SOMAFCO, often found themselves sleeping as many as 20 to a single room in houses in Dar es Salaam and elsewhere. The organisation struggled to feed and support them while searching for ways of harnessing their energies. This was not a simple question, given differences in maturity, physique, and in levels of political consciousness and education. There was no question of recruiting them en masse for Umkhonto we Sizwe (MK).

The township uprisings presented complex questions. Brave confrontation of the police in South Africa did not always translate into disciplined zeal in exile. Many found themselves at Mazimbu, in the words of John Pampallis, 'by historical accident'. Some drifted between the ANC and PAC. Attempts, sometimes heavy-handed, to inculcate discipline could lead to resentment of, even hostility to, the ANC. At worst, some took to a life of criminality. People who would probably never have chosen to mingle were forced together in the extraordinary context of exile; 'nobody', says Mzwandile Kibi, 'was truly happy at SOMAFCO, though there were many memorable moments'.

On one level, many young people were indeed potential recruits for the armed struggle against the South African state. However, the ANC was involved in much more than an armed uprising, and it wished to demonstrate that the struggle against apartheid was multi-faceted, involving the remaking of a society and not just the overthrow of a government. The opening of a school by the ANC gave institutional expression to this policy, and provided a focus for aid from countries and organisations that were sympathetic to the movement while unwilling to support armed insurrection. The very fact that a school is not at first sight an overtly 'political' entity implied that the ANC was bidding to lead and mould South African society in a comprehensive way, and signified that it intended to re-establish itself as a decisive force in contemporary South Africa.

A SOMAFCO chronology

Though SOMAFCO existed for only 15 years, it changed considerably during that time, and statements made about one period may not be true of another. This book is written thematically, and a brief chronology will help to anchor the account in time.

In 1977, the first groups of young people from among those who had fled South Africa in the aftermath of the Soweto uprising arrived at Mazimbu. At this early stage, Mazimbu was a refuge for the new arrivals rather than a school, though some informal classes were held. However, construction of the school, at this stage envisaged as a secondary-level institution only, began under Oswald Dennis. The nature of the school was debated vigorously at this period in the various centres where the ANC had a presence, particularly London. The following year, teaching started under the first principal, Wintshi Njobe. In October 1978 the first Joint Committees' Meeting, later called the National Education Council (Neduc), was held in Mazimbu.

On 6 April 1979 Solomon Mahlangu, the young MK soldier after whom the school was named, was executed. Also in that year, in response to the increasing number of infants and young children, a temporary crèche and a nursery school were started in the nearby town of Morogoro. In 1980 the primary school was founded, under its first principal, Terry Bell. Bell left in 1982, and was succeeded by Dennis September.

Meanwhile, supporting institutions multiplied, such as the Vuyisile Mini Furniture Factory, founded in 1980, and this broadening of functions became even more pronounced with the establishment, in 1982, of the Dakawa Development Centre, 55 kilometres to the north of Mazimbu, under its first Director, Mary Thuse, later succeeded by Jackie Morake. The increasing complexity of the ANC settlements demanded a more elaborate administrative system. As well as the secondary school principals who followed Njobe (Tim Maseko 1981 to 1985, Andrew Masondo 1986 to 1990, Don Ngakane 1990 to 1991 and Ray Marutle 1991), supported throughout by the Vice-Principal, Slim Zindela, the post of Chief Administrator, later Director of Schools, was created. Mohammed Tikly held this position from 1982 to 1986, succeeded by Tim Maseko until 1988, and Alpheus Mangezi until 1991.

The 1984 Nkomati Accord between South Africa and Mozambique, which led to the expulsion of ANC cadres from that country, and the increasing violence in South Africa itself in the 1980s, led to a further influx of South Africans to Mazimbu and Dakawa. At the same time, the campus was steadily growing. In 1984 the Charlotte Maxeke Children's Centre was completed, and the ANC-Holland Solidarity Hospital in Mazimbu opened. In 1985 a new primary school building was completed. This was also the year of the official opening of SOMAFCO by Oliver Tambo, the President of the ANC.

In February 1990 the ban on the South African liberation movements was lifted, and Nelson Mandela was released from prison. He visited SOMAFCO soon after and declared that the exiles should prepare themselves for returning home. On 9 September 1992 SOMAFCO officially closed and the complex was handed over to the Tanzanian government.

CHAPTER 2

Origins and early years of SOMAFCO

'Tell my people that I love them and that they must continue the struggle.
My blood will nourish the tree that will bear the fruits of freedom.'

These are said to have been Solomon Mahlangu's last words, to his mother, before his execution. They seem strangely, touchingly rhetorical for a young man whose life was about to end brutally on the gallows. Nevertheless, they are an apt slogan for a school which had always to be more than simply a school, and which, even while it implemented the sometimes mundane educational routines familiar to teachers and learners everywhere, was also a highly-charged symbol of the struggle against apartheid.

Mahlangu represented the generation that fought the apartheid state in 1976. He left South Africa in the aftermath of the June 1976 uprising. According to Siphiwe Nyanda, now head of the South African National Defence Force, after training as an MK soldier Mahlangu returned on a mission early in 1977, with the aim of protecting students against the police and military. In June the police engaged him and two comrades in combat in Goch Street, Johannesburg. In the ensuing gun battle two whites were killed. He was tried, found guilty of murder, and sentenced to death on 8 March 1978. The UN called on the world community to take urgent steps to save Mahlangu's life, even declaring 7 February 1979 a Day of International Action for Solomon Mahlangu. Organisations worldwide were involved in protests against the planned execution. Despite these efforts, he was hanged on 6 April 1979. The editorial comment of the June edition of *Sechaba*, the ANC journal, headlined 'Hamba Kahle Solomon Mahlangu', declared that 'he went to the gallows courageously and confidently. He was aware that the black people of South Africa … were behind him and indeed the whole of progressive humanity supported him.'

This is why, after initial suggestions that it might be named the Albert Luthuli Institute or the ANC Freedom School, the school near Morogoro in Tanzania was given Solomon Mahlangu's name. It was a way of preserving the memory of a young hero and of furthering the educational cause of the South African people. In other words, the complex was intended to nurture and, as far as possible in exile, realise the educational aspirations of a free South Africa.

The reality that faced the planners of the ANC's liberation school, however, was logistically and educationally daunting. Its foundation meant that the educational ideas of the movement suddenly became not speculative issues for the indefinite future, but matters requiring immediate and urgent attention. The school was not just for those young people who happened to be at Mazimbu in the wake of the events of 1976. Clearly, whatever the ANC might do had to be in line with the movement's policies towards education in a future liberated South Africa. Developing the facility for exiles needed to go hand-in-hand with developing a blueprint for an educational system for a free South Africa. The school, it was argued, would act as a laboratory where theories as to how a dynamic education system, accessible to everybody, could be put to the test, and being an integral part of the liberation struggle, its curriculum and organisation would be those of a revolutionary school. The question was: what in fact was a revolutionary school? The Freedom Charter stated that 'the doors of learning and culture shall be opened … . Education shall be free, compulsory, universal and equal.' How should this aspiration be translated into action?

Debates leading to SOMAFCO

The idea of a school for exiles was not new within the ANC or in the broader southern African liberation movements. In the early 1970s Mazisi Kunene and Mendi Msimang were assigned by the ANC to start schools for vocational training. The Zimbabwe African National Union-Patriotic Front (Zanu-PF) founded schools in Mozambique. During the struggle against Portuguese colonialism, Frelimo had a school in Bagamoyo in Tanzania, later moved to the liberated areas in northern Mozambique. The South West African People's Organisation (Swapo) had a different model. The UN had inherited the responsibility for the ex-German colony of South West Africa from the League of Nations. The League had allocated the mandate over the area to the then Union of South Africa, and the UN was, therefore, able to involve itself more closely with Namibia than it could with South Africa itself, or with Rhodesia, later Zimbabwe. The foundation of the Namibia Institute in Lusaka was part of the UN's involvement. Here, personnel were trained for a future free Namibia, with the UN providing generous support, including staff salaries at international level. This option was not open to the ANC, and it is unlikely that it would even have been considered desirable since it involved substantial external control. Closer to the ANC model, in the mid-1980s when SOMAFCO was already flourishing, the Namibia Secondary Technical School was set up at Loudima, Congo (Brazzaville), with Norwegian and other support.

The outflow of young exiles from 1976, therefore, made it possible to implement an idea that was clearly already in the air. Even so, the foundation of

SOMAFCO was a bold move, and might never have succeeded but for the consistent support of Oliver Tambo. Henry Makgoti, the ANC secretary for education, described the basis of SOMAFCO in his report at the official opening and naming of the school in 1985, a full seven years after the actual commencement of the institution:

> Solomon Mahlangu Freedom College is a cadre-training centre of the ANC. The problems posed by the freedom struggle in South Africa are extremely complex and the successful consolidation of that struggle demands cadres of a high quality. Here at SOMAFCO the ANC is making a modest effort to meet that challenge.

This explanation outlined one core element of the school. It was intended to anticipate a liberated South Africa, which at the time seemed far from realisation, and to be a symbol that would keep morale high within the ANC. The leadership needed to generate optimistic statements, particularly in the aftermath of 1976 when volatile young people had to be kept loyal to the movement while being brought to realise that the revolution was not, it seemed, going to come in the immediate future. Endurance would be as necessary in its service as impetuous zeal. It was a delicate balance: these young people had experienced extreme brutality and any wavering by the leadership would have led to severe setbacks in terms of organisational focus and political commitment.

On another level, the opening of the school strengthened the bond between the exiles of the 1960s and earlier – the 'old guard', the *umgwenya*, who had left the country in the 1960s to join the ANC and especially MK – and the 'young lions' of the 1970s, many from a background influenced by Black Consciousness. With the creation of the school, the ANC became the natural home of the recent youthful exiles, reinforcing its claim to be the leading organisation in the struggle for freedom in South Africa. The educational initiative also justified continued support for the ANC by donors, at a time when various South African political organisations were struggling for international recognition.

Specifically the school was characterised as an institution:

> where academic studies and vocational training and labour would be equally respected – a counter to Bantu Education – where children would get the best possible tuition, be free to learn the culture of their own people and subsequently have the opportunity to take up scholarships in universities and colleges in different parts of the world. Finally, they would be practically and intellectually equipped to make their contribution in the present phase of the struggle in which they are eager to participate, and to take their rightful place as citizens in a free and democratic South Africa of the future.

This did not begin to describe the work that had to be done in planning, organising and actually starting the school. To get the project under way, the Tanzanian government offered the ANC 1 000 hectares of land at Mazimbu near Morogoro, for the purpose of setting up a secondary boarding school, which was all that was envisaged in the beginning. This land had previously belonged to a Mr Anatoglu, a Greek farmer, whose land had been nationalised under the Arusha Declaration of 1967. Some of the estate workers asked the government if they might remain on the land, and a Sisal Estate Union, chaired by a man named Mnemba, was formed to press their case. Some local residents say they were not happy that land they considered theirs was granted to the ANC, and they sent a representative to deliver their grievances to parliament at Dodoma. The representation bore no fruit. Some then refused to leave, and to bring pressure, the ANC withheld the offer of jobs until they departed. It should be noted, however, that some claimants may have occupied land after the demise of the estate, and that land was not a scarce resource in the vicinity.

Organisational framework

The ANC Education Department wanted to mobilise as many members and supporters as it could in support of the new school. At the same time it wanted to co-ordinate this mobilisation so as to avoid duplication and waste.

Since the mid-1970s, education committees had come into existence in different parts of the world where the ANC had a presence. They were relatively informal and usually consisted of individuals who were willing to volunteer their time aside from their regular jobs. It should be remembered that the ANC only began to develop a functioning, record-keeping bureaucracy in the late 1970s. For a time, unstructured methods of operation existed parallel with the beginnings of something like a government-in-exile, mirroring the ministries and departments that constitute the apparatus of a modern state. In 1976 and thereafter, these committees were mobilised to do what they could to help in the new situation created by the students' revolt, for instance assisting co-ordination with international donor agencies, which wanted to give immediate help in the form of books, advice, supplies and monetary contributions.

The committees thus came to be directly linked to the idea of the school. Part of their brief was to develop syllabi and teaching materials. Committees were located in London, New York, Dar es Salaam and Lusaka. The main centre was London, where curriculum development, organisation of resources, policy discussion and material dissemination took place.

It was clear from the growing complexity of its involvement with education that the ANC had to inaugurate an Education Department, separate from the previously existing Department of Professional Bodies. Explaining the reasoning behind the fully-fledged department, which came into existence in 1978, in August 1979 *Sechaba* said:

> Reacting to the crisis that is taking place within the country, the ANC has decided to streamline its machinery, departments and sub-departments dealing with various aspects of our work. The creation of the Department of Education and Culture was one move. With South Africa embroiled in an educational crisis, it was created to meet the demands of our people. The formation of this Department is an attempt to meet this challenge and to create an alternative to Bantu Education. The decision of the NEC of the ANC to establish last year the Department of Education and Culture is symptomatic of the new revolutionary phase of the struggle against apartheid, heralded by the armed struggle and the adoption in 1969 of 'The Strategy and Tactics of the South African Revolution' [that is, the Morogoro Declaration].

At the same time, further committees were established, geared to achieving the overall aims of the school, and, through the school, of the ANC as a whole. For accessibility, these committees, which concerned Basic Planning, Co-ordination, Education, and Political Issues, were to be based in Dar es Salaam. The Basic Planning Committee was allocated issues such as basic education, extramural activities, political education, catering, domestic work and social welfare. The Co-ordination Committee was to co-ordinate the activities of the other committees and guard against duplication of effort. It also looked at construction and building materials, staffing, curricula, teaching materials, and students. The Education Committee had overall supervision of the work of the committees, being responsible for bringing all the proposals into one coherent scheme. The Political Committee was responsible for the political direction of the school. These were their functions on paper, but predictably, in a project of this complexity, roles tended to overlap in practice.

The organisational structures were also the framework within which the nature of the school was debated. Through these committees, attempts were made to examine all the contentious issues crucial to the operation of the school. The overriding point in all these proposals was that education should be seen as a political issue, which meant rejecting the idea that education is a 'technical' matter best left to educational experts. It followed that the school must be directed above all towards the political education of its students. This insistence was an attempt to stamp out calls from some sections of the ANC that the school serve the conventional requirements of providing basic knowledge, simply preparing students for work or tertiary education.

It was one thing to theorise about the necessity for a 'cadre school', and another to actually implement the idea, and this question was vigorously debated, leading to some tensions and disagreements. From the first Neduc meeting of the ANC, held from 1 to 3 October 1978, there was an intense debate centred on the complex issues of the political versus the technical approach to education. At times the issues were explicit and at times implicit. In relation to certain questions there was immediate agreement. In other instances, particularly where the political content was implicit – for example in questions of relations between staff and students, and in relation to the organisation of the school – an assumption of the non-political nature of the school and of education tended to assert itself. These debates had many implications. There was controversy on payment of ANC teachers, for example, with some fearing that conventional salaries would create an elite class. At least one teacher refused even the meagre payment that was offered, preferring to rely on the comprehensive, if frugal, support and welfare system available at Mazimbu. Others felt that only through adequate payment would the crucial teachers of quality be attracted.

Though salaries for ANC teachers remained low, in general the concept of SOMAFCO as a school, strongly supported by Oliver Tambo, tended to win out over the concept of the institution as a training-centre for cadres, advocated particularly strongly by the London Committee. The first Neduc meeting laid down specific aims, which asserted the predominance of politics. The main objective was to 'prepare cadres to serve the national liberation struggle of the people of South Africa in the phase of the struggle for seizure of political power'. In serving economic, educational, scientific and other objectives, priorities would be dictated by the needs of the liberation struggle. By the second Neduc meeting in April 1979 it was obvious that there were major deviations from earlier decisions, specifically on the political outlook of the school. Some delegates felt that a number of decisions adopted at the first meeting had been reversed without adequate discussion. Points of contention included staff recruitment, the role of political commissars, and student discipline.

How these differences were manifested in practice is reflected in tensions over recruitment. For example, the London Education Committee registered its concern about approaches that had been made to two applicants, though they were known to have had connections with a political movement hostile to the ANC. They also referred to one teacher appointee as having 'a very non-political approach to education and [she] operates within a conventional, authoritarian relation with pupils'. There was a clash here between political orthodoxy and the desperate need of a functioning school for competent teachers who could begin to extricate pupils from the shortcomings of Bantu Education.

The question of political commissars also concerned student discipline. The second Neduc meeting dwelt at length on the relationship between the ANC Youth Section and the Education Department, and the assumption developed that the Youth Section had a political role in recruitment and the Department a technical role. Some people's concern was that this again revived the conception of education as apolitical, contrary to the policy adopted at the first conference. At the second meeting wardens or 'house-masters' were instated. The London Committee thought that this reflected a further retreat from politics, downgrading the role of the political commissars who were attached to each residential block and were supposed to play an important role in nurturing political discussion in the dormitories. Similarly, the first meeting had rejected the idea that a social worker be appointed to look after the discipline of the students, instead stressing that as part of their political development, students were to devise their own structures dealing with matters of discipline. Some, therefore, considered the appointment of a welfare officer for students as contrary to the earlier decision. Such disagreements emphasised that conditions on the ground did not necessarily comply readily with political ideology.

Building SOMAFCO

Starting the school depended on recruiting teachers and builders, and on the presence of young people of secondary school-going age. The Planning Committee set out ground rules for the recruitment of workers and volunteers. The ANC offered transportation to the school for prospective teachers and their families; accommodation; basic supplies, such as food, toiletry and pots and pans; a meagre monthly allowance; and an undertaking to provide for annual visits to relatives or to receive visits from them.

There would have been no school and no settlement without the people who planned and designed the settlement and its buildings, and who organised the work force. Key people were co-opted or recruited. For the critical purpose of overseeing the development of the initial infrastructure the ANC secured the services as project manager of Oswald 'Ossie' Dennis, who had qualified as a civil engineer in the German Democratic Republic (GDR). The architect, Spenser Hodgson, later joined him. With only six other workers at first, Dennis started work in Mazimbu in July 1977. Much of the site donated by the Tanzanian government consisted of an old sisal estate, and on this stood several dilapidated structures, without windows, doors, ceilings, running water or electricity. From these inauspicious beginnings SOMAFCO grew.

There were many problems, often stemming from difficulties in keeping supplies flowing regularly. Tanzanian firms contracted to provide crucial building materials sometimes delayed inordinately. Dennis and his colleagues

2. Buildings under construction in Phase 2 of the school's development

wrote repeatedly to suppliers, drawing attention to the inconveniences caused by their delays. Dennis also had to consult widely with ANC structures on progress at the school and on his requirements for skilled workers. In a typical letter to Rusty Bernstein in London in 1981, he reported on the magnitude of the work at Mazimbu, saying he 'estimate[s] the finished complex including vocational training, workshops, etc. will be in the region of 10 million dollars'. He added, indicating the complexity and variety of the responsibilities placed on people leading the work at SOMAFCO, that 'apart from architectural and building work, we have over 200 students in great need of political education. There is also a great deal of artistic talent amongst the students, which needs to be developed.' Progress reports such as this had to contain as much information as possible to sustain everybody's interest. The more they contained and the more constituencies to which they appealed, the better the chances of convincing donor agencies of the need for help.

The first students arrived in SOMAFCO in 1977, at the inception of the project. They were also instrumental in clearing the land upon which SOMAFCO was to be built. Amongst them was a student named Titus, who arrived in East Africa in 1977:

> I came straight to Mazimbu when I arrived in Tanzania. There was just bush everywhere. About fifty of us, all students, went to work clearing the bush and helping in the renovation ... We improvised a school. Those of us who had completed their matriculation levels at home assisted ... [in] teach[ing] the junior students.

Such were the beginnings of the secondary school. Systematic construction of the complex started in 1979 and late in that year students and staff were able to move into the first completed dormitory block. In these conditions some rooms were used as classrooms and others served as accommodation for both staff and students.

Though originally only a secondary school was envisaged, the primary school then came into existence because, in the words of a 1983 report, 'the population became aware of the fact that there were some 20 young children who should be at school. A "teacher" took them in hand early in 1980 and a school began to take shape.' The nursery school, daycare centre and adult education facility followed the same pattern. It was also realised that if the system were to move away from Bantu Education, vocational schools offering technically-based learning would have to be developed alongside academic education. This in turn implied the need for practical training, which eventually resulted in centres at Mazimbu and Dakawa which were partly factories and partly vocational training facilities: garment and leather-goods factories; mechanical and carpentry workshops; and similar enterprises.

It thus quickly became clear that a school of the sort envisaged could not survive unless supported by various facilities that were not strictly educational. In addition, there was complete uncertainty as to when those involved with Mazimbu would return to South Africa: it was necessary to prepare for that day rather than wait for it passively, and investment in the school was part of this process. It was not surprising, therefore, that it tended to take on a certain permanence in their minds. Furthermore, the ideology of self-reliance that was such an important aspect of the institution also implied a degree of continuity. This worried some participants. John Carneson remembers Jabulani Nxumalo (Mzala), who was at SOMAFCO for about a year and also worked for the ANC's Radio Freedom, playing with the much-used phrase that it was time to return to the 'promised land', commenting ironically that 'you people are building pyramids in Egypt'. Such scepticism notwithstanding, the development of this quasi-permanent complex required a many-sided plan that would permit material security and modest comfort, and help to make the complex, as far as possible, independent of the uncertainties of supply in an impoverished country where growing economic problems in the 1980s encouraged the spread of corruption, theft and bureaucratic inefficiency.

Supporting the school: building, farming, health, manufacturing

During SOMAFCO's early phase, design and construction capacity was installed, including departments devoted to planning, programming, purchasing, stores, construction and site supervision. This was sponsored mainly by the United Nations Development Programme (UNDP). By 1980, the site had been cleared and seven existing houses renovated, temporary water supply and sewage systems were in place, and Mazimbu had been linked to mains electricity. There was a poultry unit for 100 layers, maize had been planted, and a vegetable garden and orchard had been initiated. The construction of 3 dormitory blocks for 144 students and of 4 teachers' houses was in progress. There were further plans to construct more dormitory units, houses, a kitchen, dining block and other facilities, all in conjunction with on-site training of carpenters, masons, electricians, plumbers and painters. Various donor agencies had been identified to assist in areas in which they showed interest or had particular competence. For example, the World Health Organization (WHO) was to be approached to assist with a water and sanitation project and a health centre, whilst the United Nations Educational Scientific and Cultural Organization (Unesco) would be asked to support educational projects and the building of a library. Such initiatives set the pace for future project developments.

For ideological and practical reasons, it was crucial that food production be stabilised and regularised. This meant that the development of the farm was a priority. Self-reliance also depended on a healthy community, necessitating high-quality healthcare for the exiles, unused to the tropical Tanzanian environment. Continued construction required that as much as possible of the material to build, maintain and equip the complex be produced on-site. This led to the formation of a Construction Department team specialising in the manufacture of structural components such as beams and roof trusses, and a factory to make furniture.

For all these purposes, in 1980 the ANC initiated a Project Management Department (PMD) to 'provide effective and efficient administration and co-ordination of projects undertaken by ANC departments and maximise donor assistance'. The PMD's brief was to concern itself with all ANC projects in Tanzania, the biggest being SOMAFCO, where it was to co-ordinate the different sub-projects that would make up the Mazimbu complex. The underlying vision was that of providing an opportunity for South Africans to control their environment in a way that was impossible at home, in a non-discriminatory, communal way. It was also intended to provide experience in organising and managing a large community and its social services. All this required the training of masons, carpenters, electricians, sanitation engineers and community planners, amongst others. It was also felt that, in the spirit of self-reliance, there was a need to educate everybody in basic building skills, and to inculcate concern for the environment and commitment to community organisation.

This programme had to be carried out in difficult circumstances where the ANC relied on foreign donors and suppliers. As so often with donor money, it was easier to find assistance for building than for running costs and supplies, and even supplies, when they arrived, frequently came in the wrong qualities or in excessive quantities. John Pampallis comments that, thanks to Polish generosity, SOMAFCO had 'pencils to supply the whole continent'. At one point 100 lorry-loads of Russian timber for furniture arrived, rather than the four loads of building timber requested. Voluntary solidarity groups in Europe and elsewhere, especially when informed by returning volunteers, often responded more flexibly and appropriately. However, they would not have been able to supply all the needs of the school.

The Mazimbu farm project was intended to be an important support to the school. Indeed, relying on generous aid from abroad, it eventually achieved a level of mechanisation and productivity in animal husbandry and agriculture among the best in Tanzania. The ANC spelt out the aims of the project as being:

> to achieve a standard whereby the whole complex would be self-reliant to maintain a population of approximately 2 500 people through development of crop and animal husbandry production and related manufacture of products. To develop and manage the farm to a standard which can provide up to date training for ANC cadres in all aspects of agricultural activities. The farm … [will] not only feed the community in Mazimbu, but also generate funds to pay for running costs, seeds, fertiliser, fuel etc. for subsequent years. The agricultural activities are divided into three main sections: crop production, livestock, and agricultural planning and implementation.

To launch the project, a farm consultant, Hans Jurgen, was provided by the Swedish International Development Agency (Sida). He was to advise the Agricultural Department, co-ordinate agricultural activities and advise on long-term planning and development through a Farm Committee, which was to meet monthly. By the time Jurgen arrived, the Tanzanian government had allocated 1 000 hectares of land at Mazimbu to the ANC, the bulk of which was intended for crop production and animal husbandry. There was already a piggery with 600 pigs, a poultry unit producing regular, but still inadequate, supplies of broilers and eggs, and approximately 150 hectares under crops. The construction of a complex that included an animal feed mixing plant and a grain storage unit was in progress.

With Jurgen's guidance, a comprehensive proposal for a modern farm, *ANC Farm for Self-reliance*, was submitted to the United Nations High Commission for Refugees (UNHCR) in 1981. Among the objectives were that by 1984 the farm should achieve a level of self-reliance and standard of living for a community of 2 500 ANC members identical to that of the surrounding population: in fact, the South African standard of living was always above that of the surrounding Tanzanians. For 1982 the target was that 400 hectares of land would be cleared and cultivated. Grain crops, fruit trees and vegetables would be planted, the first phase of the construction of the dairy would be completed, and 50 cows would be purchased. The aim was that by the end of 1984 there would be a dairy with 100 thoroughbred cows, a beef herd with 400 cattle, a poultry unit with 3 000 layers and 5 000 broilers, and a piggery with 100 breeding sows. The following year would see the construction of fences, drinking troughs, the poultry unit and breeding pens for the piggery, and the beef herd would be augmented. In the second phase of the dairy, the other 50 cows would be installed, and fattening pens for the pigs would be built.

The modern farmyard was also to have a storage area for machinery when not in use, and several service bays and workshops, including a metals workshop for production and repair of components. Fuel tanks geared specifically for the needs of farm equipment would also be located within this secure environment. This complex would be the heart of the farm. The projected budget for this phase, envisaged to last from 1982 to 1984, was US$3 849 612. Modern, mechanised, agricultural self-sufficiency, if it can really be called self-sufficiency, was expensive. It was very different from the necessarily frugal self-reliance of the surrounding Tanzanian peasantry.

Health was a constant concern at Mazimbu. Coming from a relatively temperate climate, South Africans had no immunity to the tropical diseases, particularly malaria, that were rife in Tanzania. Road deaths and injuries were high, at times related to careless or drunken driving, and to overcrowding of sometimes badly maintained vehicles on the hazardous Tanzanian roads. A visit to the graveyard at Mazimbu shockingly demonstrates the high mortality rate of South Africans of all ages. It was also necessary to create an effective healthcare system so as not to put undue pressure on the fragile Tanzanian medical system, and to demonstrate the self-reliance of the ANC.

Mazimbu became the main health centre for the ANC in East Africa as a whole, and the foundation of the health unit there should be seen within the context of overall ANC health policy at the time. A meeting in Lusaka on 27 August 1977 that included the Secretary General, Alfred Nzo, and the Treasurer General, Thomas Nkobi, set up a Health Committee comprising people within the ANC who had medical backgrounds. Peter Mfelang was chosen as Chairman, Manto Tshabalala as Secretary, and Nomvuyo Nokwe and Fiki Radebe-Reed as additional members. In December the committee was re-designated a department, with a secretariat made up of Mfelang and Tshabalala, together with elected delegates from health teams located wherever there were ANC settlements.

In 1981 it was decided that members of the ANC in the medical professions, from doctors to medical aides, within centres, localities and regions, were to constitute themselves into health committees that would meet at least twice a year and oversee medical and social welfare matters. They were to develop publicity strategies, especially briefing the solidarity groups whose assistance was vital in obtaining equipment and medicines. In essence, the Health Department was called upon to analyse the health status of those for whom the organisation had some responsibility and to analyse the healthcare delivery system. In January 1982, Peter Mfelang, summarising the ANC's approach, said that:

> We were to generate awareness amongst ourselves and the ANC membership at large, on the close relationship between health and the prevailing socio-economic, political, cultural and any other related factors. Medicine could no longer operate in isolation, but was an integral part of the very tapestry of the existence of humanity. Health programmes and activities had to be geared towards the reduction of human suffering … The department was therefore to identify the health needs of our people, and promote and support good health. More than that it had to develop a high level of organisation and commitment in the delivery of health care to our people.

However, the harsh reality was that the Department was in a precarious state. At a conference in Lusaka near the end of 1982, Manto Tshabalala presented a paper on *Objectives and critical analysis of the present state of affairs in the Health Department.* She said that healthcare in general left much to be desired. Health teams were unable to solve problems on the spot. Working relations with local health institutions were not being fully developed. There were insufficient skilled health professionals and their numbers were static, so the quality of healthcare to ANC communities was not improving. Other presentations commented on indifferent procedures in health education and administration, lack of transport for the secretariat, absence of adequate staff housing, and restrictions on referrals abroad, exacerbated by the fact that some patients with influence chose where they wanted to receive treatment.

Added to these problems were the difficult personal and professional relationships that often characterised the Health Department. An example of this acrimony and what could result from it is the resignation letter of Tim Naidoo, a nurse at the Mazimbu Clinic, in February 1982. She felt she could:

> no longer work where whatever I do as a health worker is seen as wrong. I simply find it impossible to work in an atmosphere of dishonesty, insecurity and non-cooperation. Explanations are not sought, we are reprimanded and condemned in stories and rumours.

When Naidoo was asked to substantiate her claims, she added that even since she had written there had been further deterioration to the extent that she felt ashamed to belong to such a society. She criticised the behaviour of the Mazimbu authorities over a cholera outbreak, criticisms corroborated by a memorandum from Terry Bell, the primary school principal, who was outraged that even while Mazimbu was quarantined busloads of primary schoolchildren from Morogoro were allowed onto the complex.

There were also many running battles in the Health Department, some focused on Mazimbu. For instance, the Regional Chairperson for Health at Mazimbu complained that the Secretary of Health turned the choice of students for the maternal and child health course into a 'one-man job'. She charged that when certain irregularities were raised with the Secretary, she took from minutes what suited her and sent copies to leadership, making it appear that she was the victim of a power struggle. The Regional Chairperson later tendered her resignation, citing conflict with the Secretary as the main reason. With this conflict in the open, in October 1982, the ANC decided to set up a commission to investigate the East Africa health team. The commission was presented with ample evidence to demonstrate that indeed power struggles and personality clashes were widespread and demoralising.

Personal conflicts did nothing to solve the many problems that the health professionals faced. There were conditions that often accompany poverty and social dislocation like malaria, tuberculosis, rheumatic heart disease, gastroenteritis, uncontrolled diabetes, malignant hypertension, substance abuse, depression and schizophrenia. Measles affected children badly. There is no doubt that malaria was the most devastating condition, demanding the greatest resources in terms of personnel, drugs and in-patient facilities. It also represented a tremendous cost to the community in terms of loss of productive capacity.

To confront this situation the ANC decided to build a hospital. Officially opened on 1 May 1984, it was named the ANC-Holland Solidarity Hospital. It replaced the clinic that had proved completely insufficient for Mazimbu's needs. A medical solidarity committee in Holland planned and financed the hospital, while the ANC was responsible for its construction. Additional equipment was supplied by a combination of Dutch supporters. At the opening of the hospital, Henk Odenk, representing the solidarity group, stated that it symbolised the support of the Dutch people for the ANC, asserting that they had financed the hospital as part of the struggle against capitalism.

Though the hospital was small, for its size it was wide-ranging in the treatment it offered, as it was intended to be the referral centre for ANC patients in the East Africa region. It offered diagnostic services, backed by X-ray and laboratory facilities; in- and out-patient treatment, both medical and

3. The ANC-Holland Solidarity Hospital under construction

surgical; mother and child services including deliveries and immunisation; dentistry; health education, and preventive healthcare. Medical opinion was divided as to the adequacy of the hospital for its purposes, but it did provide the essential backbone of medical provision for the school, for Mazimbu and for the ANC in Tanzania.

Finally, an example of the sort of enterprise that contributed to the development of SOMAFCO in the sphere of manufacturing was the Finnish-financed joinery and furniture works founded in 1980, named the Vuyisile Mini Furniture Factory in honour of the Port Elizabeth labour leader and MK soldier executed by the South African state in 1964. It was intended to support the construction programme in Mazimbu, and later at Dakawa, and doors, window frames, furniture and other wooden products were supplied from it. Broken furniture was also repaired at the factory. Oswald Dennis, writing to the resident UNDP co-ordinator in January 1982, described its importance in the context of the arrival of woodworking machines:

> The factory is of considerable value to … our construction programme since it provides the building site with all joinery parts and fixtures required. The coming online of these machines will represent a substantial saving since it means we can dispense with the services of contractors … In the future, as our building programme nears completion, the factory can begin to produce for the market, thus providing funds for the maintenance of our complex.

This is indeed what happened, and the factory supplied high-quality furniture in attractive, functional Scandinavian-influenced designs not only to Mazimbu, but also to the wider Tanzanian market.

CHAPTER 3

Teachers, administrators and students

Though South Africa has had a long history of social, ethnic and political division and conflict, it has also had long experience of coexistence and co-operation, especially within the ranks of the liberation movements themselves, notably the ANC. United, sometimes tenuously, by the ideal of a free and non-racial nation, the ANC and supporting organisations brought together blacks, whites, Indians and coloureds; Soviet-leaning and Trotskyist communists; social-democrats and liberals; rural and urban workers and members of the middle class; the highly educated and those struggling with illiteracy. The new South Africa, with its tensions and misunderstandings, but also with its conviction – in the vocabulary of the negotiations of the early 1990s – that 'sufficient consensus' was absolutely necessary for survival, was forged long before 1994 within the liberation movements themselves. At its best, SOMAFCO, in the ANC tradition, epitomised the spirit of a shared South Africa embedded in the diversity of its teachers and the students that they taught. This chapter gives a necessarily selective sample of this diversity, as reflected in some teachers, administrators and students.

Recruiting teachers

In the early days of the school there was as yet no established source of funding. Teachers and others at Mazimbu needed to have a commitment to ANC ideals that could survive great uncertainty. As those who worked there at the early stages emphasise, conditions were tough and unforgiving, but often there is also an underlying pride in the resilience and capacity to face challenges which set such people apart.

In recruiting teachers, the ANC sent out communiqués to all its missions, encouraging people to join the school. Initially, those of South African origin were targeted, and invitations were even sent to internal underground structures within South Africa. The principle laid down by the third Neduc meeting in August 1980 was that all recruits to the new school should be:

> committed to the role of the ANC as a liberation movement whose only resources derive from the sacrifices and selfless devotion of the oppressed South African masses themselves. Services to SOMAFCO therefore must be seen not as a favour to the ANC but as a modest contribution and privilege to serve oneself and one's own people.

This meant, in short, that anyone going to Mazimbu should not expect material rewards, but should rather serve willingly as his or her contribution to the struggle.

In an attempt to systematise the recruitment criteria, the same resolution gave priority to ANC members who were professionally qualified, followed by members who had no professional teaching qualifications. Lastly, non-South African supporters who had appropriate professional qualifications would be considered. The first category comprised the ideal candidates. The second acknowledged that whilst the ANC had a large pool of educated supporters, they were not all trained teachers. It implicitly also acknowledged that by 1980 there was a substantial number of students at SOMAFCO who had matriculated, and, while awaiting scholarships to study abroad, and in view of the dire shortage of teachers, could help with teaching. In targeting the third category the ANC set out to utilise its support base amongst solidarity groups throughout the world. The ANC wished to promote the 'hard' sciences, which the apartheid government had discouraged amongst blacks and in which there were few South African teachers from backgrounds likely to be sympathetic to the liberation struggle. Therefore, the most likely recruits would tend to be drawn from foreign supporters with a solidarity background. Overall, Neduc stressed, teachers and their work were 'the very pillar' upon which achieving the aims of the school rested – SOMAFCO's success or otherwise depended on getting the best possible people who would be able to transcend decades of inferior education and instil new ideals and goals whilst building students' confidence.

From the beginning, the impermanence of the teaching staff was a problem. John Pampallis remembers that when he went to England in 1985 to write a history text for use at SOMAFCO, there were 26 teachers at the school: only six of these were still there when he returned 15 months later. To mid-1982, most of the staff was composed of South African exiles and members of the ANC. Few were qualified teachers, many being graduates without teaching qualifications. About half were post-matriculation students awaiting scholarships in other countries. Eventually some volunteer teachers, carefully selected on the basis both of their qualifications and of their commitment to the South African struggle, were recruited from the Netherlands, the Nordic countries and the United Kingdom to teach the natural sciences, English and geography. This eased the shortage of teachers, but had the potential to create problems of a different kind, when, as sometimes happened, the culture of the school and that of the western European teachers, raised in a different pedagogical tradition, did not match. Another important group of teachers, particularly of science and mathematics – valuable because they were highly qualified and regularly replaced – was from the GDR. Particularly towards the end of the 1980s, there was an increasing number of non-South African African teachers, from Nigeria, Tanzania, Zambia and elsewhere.

Some individual profiles, highlighting the early South African teachers who had to play the difficult yet creative pioneering role, will help create a picture of their motivation, their various reasons for being in exile, and the processes involved in their enrolling as teachers at SOMAFCO. This is an illustrative selection: there were other remarkable teachers, like Farida Mussagy, Mzwandile Kibi, John Carneson, Mohammed Jatham, and many more, who played outstanding roles as teachers and mentors. Many were members of the ANC, but were not actually working for the organisation before they came to the school. Others had histories of closer political involvement, and were redeployed to the school from other sectors of the movement. Interviews revealed the striking sense of adventure in the face of difficult conditions among the mostly, though not always, young people of all races that made up the first batch of teachers.

Some recruits had long taken their stand against apartheid education. Mrs Makho Njobe was amongst these. She and her husband left South Africa in the late 1950s, a few years after the promulgation of Bantu Education. As a trained teacher with university education, she had watched as the state set about systematically breaking down the structures of black education, putting in its place crude scraps considered appropriate for second-class citizens. Finding it hard to endure this onslaught, and with her husband increasingly in trouble with the law, they realised they had to look elsewhere if they wanted to continue teaching with integrity. At this time Dr Kwame Nkrumah was seeking qualified African teachers to assist in the building of the recently-independent Ghana. The Njobes took up that challenge and moved to West Africa. Over the years they went on to teach in other African countries like Nigeria and Zambia. Mrs Njobe's experience in these places made her yearn to be part of the SOMAFCO experiment. 'Having come across children who had grown up having never experienced racial oppression ... who were free thinking and encouraged to exercise their faculties to the fullest,' made her, she says, 'think of these displaced South African children at SOMAFCO.' Thus she took up a place in the school as a biology teacher in September 1979, a few months after tuition started.

André Proctor's route to SOMAFCO was different. His time as a student at the universities of Cape Town and the Witwatersrand had exposed him to radical political ideas, and in the process he realised that he could not accept the status quo. The deciding factor for him was the arrival of his draft papers ordering him to report for duty to the South African Defence Force. In response, he crossed with his wife to Botswana. Here he became part of the small South African exile community, and formally joined the ANC. After some years in

Botswana, he heard of the opening of SOMAFCO and arrived there at the beginning of 1980.

Like André Proctor, Richard Jürgens came from a relatively comfortable background, also leaving South Africa clandestinely with his wife. He joined the school in 1986. He described his reasons thus: 'It came down to a very simple choice about South Africa, and that was either live and not partake any more of this … unwanted privilege, rather go and be poor somewhere else, or do something about it, and then I was offered this opportunity or asked or recruited or caught in the web … and it came together at that moment.' Jürgens was motivated by conscientious objection to the excesses of apartheid privilege, which others took for granted. His experience, about which he is in some respects ambivalent, and which he describes in the only reminiscences published so far by a SOMAFCO teacher, also raises the important role of the underground ANC structures in universities where the left tendencies of some students were utilised to convince them to assist the mass democratic movement, and combat government propaganda. There is a certain irony in the privileged products of white liberal universities, mostly from well-to-do families, turning towards an institution dedicated to the overthrow of the educational status quo. Social privilege, it is clear, does not always determine political action.

John Pampallis was also called up by the army. He went through basic training and the usual routine of army life, but was constantly aware of the misdeeds of the apartheid regime. This prompted him to leave South Africa, first to teach in Botswana for a year and then to move to Canada, his fiancée Karin's home country. In Canada he joined the anti-apartheid movement and the ANC. After four years in Canada, he heard of the opening of SOMAFCO and the call for teachers through his ANC unit. He moved there with Karin, now his wife, in early 1980. Proctor, Jurgens and Pampallis, like Mrs Njobe, were highly qualified professionals, with honours and masters degrees, who could have lived comfortably anywhere in the Western world, but they chose the uncertainty of SOMAFCO.

Most of these individuals were accompanied by their spouses who also played an important part in the project. Mrs Njobe's husband, Wintchi, was the first principal of the school and John Pampallis's wife, Karin, also worked at the school. Initially she was Secretary of the Scholarship Committee, where she helped the principal interact with other ANC bodies in the difficult task of apportioning scholarships to students who graduated from secondary school. Later she joined the construction office as Secretary to the Project Manager, Oswald Dennis. In this capacity she ran his office, taking care of orders, correspondence, filing and all office work. Her contribution was so substantial that her post was later upgraded to that of full assistant to Dennis.

Due to recurrent ill health, Proctor's wife, Elsbeth, could not be employed at SOMAFCO, and her illness meant that the couple's stay in Mazimbu was short. Like Elsbeth Proctor, many SOMAFCO recruits had to battle bouts of debilitating illness, more often than not malaria, to which they had no acquired resistance, and, like her, a number were forced to leave as a result of health problems. Recruits were also shaken by the continuous ill health of their children. In addition, at these earliest stages food was prepared in the open air, under trees, in essentially unhygienic conditions.

The ANC drew on the diaspora of exiles for its teachers. Amongst these was Douglas Ramaphosa. He had been swept up in the 1976 wave of resistance to apartheid and, like thousands of others, he found himself in detention, spending time in the cells of John Vorster Square police station, in Johannesburg. Imprisonment raised his political awareness; in cases such as his, brutality at the hands of the police often brought detainees closer together and made them even more committed to the ideal of a free South Africa. Though after detention he was able to resume his life and find a good job, his contacts with the ANC underground encouraged him to abandon his cover and flee the country, ending up in Eastern Europe. Even though he was not a qualified teacher, he heard of SOMAFCO's pressing need for staff, and decided to go there.

Patrick Mtshaulana came from a poor Transkei family. He graduated with a B.Juris. from Fort Hare in 1975 and became a public prosecutor in Bizana, Transkei. Becoming convinced that the system for which he was working was not neutral, and that most of the crimes with which he was dealing were in reality the product of an unjust social system, after the events of June 1976 he decided to give up his job. For him, 'It was clear that the time had come for young people of my age to join the struggle, to join the ANC which was leading the struggle, to avert and avoid that people should spontaneously rise up as they were doing in Soweto, without leadership, which cost so many lives.' He convinced a magistrate to give him a travel document to visit relatives in Swaziland, and left South Africa in September 1976. From Swaziland he went surreptitiously to Mozambique where Frelimo brought him into contact with the ANC. In the ANC he joined MK as part of the June 16 Detachment, the first big group of trainees after 1976, and, because of his education, was made a political instructor for new recruits. In 1980 he was recruited for SOMAFCO, to teach history of the struggle.

Thami Mali's exile was precipitated when he found himself facing trial in two different cases. In the first case he was charged, with Albertina Sisulu, with contravening Section 6 of the *Terrorism Act* by furthering the aims of the ANC, a banned organisation. He was found guilty and sentenced to five years imprisonment. While appealing against this sentence he was arrested on another unrelated charge. On being released on bail in 1980, facing the prospect of a long jail term, he decided to leave the country. He made his way to Lusaka, where, after debriefing, he joined a military training camp at Pango, in Angola. In 1987, he returned to Lusaka to work in regional military logistics. A year later he was asked to leave the army and join SOMAFCO, since in his previous life he had been a teacher. Though reluctant to leave MK, he agreed and arrived at the school to teach history and English in February 1988. This was a time when there were many upheavals at SOMAFCO. Students who arrived after the 1985 wave of unrest brought with them elements of divisiveness. Thus he was also appointed Political Commissar of the primary division, in the hope that he would inculcate the motivation and discipline said to be intrinsic to military life, inculcate deeper political understanding, and dispel rivalries and prejudices emanating from South Africa.

Volunteer teachers came from the Scandinavian countries, the Netherlands and elsewhere. One was the Dutch mathematics teacher Wilma Schavemaker. She taught in Botswana in 1980, and became involved in the Dutch anti-apartheid movement where she met many South Africans. In May 1983, supported by the Dutch government and with her political credentials approved by the anti-apartheid movement, she arrived at SOMAFCO where she spent two years and six months. She taught mathematics – with the few and inappropriate textbooks available – to students eager to learn but conditioned by Bantu Education to believe that mathematics was 'something impossible'. She experienced Mazimbu's easy relations between teachers and students, which did not interfere, however, with classroom professionalism. She was horrified by the many deaths on campus and elsewhere, for which life in Europe had not prepared her, and was dismayed by policy on pregnancy amongst students who were often in their twenties. 'You can't talk about girls and boys,' she says, 'I've always talked about women and men.' She shared the widespread scepticism about 'education with production'. Volunteer teachers, she says, were 'incredibly enthusiastic', though, when the many underlying problems appeared, they could become 'very negative. Only now … do you see that the problems were inevitable.' She shared a house with another single person and a couple. As anywhere, both tensions and lasting friendships could and did result. In allocating accommodation no account was taken of race, nationality or social background, a policy that broke radically with the norms of contemporary South Africa.

There had been a debate about the wisdom of accepting volunteer teachers, and there was continuing resentment amongst some teachers of the preferential treatment received by volunteers who did not belong to the movement, often combined with a grudging acceptance of the necessity of this policy. That volunteer teachers received better remuneration than their ANC counterparts was often viewed as institutionalised elitism, skewing living standards among a group of people doing the same job. However, those on the left viewed complaints about salaries as mere whining. Terry Bell, for example, felt that ANC teachers had an obligation to serve the school in the spirit of revolutionary dedication and equality, whatever the conditions of service of volunteers from outside the movement.

Administrators

SOMAFCO was administered in the context of the settlements of Mazimbu and, later, Dakawa. Many important figures in the administration are mentioned in other chapters. Three diverse individuals who illustrate the range of personalities in the SOMAFCO administration are singled out here.

Mohammed Tikly was a key figure in the development of SOMAFCO. In exile for 30 years, 20 of those in Britain, he was a teacher and educationist in London and an ANC and anti-apartheid activist. With the foundation of Neduc, a network of supporting ANC education committees was set up in various parts of the world. The London committee, formally created in 1977 but mooted earlier, and chaired by Tikly, was probably the most active. The first task of these committees was to support SOMAFCO, and in 1981 Tikly was asked to become the Director of the new school. He agreed, and arrived in Tanzania in 1982, where he remained until 1987.

Tikly thought his job would be primarily that of head teacher. It quickly became obvious that, as well as the educational responsibilities, leadership of the school and its supporting facilities would involve numerous administrative, political and diplomatic demands. He rose to this challenge and, under his directorship, Mazimbu became a major centre that served the ANC capably and provided a compelling image of educational commitment to the international community. Though answerable to Neduc and ultimately to the National Executive of the ANC, after the school's initial phase many educational and other decisions were taken at Mazimbu. Tikly co-ordinated the interaction of the school and settlement with the movement as a whole.

One of Tikly's most time-consuming tasks was that of building relations with donors. This was crucial for the survival of the institution, creating a worldwide network of supporters and lobbyists committed to concrete support of the educational work of the ANC. Urbane and persuasive, Tikly was an ideal person to represent the school in the complex international arena where, in some quarters, suspicion of the movement was widespread. He led the school and settlement from struggling obscurity to a role of considerable actual and symbolic significance to the ANC.

In 1987 Tikly was transferred to Lusaka where he took on the post of administrative secretary of education for the movement. From there he remained closely in touch with SOMAFCO, and continued to contribute to its development. Even when the school closed in 1992, he continued his involvement, working with the Batlagae Trust for the education of exiles during and after their repatriation to South Africa.

Alpheus Mangezi was educated at the Swiss mission at Lemana, Northern Transvaal. He left South Africa in 1960, after qualifying as a social worker at the Jan Hofmeyr School of Social Work. Nearly 30 years later he became the last Director of Schools at Mazimbu. When he left South Africa, Mangezi became a trainee psychiatric worker in the Glasgow slums, where he became aware that the sort of social divisions he encountered there also underlay South African preoccupations with race and colour. He gained further qualifications in social work and sociology in London, at Ibadan during Nigeria's civil war, and in the Netherlands and Sweden, culminating in doctoral studies in Copenhagen, Denmark. He worked in Zambia, England and Denmark. In 1975 he took a post at the Centre for African Studies at the university in Maputo, Mozambique, where he spent, as he puts it, 12 'wonderful years, terrible years'. He was a colleague of Ruth First until her assassination in 1982, their sociological and historical research woven together with their political work. Mangezi had also been part of the ANC education committee in Maputo.

As a South African with a formal job contract rather than with the status of political refugee, Mangezi was not obliged to leave Mozambique after the Nkomati Accord. He was thus able to assist with the relocation of the bulk of ANC supporters that followed that agreement, many of them to Mazimbu and Dakawa. In 1989 he was requested to become the Director of Schools in the Tanzanian settlements. He moved at a time when momentous changes were about to take place in South Africa, with far-reaching results for SOMAFCO. A gentle and sensitive man, his difficulties were compounded by the fact that, although he was a long-standing ANC member, he was in a sense an outsider to the SOMAFCO community. Nevertheless, he dealt capably with the extraordinarily difficult task of managing an institution that continued to receive new students to the end, while gearing it down to the point where it ultimately closed in 1992.

Andrew Masondo graduated with a B.Sc. from the University College of Fort Hare, and then took honours in applied mathematics at the University of the Witwatersrand in 1959. In the same year he returned to Fort Hare for a diploma in education, and stayed as a lecturer in applied mathematics from 1960. While at Fort Hare, he joined the Communist Party, worked as a rural organiser under the ANC stalwart Govan Mbeki, and became an MK commander in the Eastern Cape. He was arrested for sabotage in 1963, and spent many years imprisoned on Robben Island, before being released in 1976. Banished to Umlazi in Natal, he soon slipped out of the country and joined the ANC leadership in exile, going to Angola after military training in the Soviet Union. From 1977 to 1985 Masondo served as National Political Commissar of the ANC, in which capacity he was held responsible for abuses and executions of suspected informers in military camps.

Masondo's assertive and authoritarian style, and his experience as soldier, ex-Political Commissar and educationist, gave a particular imprint to his time as principal of the secondary school from 1987. He worked closely with the security division, and became involved in clashes with some colleagues and students. He conflicted in particular with some from a Black Consciousness background. He said to students, 'Outside the classroom we're all comrades; inside the classroom the teacher is the supreme comrade,' though he put this in the context of respect, not fear. Where he felt it was justified, people he suspected of anti-social or subversive behaviour were locked up, and he was not averse to physical punishment, though never for academic failings. People were sometimes beaten, he says, 'but not in a sadistic fashion'. He describes his policy at SOMAFCO as 'firm without being cruel; kind without being weak'.

Masondo left SOMAFCO early in 1990, and went to head the ANC's Lusaka office at a time when the movement's top leaders were returning to South Africa. Subsequently he became a general in the new South African National Defence Force, and was involved in the organisation for returned MK members. He testified before the Truth and Reconciliation Commission on his role in the camps in Angola, and applied for and was granted amnesty.

Masondo was a tough and sometimes ruthless soldier, but not just a soldier: there is no doubt that this larger-than-life personality brought real pedagogic and academic skills to SOMAFCO. He was, for example, a determined advocate of mathematics and science education, and stood firmly against arguments that, he considered, weakly acquiesced to the consequences of miseducation in these spheres under Bantu Education. He was, nonetheless, a controversial choice as school principal, representing an authoritarian approach that sat uncomfortably with the more inclusive and accommodating traditions that also existed at the school.

Students

It was not easy for teachers at SOMAFCO to operate within what was intended to be a revolutionary school. There were no facilities that trained teachers for such an environment. They needed to approach their work creatively, deconstructing previous rigid, hierarchical and authoritarian approaches to student-teacher relations, and accepting that their students came from a wide variety of backgrounds. A 1980 Neduc report categorised the SOMAFCO student community as coming from four backgrounds: those with a history of direct political involvement; those influenced by a political environment; those with parents so involved; and the non-committed.

The directly involved referred to those who had recently left South Africa with first-hand experience of the apartheid system. These tended to be the most amenable to political education, though some had behavioural problems stemming from their often-traumatic experiences. Those in the second group, who had grown up in places like Lesotho or Mozambique, were influenced by local politics and had an insight into the conditions of the liberation struggle. Those with involved parents had grown up in exile, and knew something about the ANC, but could be quite detached from the country and its problems. The non-committed group was deemed to be those students who knew virtually nothing about South Africa and the ANC. They usually came from families of which only one parent was South African. They came to SOMAFCO for family and educational motives, but often had little affinity with or knowledge of the objectives of the movement.

These categories, however, cover and partly conceal numerous individual stories. The young people who fled Soweto in the aftermath of the events of 1976 often arrived strongly influenced by the Black Consciousness philosophy, but frequently tended to gravitate towards the ANC, the organisation most capable of harbouring and utilising them. They were angry and militant, and it was difficult to persuade some of them that they could serve the cause as effectively by continuing their studies as by joining MK.

Some students, like Wandile Kalipa, whose *nom-de-guerre* was Boyoyo 'Boss' Seseseko, were the children of ANC stalwarts. Boyoyo was involved in the student revolt of 1976 in Soweto, thereafter fleeing to Lesotho, where he contacted the ANC. He was the victim of a bomb concealed in copies of *Sechaba*, the ANC journal, posted to the ANC in Lesotho. After treatment in the Soviet Union for his severe injuries, he went to Mazimbu where he resumed his studies. Phumeza Ngxala, from the Eastern Cape, a Congress of South African Students (Cosas) member, also left South Africa in the wake of the events of 1976. She was 16 at the time, and had already been detained for 3 months under the *Terrorism Act*. She hid in the home of a sympathetic white family in Crown Mines in Johannesburg, and then, fearing that the family's maid would inadvertently reveal her presence, she slipped into Mozambique through Swaziland with many difficulties and hardships, including a lengthy trek without shoes through dense thorn-bush, finally arriving in 1981 at Mazimbu.

Andrew Mohammed, a pupil at St Barnabas, a Johannesburg private school, was involved in the uprisings in 'coloured' schools in 1979 to 1980. He left South Africa through Botswana, spent some time at the Dukwe camp, and then, arriving in Zambia, was persuaded to study rather than join MK. He came to SOMAFCO in July 1980, where his relatively high level of education meant that he was for a time both teacher and pupil, passing on his knowledge in areas where he was competent, while sitting in class as a student where he was less so. Mercedes Seete, who arrived in May of the same year, followed her brother who was among the first students at the school in 1979. Jabulile Maphisa's family sent her to relatives in Swaziland so that she might avoid the educational chaos in South Africa. She studied there for some years, succeeding in her O-level examinations. In spite of her mother's opposition, because she wished to study further, she left for Mozambique and then Tanzania where she completed her education at SOMAFCO before leaving on a scholarship to Ethiopia. Like Andrew Mohammed and many others in the early days of the school, while studying she also taught, in her case in the primary school.

Some students came as very young children. Steven Nhlebeya was seven years old when he left South Africa in 1978 with his mother, who was an ANC underground worker. Mother and son travelled from Mozambique to Dar es Salaam, where he stayed with her for some years. When he was 12 or 13 years old she left on ANC business, and he went to SOMAFCO, where he stayed until 1990. Oscar Majola's mother was also an ANC worker and he was born in exile, spending his early years in Dar es Salaam with his mother and brother, and moving to the primary school at SOMAFCO in 1983 at the age of seven. Sasa Zikalala's parents were both 1976 student exiles, and she was born in exile and sent to SOMAFCO. Pule Matsebe's father left South Africa in a much earlier wave of exile, and met Pule's mother outside the country. Pule was born in Morogoro, and was one of the first primary school pupils in Mazimbu. In contrast, many students were adults. An example is Helen Radebe, a pre-1976 exile, who worked in the office of the Military Communications Department of MK in Lusaka. She had no secondary education, and enrolled in Form 1 in SOMAFCO on 9 August 1980.

Joe Mukwalo's father and mother were ANC members, and Joe was born in Zambia where his father worked on the copper mines. He did part of his early education in Zambia, and part in Uganda, and returned to head the ANC youth movement on the Zambian Copperbelt. Then in 1980 he went to SOMAFCO to complete his secondary education, where he was one of the first O-level candidates. Nana Masusu's mother was one of the group of 21 South African nurses organised by the ANC to come to Tanzania in 1962 as an act of solidarity with the newly-independent nation. Nana's father was Tanzanian, and she was born in Dar es Salaam and did her early education there. In 1980 she joined 5th grade in the primary school in SOMAFCO, where she underwent all her subsequent schooling. Like many other SOMAFCO students in her position, Nana never set foot in South Africa until the banning of the ANC had been lifted and moves towards majority rule had begun.

CHAPTER 4

The Charlotte Maxeke Children's Centre

The origin of the Children's Centre

SOMAFCO was conceived as a school for students whose secondary education in South Africa had been disrupted by political activism and exile. However, it quickly became obvious that there were other educational needs that the ANC also had to address. There were increasing numbers of children born to those already in exile, including many to parents of mixed nationality. The children of parents who were studying overseas, or who had been sent abroad on political missions, had to be catered for. There were also children resulting from relationships between people who were not married or perhaps not even living together as couples, some of them school pupils, some from elsewhere, including combatants from MK. Caring for children would clearly divert the attention of activists, particularly women, from their duties within the movement. Also, many of the mothers were young and unprepared for parenthood, especially since they were far from supportive family networks. All this implied that there was a demand for care and education for children who had not yet reached the age for secondary education, 140 of them by late 1981. As an ANC document put it, it became vital to establish a centre 'where all our children born to the ANC cadres could be brought up within a collective while their parents pursued their revolutionary tasks'.

The ANC at Mazimbu thus found itself catering for a much wider range of educational needs than had been originally anticipated. Primary education was one such need. However, it was also necessary to cater for very young children. This chapter deals with the care and education of these infants to the age of approximately six, when they became the responsibility of the primary school. Such infants were with their mothers, spending some time in a crèche for their first two years, and then moving to the nursery school. Known as the Charlotte Maxeke Children's Centre, this complex was named after the woman activist who, in 1918, founded the Bantu Women's League. This later became the ANC Women's League. The aims of the complex were to provide facilities and education for infants, thus freeing mothers to pursue other activities for the movement. Also, as a planning document said in 1979, though the children were so young, the centre aimed to teach 'the children born in exile about the South Africa they had to know'. The ANC's Women's Section (WS) undertook to raise funds to build the centre.

Early days: from Morogoro to Mazimbu

In 1979, before facilities had been built at Mazimbu, a temporary crèche for infants up to the age of three, which included facilities for mothers, and a nursery school for children from three to six, were started in the town of Morogoro, six kilometres from the ANC complex.

The crèche in Morogoro used three separate buildings. Members of the WS like Ma Mercy and Mable Choabi were recruited to help the young mothers. Some of the women were from ANC bases in Angola or Zambia, and some were SOMAFCO students who had become pregnant. Some had more than one child. Not all mothers were present, however, and infants whose mothers were working for the ANC in various parts of the world were also cared for. In 1982, the crèche was moved to a part of the Mazimbu campus known as Tabora, after a town in Tanzania.

At first the nursery school children were also accommodated in Morogoro. As a temporary measure, Oswald Dennis found a garage in the town that was renovated to create an adequate environment for the children. Jane Dumasi was put in charge of the nursery school, assisted by, amongst others, two teachers from Sweden and Denmark who arrived in 1979. However, though there was a core of excellent teachers, physically the nursery school was inadequate. Children had to be transported daily to the converted garage from the ANC residences in Morogoro and from Mazimbu. On days of heavy rain, children from Mazimbu could not be transported to town because the fast-flowing Ngerengere River made the old wooden bridge – replaced by a modern structure in 1981 when the old one was swept away in a flood – unsafe. The nursery school was cramped, and did not provide sufficient room for the children to play. Teachers like Jane Dumasi were also haunted by the danger of accidents as the children were transported to and from the temporary nursery school through the erratic Morogoro traffic. Therefore, in 1981, even before the new buildings were complete, the nursery school moved to further temporary accommodation in a renovated sisal estate house at Mazimbu.

While the crèche and nursery school were operating in temporary accommodation, the WS had been working with the architect Spencer Hodgson and Project Director Oswald Dennis to build a centre at Mazimbu, financed by the Swedish Teachers' Union, which would accommodate both facilities. In 1984, the Charlotte Maxeke Children's Centre was completed, and the children and staff moved into the new premises, which were equipped with everything necessary to make the play and education of children productive and enjoyable.

Continuing the previous pattern, the centre was divided into two sections, the daycare centre or crèche and the nursery school or pre-school. The crèche consisted of three units each accommodating 18 children, and each with a playroom, covered verandah, garden, toilet facilities, and a two-bedroomed flat attached. In addition there was a sick bay for the children. The nursery school consisted of four units, each of which had a common room with tables for meals, an activity room which could serve as a classroom and playroom, a sleeping area, art room, verandah, a garden and toilet facilities. The four units could accommodate 36 children each and were grouped around a common playground equipped with swings and other playing facilities. Activity areas within an open-plan layout were agreed upon, with movable walls and shelves that could act as partitions allowing maximum flexibility. Oswald Dennis and his department had created a cheerful modern structure, in excellent surroundings.

The boarding sections of the new centre had matrons who lived on the premises in their own accommodation. They were assisted with cleaning, washing and cooking by Tanzanian women. The children who stayed in the boarding sections were those whose parents were either studying or deployed in other countries by the ANC. Some of the children were orphans who had lost their parents in exile. Children whose parents were at Mazimbu lived with them, except for those whose parents were secondary school students in the boarding section.

'The Charlottes'

When the crèche moved to its new premises in the Children's Centre, mothers from SOMAFCO, from MK camps or elsewhere continued to live at Tabora in what was called the Charlotte Maxeke Mother and Child Centre. Children who were old enough were brought across the campus to the crèche at the Children's Centre each day. The Mother and Child Centre, 'the Charlottes' as it became known, was partly staffed by the young mothers themselves, and partly by older women who were intended to give the support that would have been supplied by mothers and aunts at home in South Africa. The mothers stayed at the Charlottes until they gave birth to their children, and continued to live there until the child was two years old.

While the Charlottes was an attempt to provide as normal an environment as possible for the mothers and their children, there was much debate and dissatisfaction about the policy of removing women from formal education when they became pregnant. Mothers were expected to spend at least two years at the Charlottes before resuming previous activities, but in fact rarely resumed their education thereafter. Fathers were also removed from school and sent for an equivalent period to what was known as the Rehabilitation

4. Entrance to the Charlotte Maxeke Children's Centre

Centre at Dakawa, an isolated ANC base north of Mazimbu, to the farm, or elsewhere. The rationale was that the father would contribute his labour towards the upkeep of the movement that supported the child. However, another reason for sending such students to Dakawa was that teachers tended to want only current students in the school dormitories, so as to safeguard the atmosphere of study. Since the ANC automatically deregistered those who had impregnated their partners, it followed that they should not remain in the dormitories. However, an internal report in 1986 considered that the Rehabilitation Centre at Dakawa was 'not capable of maintaining the student life desired by SOMAFCO', and for the men concerned, as for the women, this policy seems to have severely disrupted educational progress.

While no official stigma was intended by this policy, there was undoubtedly an unofficial one. Two years in the Charlottes or at the Rehabilitation Centre was regarded by some as, if not a form of punishment, at least a way of isolating those who had behaved in an unacceptable way, while caring for them and their babies. For some, this policy affected their view of the whole educational enterprise. For instance, according to Bessie Netsianda, a young woman who arrived at SOMAFCO in 1981, speaking of mothers who became pregnant in countries like Angola, 'most used to think that if you go to Tanzania, you are going to serve a punishment.' However, she reflects an ambivalence experienced by many in this situation when she adds that two years in the Charlottes could not really be considered a punishment as a woman, after all, has a duty to look after her child.

It could be said that the ANC acted conservatively in this sphere. There was controversy about this within the organisation. Some saw it as a necessary and egalitarian policy that treated young men and women equally. Others saw it as originating in a complex of hierarchical and moralistic South African attitudes, censorious of the sexual freedom of young people and vindictive towards potential young couples. This remained one of the unresolved issues at SOMAFCO.

Learning

There was a conscious attempt to educate in both the crèche and nursery school. Pre-primary school children were introduced to various subjects and skills, ranging from those close to play, like identifying colours and drawing, to those that laid the foundation for primary school education, like elementary arithmetic, writing and reading. The primary school principal had frequent meetings with his counterpart at the nursery school to discuss the relationship between programmes at the two institutions. It was expected, for instance, that children should have basic skills in writing, English language and arithmetic when they moved up to the primary school. This was more than was demanded by the Bantu Education system at this stage in a black child's education.

Much of the routine of good early childhood education took place at the two divisions of the Children's Centre. There was storytelling with older people from the Mazimbu community invited to share stories with the children, creating a bond between adults and the young and broadening the child's knowledge. These stories were told in South African languages, helping children become familiar with languages that they might otherwise not have heard in the exile environment. The SOMAFCO cultural group would often visit the nursery school to demonstrate South African dances and other activities. In these ways, the children were introduced to aspects of the life they would face on return to their homeland.

The nursery school was equipped with tricycles, balls, and all the usual material of a well-equipped nursery. Full use was made of the outside play area. There were also more directly educational toys, such as puzzles of various kinds. As the children pored over them, music was played. Individual activities such as this allowed teachers to estimate the skills and level of development of children, and react accordingly. With small groups and a caring, participatory style of teaching, it was common to see a teacher intervening when a child needed assistance, through, for instance, herself doing whatever simple task was requested of the child. Teaching by example and learning by emulation were at the heart of pre-primary education at SOMAFCO.

The visual approach was emphasised, and there was extensive use of equipment such as overhead projectors. Education shaded into entertainment when videos were shown to the children on Fridays. *Sleeping Beauty*, *Town Mouse*, *The Lion*, *Tales of the Sea* and *The Little Prince* were favourites. Occasionally, mistakes were made, as happened in April 1987 when the children were shown the war film *Dirty Dozen*. SOMAFCO Education Co-ordinator Marius Schoon protested vehemently against the showing of this gratuitously violent film to small children, some of whom had been traumatised by the military activities of the then South African regime.

Indeed, trauma was not unusual among people in exile, including children. Some nursery school children had undergone horrific experiences. Some had witnessed the killing of their parents in bomb explosions, or had experienced events like the Lesotho raid of 1982. Others had witnessed 'necklacing', that is, people being burnt to death with a tyre and petrol in a form of mob retribution. According to Jane Dumasi, such children tended to be emotional and aggressive, behaviour that was often noticed in a child's play, when his or her suppressed anger and frustration might be directed against a toy.

Apart from the obviously traumatised, there were other young children who seemed withdrawn at school, such as those whose parents or parent had left them at SOMAFCO in order to undertake ANC missions elsewhere, as students or otherwise. Such children tended to be difficult or upset as a result of separation from the mother and father, at least at first. Eventually, in most cases they got used to the situation, became attached to the caregivers and behaved normally. Such children were constantly reassured that the separation from their parents was only temporary.

As everywhere, there were dysfunctional families at SOMAFCO, in which children suffered in a cold and unfeeling environment, or even through physical violence. Teachers observed the children and if they identified any who were isolated or lacked concentration they made further inquiries. Such children were sometimes removed from their parents by the school authorities and placed in the boarding section of the school. The parents concerned received counselling and their child would return to the family environment when there appeared to be a change of attitude.

SOMAFCO teachers received formal training in the education of pre-school children, and in dealing with those needing special attention. The ANC had access to such training at Mindolo Ecumenical Training Centre near Ndola, Zambia, and in Sweden. At Mindolo, pre-school teachers, women and men, studied various subjects in the theory and practice of infant education. While some practical teaching experience was done in Zambian pre-schools, trainees at Mindolo were often allocated to the Children's Centre in SOMAFCO for their main practical teaching experiences, with their supervisors travelling from Zambia to evaluate them. Even teachers who trained in Sweden did their main classroom practice sessions at SOMAFCO. This allowed the trainee teachers an opportunity to put into practice what they had learned and also enabled them to re-establish contact and exchange ideas with the SOMAFCO teaching staff, and meet with the children whom they would eventually teach.

Mindolo also enabled ANC trainee teachers to broaden their political horizons. Pre-school teachers from Swapo, the main Namibian liberation movement, also studied at Mindolo. In this way the political and educational ideas of the two liberation movements fighting the South African regime were explored. Mindolo also exposed trainee teachers to religious concepts. The ANC was happy to send its teachers to Mindolo, an institution with a definite Christian ethos. Though they came from a secular institution with many Marxist influences, SOMAFCO student teachers at Mindolo studied Christian Living as part of their curriculum.

Some of those sent to colleges like Mindolo to acquire expertise in pre-school education were males. Farida Mussagy, the former principal of the nursery school, remembers four male teachers being sent to training colleges. This perhaps helped to replace the absent father figure in the lives of some of the children, and contrasts with Bantu Education, which removed male teachers at primary level, and left pupils without male role models.

Mussagy herself undertook international trips, visiting institutions and individuals with expertise in pre-school education. Her first trip was to the GDR in 1987, where she spent three weeks visiting pre-schools. In return, a German expert spent six weeks working with the Children's Centre staff at SOMAFCO. There followed another trip, this time to France, where she studied school administration. She also familiarised herself with pre-school teaching in Tanzania. Experiences such as these provided her with valuable insights and expertise.

The school attempted to widen the outlook of the children to the maximum extent. Learning about and caring for their world started at the children's centre itself, where the youngsters were encouraged to take as much responsibility as possible for the upkeep and tidiness of the complex. Excursions beyond their immediate environment formed an important part of the learning process. These were both within the extensive boundaries of the Mazimbu settlement and to places elsewhere. On the campus, children were taken to visit and learn from the farm, the furniture factory and all the other institutions scattered around the complex. Other trips were purely for entertainment. There were picnics, for instance, usually held at the foot of the mountains west of the Mazimbu complex.

There were also excursions away from Mazimbu, to Morogoro and Dar es Salaam, and to game reserves, parks and beaches. In Morogoro, which was six kilometers from Mazimbu, there was a resort called 'Rocky Gardens', which had lawns and what one ex-teacher calls a 'small waterfall'. This was a popular site for excursions by SOMAFCO students at all levels. An example is the nursery school expedition to the Rocky Gardens on 3 and 4 October 1987. Because there were about 100 children, they were split into Saturday and Sunday groups. Snacks – soft drinks, bananas, ice cream – were prepared for the children. The school provided everything, including the entrance fee.

There was an excellent game reserve at Mikumi, in the Morogoro District, some 100 kilometres to the southwest of Mazimbu. The nursery school children were taken there for visits. The children were also taken now and again to beaches along the Indian Ocean coast, as well as to places such as the airport in Dar es Salaam.

Play

Play is crucial for children everywhere. It helps the child to integrate with others and learn about his or her abilities and limitations. Every effort was made to foster such behaviour, and the environment was as encouraging as possible. SOMAFCO children had access to many toys. There was an extensive playground for the children with facilities including swings and paddling pools, welcome in a hot country such as Tanzania. The primary school children were also encouraged to make use of the outside facilities of the pre-school. This pleased the pre-school children as they got an opportunity to mix with older children and it enabled them to learn from the older ones. The children also had their own small gardens behind the pre-school, where, with the assistance of their teachers, they grew flowers and vegetables.

Children at SOMAFCO were exposed to a variety of languages, including Zulu, Sotho, Swahili and English. Although in class children were taught in English, in the playground they used African languages, unlike the secondary school where students were expected to talk English even outside class. Zulu was the dominant language at the Children's Centre, though most children also knew how to speak Swahili.

SOMAFCO, including the Children's Centre, was a racially mixed society. Farida Mussagy remembers twin white boys at the nursery. Some volunteer workers from countries like Holland and Denmark also came with their children to SOMAFCO. She asserts that children of pre-school age never thought of

5. In the playground of the Children's Centre

themselves as white or black. Diana Cumberledge, the mother of the twins, was a primary school teacher who came to SOMAFCO in 1983. As her boys settled into the Children's Centre, they mastered the Zulu language, so that even at home they sometimes responded in Zulu when spoken to in English, and in some instances mixed the two languages. The contrast with the educational situation in the South Africa of the time is clear.

Despite these undoubted successes, the Children's Centre had its problems. Staff meetings discussed the numerous issues that confront any such institution, such as the various activities conducted by teachers in class, the physical and emotional needs of the children and problems concerning illness. However, a major source of concern and constant subject of anxious discussion were staff shortages, and the resulting overcrowding. Teachers would sometimes be called for duty elsewhere by the ANC without being immediately replaced and without, the teachers often felt, sufficient concern for the welfare of the children. The remaining teachers were then left to grapple with large groups. According to Jane Dumasi, overcrowding was exacerbated because the ANC often required children to be left behind when parents were sent on missions for the organisation. Adults who went for studies were rarely, if ever, allowed to bring their children with them, and these children generally ended up for lengthy periods as the responsibility of the Children's Centre or the primary school.

One way of dealing with staff shortages was to ask other departments to assist. For instance, students awaiting scholarships played an important role as temporary teachers at the Children's Centre. Thuse Kabileng, for example, reinforced the nursery staff in 1985 whilst awaiting a scholarship. Though this was a help to the pre-primary school, such people were untrained. Even where they had a talent for dealing with young children, they were unlikely to make an excellent job of it, and the professional staff had to spend valuable time, which might otherwise have been spent with the children, in mentoring them.

CHAPTER 5

The primary school

Like the crèche and nursery school, the primary school at Mazimbu was not part of the original plan for the complex, and in the beginning the ANC did not realise that there would soon be a need for schooling at this level. The exiled young people from 1976 were mostly of secondary school age and level, though some of the first primary school children aged between 7 and 16 came on their own from South Africa. The primary school, therefore, was created in an ad hoc manner to answer pressing needs, and in some ways remained the poor relation in the Mazimbu family of educational institutions.

The formation of the primary school

Once the ANC began to consider the question of an educational institution, it was realised that, apart from the influx of youth from South Africa itself, there was also a problem in providing for the children of ANC cadres who had left the country as early as the 1960s and who had often married Tanzanians. Those in the Morogoro area tended to live in the town or the surrounding villages with their wives and children, some of whom were of school-going age. In other circumstances, such children would probably have simply become part of the surrounding Tanzanian population. The creation of the primary school, however, made it possible for these families to cling to and elaborate a South African identity. A perplexing issue was when some Tanzanian wives of South Africans enrolled children that the ANC suspected were not their biological children.

Terry Bell and his wife, Barbara, were key figures in the early history of the primary school. Bell, a South African member of the ANC based in New Zealand, was asked by Oliver Tambo to take on the task of organising the primary school. The Bells left New Zealand in 1980, followed soon by a container stocked to the brim with educational materials that they thought would be of use in Tanzania. Construction at SOMAFCO was at its early stages, and teaching began in one of the old sisal estate houses. The house was renovated, though the space was not sufficient and a tent was erected to serve as a fifth classroom. Even this did not solve all the problems, however, and overcrowding meant that in the early days some of the children had to attend local Tanzanian schools.

Overcrowding was not the only problem that faced the primary school at this time. Language was also crucial. At first most of the children at the primary school spoke Swahili because of their background in Tanzania. Swahili was widely spoken on campus and at home, and naturally the primary school children resorted to what was in fact their mother tongue. Thus English was spoken in class only during school hours. Among other languages spoken in the school were Xhosa, Zulu, Sotho, Tswana, Portuguese, Bemba, Nyanja, Afrikaans, Danish and English, and these languages were mixed and borrowed from in a rich linguistic pattern.

Although Swahili can be said to have dominated in the early days, Zulu later overshadowed it, though more slowly at the primary school than elsewhere. One reason for this is that as more and more South Africans came to Mazimbu, the complex began to reflect the immediate South African background rather than the mixture of South African and Tanzanian elements that was characteristic of those who had been in exile for longer. This linguistic and cultural mixture was strongest and lasted longest at the primary school, where many children were from such backgrounds. The secondary school, however, was more oriented towards the South African environment from the first, because of the predominance of recent exiles, who had not established strong ties with the local community.

The language question was a concern throughout the life of the primary school. The difficulties of linguistic diversity were circumvented by concentrating on the English language. Thami Mali, for example, who joined the school in 1988 from MK, says language problems were tackled by assisting pupils with English, through remedial classes where necessary.

Terry Bell's educational philosophy

SOMAFCO was a complex educational experiment, moulded by many practical and ideological considerations. It was intended to be a challenge and reproach to Bantu Education; nonetheless, many of the staff had been taught in precisely that Bantu Education system, or earlier, in Christian mission schools, which, despite their opposition to and eventual destruction by the apartheid system, were not often progressive in their educational thinking and practice. On this basis were laid various streams of educational thinking, generally from the left of the educational and political spectrum. These streams of thought were themselves far from uniform. They included models derived from Soviet educational practice, generally didactic and authoritarian, with the aim of creating what was often referred to, with a complete disregard for gender sensitivity, as the 'new man'. The 'new man' also appeared in the educational discourse at SOMAFCO. However, less hierarchical and more libertarian educational ideas stressing freedom and equality, and stemming from thinkers and practitioners as diverse as Rousseau, John Dewey, AS Neill and Paulo Freire, also echoed through the ANC's educational 'broad church'. The early days of the primary school provided a laboratory for some of these ideas.

Terry Bell believed that children were not empty vessels waiting to be filled with information, but should be seen as individuals who would be helped to learn for themselves. They had to discover things on their own with the teacher acting as a mentor and guide rather than as an instructor. The influence of Freire's ideas is apparent here. Pupils were to be creative and independent in thought, able to find their way as learners independently, with the teacher simply helping and guiding. Children should see the world through their own eyes and not through the eyes of a teacher.

But Bell did not only draw from Freire, nor was his theory of education based on one particular philosopher. He argues that he drew from a variety of ideas in developing his argument for democratic schooling. He mentions for example, Anton Makerenko, a Soviet educational theorist who seems out of tune with Bell's practice, but whose ideas on the abolition of examinations he found useful. Bell's school simply issued progress reports noting what the student had achieved rather than formal examinations. Thus pupils were not categorised as having passed or failed.

The third Neduc conference stipulated that a child should be exposed to different learning experiences, building him or her holistically and producing a critical person who could be expected to co-operate with others in the learning process. This co-operation between students would help to produce self-disciplined pupils and to achieve a sound learning environment within the school. The question was: how would these admirable aims be achieved in practice?

Terry Bell approached his task believing that pupils should have as much freedom and responsibility as possible. He did not, for instance, believe in the division of students into classes or grades, and in this he was drawing not only on a long tradition of educational thinking, but also his and his wife's experience of experimental schools in New Zealand which were trying to put 'democratic schooling' into practice. 'Democratic schooling' involved freedom, but with restraint, suggesting, as Bell states, that freedom to do as he or she might please should be constrained by the requirement that one person's freedom should not affect that of others.

This is shown in the following example: at one point, nine pupils asked to be allowed to go outside to play during school hours. Bell allowed this, as, in contrast to the secondary school, compulsory attendance was not required. The nine pupils were thus granted their freedom to play. But when they came back for water and later lunch, these were denied, as they had not been part of schooling on that day. They were, in other words, infringing upon the freedom of those who had remained in class. They quickly returned to school of their own accord. Bell says as a result of the policy of voluntary attendance, they achieved over 90 per cent attendance with only a few absentees due to sickness.

Everyone was considered to be equal in the primary school. This included the approach to tasks like cleaning. Teachers and pupils were expected to clean classrooms and the rest of the buildings, thus, it was hoped, strengthening and equalising the relationship between them. It is striking that children also played a role in decision-making at the primary school. The pupils voted even Bell, the principal, into power after he requested that they elect the chairperson of the school. In this spirit, Bell preferred to be called 'chairman' of the primary school, with all the democratic implications of that term. Pupils' power to make decisions even extended to the suspension and expulsion of school members, including both teachers and students. One teacher, for example, was suspended by a school meeting for refusing to take part in cleaning. A decision was also made to expel a pupil from the school for stealing, though the case was reviewed later. Clearly, issues like this raise fascinating questions about the relationship between children and adults, the purpose of education, the limits of liberty, human rights and many others.

Bell's ideas about equality extended to other areas of life as well. He was upset that the students' food ration was poorer than that of teachers. Also, when it was proposed that he would receive a small stipend of 2 000 shillings per month, his wife Barbara 1 500, and other teachers much less, the Bells decided to divide their stipends equally amongst the teaching staff of the primary school.

Learning

The test of any educational philosophy is how it operates in practice. As has been seen, Bell did not support a graded system of education in which a child proceeds annually, and, he would have said, mechanically, from class to class. His belief was that a child could achieve to the maximum only if enabled to succeed in successive tasks that confront him or her. He devised an organisational pattern that he felt implemented this belief.

Taking advantage of the accommodation available in the sisal estate house and the tent, Bell divided the students into five 'family groups', namely the Luthuli, Ngoyi, Moshoeshoe, Sikonyela and Kotane families. In turn, each family had to elect a commander and deputy commander, who were expected to lead their groups.

Bell thought that the priority was for children to acquire the English language and become numerate. These were life skills that would provide the basis for

6. Primary school children on an outing

whatever further aims an individual might wish to accomplish. Games like Scrabble were used to encourage language acquisition. This approach also applied to mathematics where quizzes were used in the education of children. Students were expected to participate during the learning process and they were given what it was hoped were achievable aims from which they would then make further advances, such as completing one set of mathematical problems or reading a whole book. Children who performed better than others were given more difficult tasks. This implies that children did not have to wait for a year to go to the next class for more challenging activities. Indeed, there were no classes for them to be promoted to, and they simply moved from educational phase to phase, tackling new tasks within a particular area and branching out to explore new areas.

In tune with the school's ideology of co-operation and mutual support, pupils were expected to assist their peers wherever possible. The characteristic role of the teachers was to assist and supplement this process; indeed, the term 'group leader' was used rather than 'teacher'. While these leaders had their own group to which they would give most attention, where possible they would also assist others with their work. When there were enough staff members available, groups would be further subdivided to provide the maximum personal attention. Any group member was allowed to join another group, though only with the approval of the pupil's group peers.

Apart from teachers or group leaders, there was a co-ordinator who acted as a floating group leader. He or she would replace absent group leaders, and was also expected to pay particular attention to individuals or small units of two or three drawn from the established groupings, where this was considered necessary. Decisions about such matters were taken at the weekly staff meetings at which group leaders presented reports about their groups' progress.

The Bell era at SOMAFCO primary school had its ups and downs. Though they stayed at SOMAFCO for only two years, they had definite achievements. Amongst these was discipline and co-operation amongst children from different backgrounds, in this way fulfilling the expectations of Neduc. Petty theft and other misdemeanours declined. As a sense of self-discipline developed, the children managed to function effectively as groups in their respective 'families' or while working as individuals. Progress was also made in the acquisition of English and numeracy, and learners were successfully introduced to the basics of subjects like biology and geography.

However, Terry Bell was criticised for how he ran the school. Tim Maseko, the SOMAFCO principal at the time, began to ask where the graded classes were and to which forms students were allocated. He also demanded to know how many of the students had failed and passed, to which Bell responded, in accord with his belief that examinations were misleading and harmful, that none had failed and none had passed. He said that all that was needed was a primary leaving certificate which one could produce to enter the secondary school, implying – in a way reminiscent of outcomes-based educational theories – that no one could claim a certain grade or position at school, only skills which one could exercise at a certain level. This sort of approach was not popular with the school authorities, and by the time the Bells left SOMAFCO they knew that their system would be phased out.

On 1 May 1982, the Bells resigned from the school for a number of reasons that included the claim that there was hypocrisy, petty corruption, use of corporal punishment and incompetence amongst the school authorities. There was also, Terry Bell said in a letter to Tambo, 'suppression of revolutionary dialogue and this gave birth to tyranny,' and he claimed that there were various abuses, such as flogging (even of women), night raids on people suspected of disloyalty, and brutality towards those accused of smoking dagga.

There seems no doubt that the Bells' educational libertarianism merged with a political outlook inimical to those controlling SOMAFCO, and that in the hothouse atmosphere of Mazimbu, political differences could merge with personal irritations and differences in lifestyle and fester into bitter conflict. Bell felt that students were not receiving the type of treatment received by teachers and adults in general on campus. When the teaching staff held parties, for instance, the Bells would not participate because they considered the party-goers were enjoying unmerited privileges. Bell even considered leading a sort of internal coup against the school authorities, but dropped the idea because he realised that this might mean, or be construed as meaning, revolt against the movement in general. It is perhaps not surprising that the Bells' stay at SOMAFCO was exciting, turbulent, and relatively short.

The new primary school

When Bell left SOMAFCO in 1982, his ideas about a school without grades and his particular version of democratic schooling also disappeared. This is not to say that the school reacted into conservatism, but rather that another, less libertarian, vision of what a progressive school should be, began to predominate. No doubt the growth in scale from the small student numbers under the Bells to 230 in 1984 and approximately 350 in the late 1980s, encouraged more conventional school organisation; arguably only such a relatively predictable framework could be expected to cope with the financial insecurity and reliance on voluntary service that increasingly characterised the school as it expanded. The departure of Bell also removed the lynchpin from a form of educational organisation particularly dependent on the force of a powerful personality.

The crucial figure at the primary school in the period after Bell was Dennis September, affectionately known as 'Babu' September. September, with his wife Hazel, inherited the educational ethos of the coloured schools of Cape Town, and that of the public schools of Canada, where they had been in exile. He had been a physical education teacher, and under his leadership sport had an important, though extra-curricular, place in the school. He also believed that teachers should know their pupils thoroughly, and he therefore emphasised continuous assessment.

Henceforth, the primary school curriculum came to be defined in accordance with the traditional approach to schooling, though content was different from that in contemporary South Africa. Teachers in all grades taught a fairly conventional range of primary school subjects. The teaching of geography shows how a subject-based approach was, however, combined with sometimes novel content. As well as teaching conventional aspects like the physical structure of South Africa and the commercial and mineral wealth of the country, some sections dealt with South Africa's political geography. In one Grade 7 test, for example, pupils were asked to name (in a diagram) the pieces of land allocated to blacks. They also had to explain the *Land Act* of 1913 and briefly define the policy of apartheid.

This approach can also be seen in the children's journals. In these, the primary school pupils often revealed their thinking about township life in South Africa, including their ideas about the terrorism against township dwellers. One pupil wrote:

> South Africa is having political and economical problems and its spending a lot of money buying weapons to kill blacks wich [*sic*] are trying their best to get freedom. Meanwhile South Africa's rand has lost its value. Many Africans are being killed and Boers care less about the killing of blacks. The SADF has no other work but to kill and arrest Africans.

Students at the primary school were now divided by grades, a return to the traditional schooling which Bell regarded as rigid, but which September considered necessary if the school was to interact in a satisfactory way with the secondary school. Generally, students were placed in grades by chronological age level. Some students in the early- and mid- teens were placed in the highest grade. It was realised later that their performance actually meant that they should have been placed two, three, or even four grades lower. In January 1984, some students who were promoted to secondary level were sent back to the primary school, probably due to poor performance at school.

The inappropriate placing of students and the shifting of some from higher to lower grades has a further implication. Most of these children were pupils during Terry Bell's era. The unstructured nature of Bell's school compared to the conventional grade hierarchy did not make it easy to know where students should be placed. It is not surprising then to see pupils being moved from one grade to another, indicating uncertainty about real levels of achievement. This may indicate the essential incompatibility of Bell's system with the new but more 'traditional' approach.

The disappearance of Bell's philosophy of education soon after his departure, and the immediate grading of classes, implies that the authorities did not support his beliefs. Support for this view comes from one of the teachers, Pethu Serote, who says that this approach was bound to create problems, as by downplaying formal organisation and grading at this early stage, problems would inevitably arise later when students confronted the reality of hierarchical education. As a result they ran the risk of not being accepted by institutions organised in this way.

However, although in the end the primary school followed traditional methods of schooling in terms of school organisation, and even to some extent curriculum, the focus on the building of a new person through education remained, with the same expectations of responsibility, co-operation, initiative, self-discipline and patriotism by the pupils still regarded as important.

These norms were inculcated by September and other dedicated staff such as Freda Katz, who arrived in 1984.

It is noticeable, for instance, that even though the school was now organised in grades, teaching methods did not alter completely from those during Bell's time. The school continued to encourage students to be critical and to work co-operatively. For example, a teacher, Thami Mali, explains that learning from and with peers was encouraged, generally through the formation of groups in class. Often, capable students were paired with those who were less competent to help uplift the weak ones. Pupils were encouraged to read ahead in preparation for taking an active part in the next lesson, and had access to the books and other facilities that made this possible. They were also encouraged to present their findings in class, with as little assistance from the teacher as possible, thus helping them to be critical, self-confident and independent, and linguistically competent. There was thus a real effort to implement what Freire refers to as 'problem posing' education.

Another teacher, Diana Cumberledge, shares Mali's views. She says that history, for instance, was taught in a way that encouraged students to see themselves as part of it. Pupils explored their own family history and how this fitted into the larger picture. In this way history was seen not as the deeds of great men and women, but rather as everyone's collective story. The idea of the teacher as narrator, preaching in front of the class, was downplayed, and attending to individual problems was stressed. This was particularly so because some pupils had serious difficulties, particularly with language, since most primary school children at the time spoke Swahili. Pupils were encouraged to acquire language skills through, for example, the use of drama.

Primary school children were to some extent introduced to 'education with production', aimed at bridging the gap between mental and manual labour, though the main focus in this area was on the secondary school students. Primary school students were encouraged to keep their own gardens, and were involved in maintaining and improving the school environment. They also established a small orchard to help teach botany in a practical way, and planted trees around the campus, though more for landscaping than in a serious effort at afforestation. In art and craft lessons and clubs, articles such as lampshades and fittings and furniture were produced for their dormitory units. The children and their teachers also renovated certain teaching areas, painting the buildings inside and out. Thus the 1984 report closes by saying that, 'in this regard we have tried to instill into our young people the dignity of labour'. However, as will be seen, as the 1980s progressed the concept of education with production was dying away and the primary school students visited places like the furniture factory, the electrical department and the farm to see how they operated, but did not themselves participate in this work.

Many oral informants indicate that the primary school was not given priority at SOMAFCO, though Dennis September and his colleagues fought hard for its interests. Diana Cumberledge, for instance, says the primary school was still developing when she joined it in 1983. There was a serious lack of teachers as well as an absence of textbooks and the school was also working on its curriculum. Some of this was perhaps inevitable in the circumstances. However, she says that though some, particularly the volunteer teachers, regarded the primary school as being at the core of education, in general it was somewhat marginalised.

The primary school shared fully the staffing problems that afflicted the secondary school. In many instances, even where a teacher was obtained, he or she would be unqualified, usually being a SOMAFCO graduate awaiting a scholarship. On one occasion, in 1984, the Grade 6 students were left without a teacher for about three months. As a result, effective teaching could not take place. When a teacher was identified for this group, he left the school as soon as he was awarded a scholarship.

Given the pressures on staffing, disruption was caused even when teachers went for further training in primary education. For example, when five experienced and qualified teachers went for training in Sweden in 1984, this had a drastic effect on the school programme. Pupils were left unattended. Though some remaining teachers helped where they could, their main responsibility was to their own pupils. For the authorities to have allowed five teachers to leave on scholarships at one time was surely a blunder.

It seems to have been assumed that a scholarship offer automatically took precedence over the needs of primary school children. Teachers who left on scholarships usually informed the administration at short notice about their departure, and often failed to leave class records behind, leaving their replacements floundering. Even when a replacement was found, it usually took some two to three weeks for a new teacher to adapt before he or she could be left alone to teach. The new teachers, who were generally untrained, were often a burden on the qualified teachers who had to help them. All this resulted in a lack of continuity, partly ameliorated by the regular appointment of teachers from the GDR and Sweden, such as the German volunteer teacher Gudrun Pilz, who was deployed at the primary school in 1987 to teach Grades 6 and 7. But the problem was never really overcome.

The primary school also faced problems of overcrowding. The movements of people in exile, many of them in essence forced migrations, made the situation worse. The case of 30 students who joined SOMAFCO from Mozambique in 1985 is an example. They were casualties of the Nkomati Accord of 1984 between South Africa and Mozambique in terms of which the Mozambican government was expected to oust the liberation movements from their country. These young people appeared at Mazimbu, were formed into another Grade 6 class and studied under trees. In 1985 the primary school moved to new premises, having previously been in two crowded and unsuitable houses, but Babu September states that they still faced overcrowding, noting that primary school numbers exceeded those of the secondary school.

Nevertheless, the primary school did a remarkable job. Perhaps the most critical area for the primary school children was not the school itself, but rather parental care. These small children, many of them with their parents away on ANC missions in other parts of Africa or the world, were accommodated in dormitories, as were the older secondary pupils. Equipment, such as the bicycles from Holland that visitors saw children riding around the compound, was plentiful, but observers agree that there was not enough of the high-quality supervision and care that might have gone some way to substitute for their absent parents. There were attempts to institute foster programmes where families took children into their homes during weekends, but these appear not to have worked very well. Certainly, these young children were, in an indirect but very real way, victims of the social disruption brought about by apartheid.

CHAPTER 6

The secondary school

The secondary school was the heart of the Mazimbu complex. It had originally been assumed that there would only be a school at this level. Even when the complex expanded, the secondary school in many ways continued to set the tone for the rest of Mazimbu.

Teaching started at the secondary school in 1978. At first, a handful of students crowded into 'Odessa', an old estate house, supplemented by tents. In 1980 teaching moved for six months to 'Luanda', the new Unit 1 area, with teaching carried out temporarily in one of the three new dormitory buildings. At this stage, the key teacher, who remained a stalwart of SOMAFCO until the very end of the school, was 'Uncle' Slim Zindela. Many other teachers at this early stage were only qualified at matriculation level, coming and going according to the many demands of the movement.

Educational activities of students and their conduct at school

Superficially, everyday life at SOMAFCO bore some resemblance to life at any British-style boarding school. The secondary school was organised into five forms. As in most such schools, students were expected to attend classes five days a week, from Monday to Friday, and could only stay away if they produced a doctor's note. This was one of the rules enshrined in the students' code of conduct, which defined the boundaries of acceptable behaviour. The archetypal battle between students and staff about smoking, emblematic of discipline and challenges to discipline, seems to have been waged as vigorously at SOMAFCO as in any conventional boarding school. Students were forbidden to smoke in the classrooms or school grounds. However, rules such as these sometimes had to be modified in the face of reality. To some extent, as all over Africa, adults were willing to be treated as classificatory adolescents and subject themselves to the sort of rules that seem to characterise institutions of this type, even where, in the case of SOMAFCO, some students were as old as 32. Some were MK cadres who were returning to school, or students who had been detained in South Africa and upon release had gone into exile to continue their interrupted education. Thus, in 1986 the concession was made that students over the age of 18 could smoke at the end of Blocks 1, 2, 9 and 10. Even here, however, everything possible was done to isolate the smokers and play down this inconsistency in school rules.

In theory, school uniform was prescribed at SOMAFCO. Students were expected to appear smartly and cleanly dressed in blue and white. Uniform tends to be associated with officialdom and a conservative type of education, as it has been and still is in South Africa, where it has long been the norm. It might be expected that it would not be prescribed in a liberation school. In practice the dress code was not rigidly established or insisted upon, but it remains interesting that this aspect of conventional schooling was reflected in the school rules. The argument that school uniform levels out differences between students from varied backgrounds surely did not apply in an environment where all were exiles, all depended on the ANC for the necessities of life, and all were at the same economic level.

SOMAFCO classrooms operated as in most schools, with teachers in a range of roles from manager to chairperson. Teachers were encouraged to vary their teaching styles, and many certainly attempted to create a learning environment where critical questioning was the norm. It is difficult to extrapolate from lesson plans and observation reports, but, on the whole, those that survive give an impression of teachers who made an attempt to teach in a stimulating way. Typical is the principal's comment on one lesson in 1990 that 'what is impressive is that the students ask and answer questions freely and in an orderly and acceptable manner'.

Students were encouraged to take responsibility for their own learning. For instance, often, during the last ten minutes of a class period, they would divide themselves into groups and elect someone who had performed well at his or her work during the period. This student would then explain to the others how he or she had managed to succeed. This classroom style was markedly different from that typical of Bantu Education, where students were expected to assimilate material passively. There were also form commanders, who were elected every year and between them made up the Commanders' Council. The job of form commanders was to represent their fellow students in all that concerned their academic work.

Apart from attending classes and using the library, the students also had to attend compulsory evening studies, which took place from Sunday to Thursday evenings between 19h00 and 21h00. These sessions were held in the lecture halls and were monitored by teachers. This gave the students time to look at their schoolwork and, unusually from the point of view of many schools, they were allowed and encouraged to consult with each other as they studied.

Of course, as in all schools, there could be rowdiness, insubordination and other disruptive behaviour, whether because of poor teaching or for some other reason. We get glimpses from the records of classes such as one in May 1990 where the teacher lost all control, with the students writing, reading and talking as the mood took them. Sometimes fighting occurred, or students used insulting language, which the school code of conduct did not permit. A letter of 10 March 1983 records that a Form 1 student attacked another for 'addressing the class in an abusive language'.

Although students were expected to be punctual, late-coming and absenteeism, and 'dodging', that is, students coming to school but then leaving before the final bell, sometimes occurred. Because students were not allowed to be absent without producing sick slips, those who were illegally absent would forge these slips to present to the school authorities. For example, two students were reported not to have attended the morning assembly on 22 July 1982. They were said to have 'spent the morning at Cde Ndlovu's store', allegedly smoking dagga.

At SOMAFCO, unlike most boarding schools, it was not even possible to get away at the end of the term. Home, family and neighbourhood friends were far away and inaccessible. In this introverted environment what might seem like small problems could fester and eventually cause serious disruption. Ways of dealing with such problems were thus vital, and it seems that the mechanisms for doing so were open and democratic, and did not unduly privilege the teachers. Meetings where the complaints and views of students were heard, chaired by the class teacher, were held to air such problems before they became unmanageable. At these meetings academic difficulties and sometimes the ineffectiveness of particular teachers were discussed, and it was the duty of the class teacher to report such grievances to the school authorities. Teachers of all forms jointly discussed matters affecting students in general in 'form meetings'.

There were formal and informal ways of defusing tension and conflict. Relations between students were oiled by what they called 'class parties', which were usually organised at the end of each term or at the end of the year. Classmates were expected to contribute a certain amount of money to buy snacks. During these parties, which were held in the residences, students would play music, dance and socialise.

Rewards and punishments

The basic incentive to succeed in class was promotion to the next level. However, to encourage good performance and keep morale high, there were awards and incentives of various kinds, not all of which were based on purely academic effort and success. They were also given for cultural and sporting achievement, the cleanliness of classrooms, and good conduct.

Once a year the school authorities organised a function to reward students for their performance in various fields. The Emulation Committee, which consisted of the principal and other members of the school administration, recommended meritorious students for awards. For example, in 1982 there was a function to reward the best students in each form from Forms 1 to 5 by giving each of them an 'individual present'. One of Nathaniel Mosipa's teachers recommended him for an award because of his cheerful personality and regular school attendance: 'He is well disciplined in class and a very simple comrade.' In 1985, two Form 3 students were recommended by teachers for awards because 'they have proved themselves to be a good exemplary [*sic*] to their entire class, source of inspiration when we come to discipline and hard workers inside the class.' Every year there was a debate between Don Ngakane, a geography teacher and Secondary School Principal from 1990 to 1991, and Slim Zindela, about rewards. Zindela disapproved of 'emulation', which Ngakane supported, and felt that the traditional notion of prize-giving was preferable. Behind this disagreement stood differing conceptions of education, as primarily a collaborative process with success measured in terms of co-operative norms, or as a competition wherein merit would be graded and rewarded.

At the end of a student's time at SOMAFCO was the lure, sometimes a chimerical one, of furthering their studies in other countries. However, most in the end did get to continue with further studies, though, as in all educational institutions, not all got to pursue what they wanted to do or where they wanted to do it. Apart from such scholarships, some students had opportunities to visit other countries on educational visits or as part of cultural performance groups. They mixed with people from elsewhere and saw at first-hand the possibilities of the wider world.

There was an official voice on what was and was not acceptable behaviour at SOMAFCO, and this was expressed in the school code of conduct. There was also a formal structure for dealing with disciplinary cases, culminating in the Disciplinary Committee. What were considered serious cases of violence, theft, sexual misconduct, insulting language and the like often ended up in this arena, as well as episodes like the smoking of dagga, which the school authorities considered serious, but about which opinions might have differed amongst at least some of the students. However, as everywhere, the atmosphere of the institution and the preconceptions of its inhabitants were perhaps better expressed in myriad day-to-day events than in codes of conduct and committees.

Teachers punished students for minor offences, such as neglecting or refusing to do their schoolwork. Typical is a punishment imposed in 1984 by one teacher, Mahlasela: the student 'is digging a hole as from Tuesday for indiscipline ... and will resume classes when he is through with punishment'. With the unerring sense that some teachers seem to develop of how to humiliate their charges, a Form 5 teacher in 1986 punished his students by making them lie on their stomachs on the grass in front of their juniors in Form 1.

Corporal punishment has been, until quite recently, an accepted practice in South African schools. The ANC, however, anxious to differentiate itself from the inhumanities of apartheid society and to adhere to progressive educational policies, and influenced by the principle of dialogue rather than punishment articulated by theorists such as Paulo Friere, took an early stand against it in its own educational institution. Oliver Tambo subscribed to this notion of dialogue. In conversation with the then Secretary of Education, Sindiso Mfenyana, he related an example taken not from some proponent of left-wing educational ideas, but from his experience of school governance at St Peter's, the mission school in South Africa where he had been a teacher. Though black institutions such as Healdton, Lovedale and St John's were sporadically involved in strikes, St Peter's, he said, was not, because the students were made to feel that this was their school and they were given a role in deciding on some of the issues that affected them.

Wintshi Njobe, a former Principal, recollecting the practice at SOMAFCO, claims that teachers never resorted to corporal punishment, suggesting that wrongdoers were dealt with through discussion and persuasion: 'We used political discussions, and when students did something wrong, it was raised up in class for discussions'. However, there is no doubt that in practice corporal punishment was at times used at SOMAFCO, and, though it was for the most part not official policy, it would appear that at least in the early days of the institution the authorities turned a blind eye to it. For instance, Snuki Zikalala, a former teacher at SOMAFCO, maintains that teachers punished students physically. Again, in a letter to Terry Bell in March 1982, a volunteer teacher, a Dane named Karen, speaks of her resignation in protest against corporal punishment at the secondary school. Diana Cumberledge speaks of a struggle to do away in reality with a practice that had been abolished in theory. The tensions are shown in the case of Dennis September, who refused to countenance corporal punishment formally or informally at the primary school. He is said to have successfully struggled with one of the teachers who would not part with his stick. On the other hand, Andrew Masondo, secondary school Principal from 1986 to 1990, personally, though not officially, supported such punishment. Chief Administrator Mohammed Tikly says that though corporal punishment was not allowed, some teachers did make use of it.

There was some limited official use of corporal punishment. The report of a Neduc meeting in 1986 says that corporal punishment had been sporadically used and that two teachers had been rebuked 'for physically punishing students'. However, it adds that corporal punishment was only carried out where 'absolutely necessary' and that 'with the knowledge of the school administration, specific individuals are given the responsibility for administering it and it is recorded.' This does indeed seem to have been unusual, at least in the later years of the school, and ex-student Nana Masusu is not aware of anyone receiving this sort of punishment. In short, though corporal punishment did occur, it was only used by a few teachers, and mainly in SOMAFCO's early days. Subsequently, it largely disappeared. It is worth adding that the Student Union, the students' own representative body, which had considerable powers, had to be stopped by the authorities from using corporal punishment against their own errant members.

The plight of a lonely or isolated student may often be more fundamentally difficult than that of a sociable individual who infringes school rules but feels at ease with his or her peers. There were students at SOMAFCO who felt themselves to be pariahs. This was a particularly tragic situation in that they, like everybody, were completely cut off from the support of family and neighbourhood. Age difference and the sense of one's individuality being submerged in the institutional culture of the school was one way in which some pupils experienced problems. Some of the adult students might even have left partners or children at home in South Africa. Humiliation and bitterness is clear in the words of an older woman student who noted in July 1983 that she intended to withdraw from schooling because 'it is being said that I am influencing the students of this school, a very old woman being a bad influence'.

The escalating crisis in education in South Africa during the 1980s was reflected at SOMAFCO. Learners coming from there were decreasingly academically qualified and competent as the decade advanced, being, in the words of John Carneson, 'weak by any formal measure of academic progress'. The school did all it could to remedy this situation, but of course it is difficult to overcome years of inadequate and disrupted education.

Academic difficulties could also cause emotional and, therefore, disciplinary problems. One of the outstanding facets of SOMAFCO is the way in which it set itself against the downplaying of mathematical and scientific studies which was characteristic of Bantu Education. The motivation and need for this is clear, but it is an irony that competence in these areas became a mark of prestige and success at SOMAFCO. Unfortunate students with a poor educational background often struggled with these subjects, sometimes reacting into hostility and rejection, and being in turn sneered at by the more successful. In student slang, those who did not like mathematics were 'vampires', though the reason for this term is unknown.

SOMAFCO was by no means dismissive of the problems of its students. Teachers carried out counselling, and assistance of a different sort was available at the hospital division. The commissar system was also intended to support students in various spheres: the college and staff commissars, who were staff members, and the school commissar, who was a student, helped to organise political discussions and other consciousness-raising exercises, and tried to encourage a sense of purpose and dedication amongst the students and teachers. All this helped at least some to deal with and perhaps even solve problems caused by the trauma of exile.

The SOMAFCO classroom

SOMAFCO students are on the whole positive about the education they received. Typically, ex-students like Jabu Mahlangu stress that the curriculum was much broader than the one they had left behind in South Africa. It exposed students to African writers. It laid stress on the sciences and mathematics. And it opened the prospect of a range of careers, including in areas like engineering – virtually inaccessible to black students in South Africa – that went well beyond the limited options of teaching and nursing familiar to academically successful students under Bantu Education. While lists of subjects say little about what happens in the classroom, they do give an idea of the scope of the curriculum, and at SOMAFCO, by 1988, subjects studied included English, mathematics, history, geography, history of the struggle, chemistry, biology, physics, agricultural science, typing, integrated science, technical drawing, development of societies, literature, and art.

Students are in many ways the best judges of the classroom, and the consensus amongst those interviewed is that their teachers were generally dedicated and skilful. Teachers also had confidence in the students. Richard Jürgens, an often critical observer, remembers the experience of teaching at SOMAFCO as stimulating and enjoyable, with students enthusiastic and determined to learn.

As has been seen, SOMAFCO was originally envisaged as solely a secondary school. Though it rapidly became clear that other levels of education would have to be added, the secondary school remained at the heart of the enterprise and received most attention. This may to some extent reflect the conservative view held in many South African schools that more emphasis should be placed on the older students as these will soon face national examinations, the equivalent of which in the case of SOMAFCO was the British-based General Certificate of Education.

The teacher John Carneson says that SOMAFCO students tended to perform relatively well at tertiary level upon their return to South Africa or when studying elsewhere, considering their disrupted academic backgrounds. Their social skills tended to be well above the average. An example is the group of students who took up places at Peninsula Technikon in Cape Town in the early 1990s on return from exile. SOMAFCO students, Carneson says, generally managed to get their degrees despite the fact that these were often done in countries where education was carried out in languages other than English. In the last years of the school some of the higher-achieving students studied at third level in Western or African countries, generally having acquired British A-level qualifications. Most, however, after their O-level qualification, went to Eastern Bloc countries, where they spent a year of preparation, particularly through studying the local language, before embarking on their substantive studies. They often had to face problems, especially racism, in the countries in which they were studying. However, SOMAFCO students tended almost by definition to be tough and socially adaptable, and on the whole they survived such experiences with remarkable resilience.

Of course, on top of the stresses that any young person may experience, SOMAFCO students were in a very untypical scholastic environment. The school was far superior to those that they had fled, but they experienced the isolation of exile, even being forbidden, for security reasons, to write to their parents and relatives in South Africa. Many had been involved in traumatic events that inevitably left their mark. For some, being in school was experienced as somewhat ignominious as compared with fighting in the armed resistance to the South African regime, the aim of many on leaving South Africa. However, it should be remembered that there was always a minority of young people at the school who had been born in exile, some with a reasonable standard of education from other countries, to whom many of these unsettling factors did not apply. This gave them a definite educational advantage on joining SOMAFCO.

Students were screened at Dakawa, the ancillary ANC centre 55 kilometres away, before being assigned to a class at SOMAFCO. The screening process sometimes displeased students, since they might be put in lower forms than those to which they had belonged in South Africa before going into exile. However, the poor standard of education to which many students had been exposed in South African township schools could make this necessary. Also, since students generally fled with the security forces at their heels, they rarely came with their educational records, and it was quite common for some to overstate their qualifications. Others again might have little political or educational motivation, having, for instance, simply followed their boyfriend, or, less usually, girlfriend, into exile. Motives and educational standards were often mixed and confused, and the screening process at Dakawa was essential.

The teachers were a major influence on the performance of students. Though there was a crucial core of teachers who stayed at SOMAFCO for long periods and provided the continuity that is important in any educational situation, the staff of the school was on the whole mobile and shifting. It was, for example, an ANC priority to educate and improve the qualifications of teachers who were members of the organisation. This had long-term benefits, but was disruptive to the teaching programme in the short term. ANC teachers might also be called away on other duties. Volunteer teachers from Europe and elsewhere left the campus after their contracts expired, leaving students to adapt to new teachers. Sickness, especially malaria, took its toll, sometimes leading to teachers being invalided out of Tanzania.

Many former SOMAFCO students say that mathematics, which was a compulsory subject, and the sciences, opened up all sorts of opportunities to them subsequently. The school managed to generate enthusiasm for these subjects, even though the students' poor grounding meant that it was a struggle for many to master them. John Pampallis notes that until the late 1980s, when volunteer science teachers from Europe began to come to the school in adequate numbers, there was always a problem in recruiting sufficient teachers for this area. Even so, from the beginning the standard was clearly well above that in Bantu Education schools, where mathematics and science were sometimes not even offered. Elizabeth Ligate, the Tanzanian director of the South African Extension Project, notes the enthusiasm of SOMAFCO students for science-related areas, though sometimes the struggle with these subjects did lead students to shift to arts-related courses. Many teachers, South African and others, also note both the determination to succeed in these areas, and the difficulties that some students experienced.

The school did what it could to assist its generally disadvantaged learners. There were special entry 'upgrading classes' to ease students into the full school routine. To attempt to grapple with problems in mathematics, from the late 1980s students could take either 'functional mathematics', or the subject at a higher level. Thembi Cele, a SOMAFCO teacher, remembers the arrival of hand-held calculators in 1984 and 1985; many students had never seen these before, and they made an immediate impact on the teaching and learning of mathematics. When personal computers arrived in the late 1980s, they were also eagerly seized upon, and students experimented with them and taught each other what they learned. According to Mohammed Tikly, they struggled, and nearly succeeded, in linking SOMAFCO online with schools in the United States, a remarkable effort at the time in this relatively isolated part of a poor African country. Thembi Cele notes the paradox of 'state of the art on one side and shortages on the other'.

Andrew Mohammed says that although students struggled with science and mathematics, they tended to succeed because they had excellent teachers. Mohammed Jatham, for example, in the school's early years, was an outstanding mathematics teacher whose pupils produced good examination results. Some students also got distinctions in science subjects. Inspired by

7. A class in progress at the secondary school

excellent teaching, the students also helped themselves by working together in study groups. However, the high level of staff mobility was a constant problem. Though 'Uncle' Slim Zindela taught at SOMAFCO from the beginning to the end, and John Carneson, Thembi Cele, John Pampallis and Mohammed Jatham were there for five to seven years, this was not typical.

As with schools everywhere, good teachers could often make a near-immediate beneficial impact. At its best, though pedagogy at SOMAFCO tended to be quite formal, it was combined with a high level of discussion and questioning. On Mzwandile Kibi's arrival at SOMAFCO in 1988 from Moscow, where he had been doing a master's degree in mathematics, he was asked by the then principal of the secondary school, Andrew Masondo, to create a 'mathematical atmosphere'. At the time, he says, there was only a 24 per cent pass rate in this subject at the secondary school. To achieve what Masondo asked, Kibi, the new head of mathematics, founded 'maths clubs' on campus, with the aim of associating the subject with the students' everyday life and the things and places around them. Maths clubs were divided into three groups at the levels of Forms 1 and 2, Form 3, and Forms 4 and 5. These groups encouraged a co-operative approach to mathematical work, and helped to make the subject a joint adventure in the mathematical world rather than a desperate individual struggle with a difficult subject. Students went to industries around the campus like the farm to do mathematics-related projects, and sometimes did practical projects, even quite controversial ones such as a study of the impact of time wasting by workers at Mazimbu. Talking to students about these maths clubs, it becomes clear that they were effective. Kibi was definitely regarded by those he taught as a positive influence. By 1990, the mathematics pass rate had risen to 64 per cent.

In SOMAFCO's early days, there was a serious lack of everything, including simple materials like chalk and chalkboards. There were even insufficient classrooms. Such shortages had a particular impact on the teaching of science, where there was, for instance, a lack of well-equipped laboratories. However, this was one area in which spectacular progress was made both in human and infrastructural terms. Science teachers came from the GDR and elsewhere, and, with overseas assistance, science laboratories were constructed which were of university standard. With such facilities, imaginatively used, students were enabled to explore the natural world, even making soap and other useful products.

Subjects like zoology had their own facilities. The secondary school had a collection of reptiles, kept for educational purposes, under the care of one of the teachers from the GDR, and students were responsible for the maintenance of this 'snake park'. As a matter of course, geography was taught in the field as well as in the classroom. The geography students ran their own weather station, and there were numerous educational expeditions to the mountains and elsewhere. As Phumeza Ngxala, one ex-student says, in South Africa, pupils would be told theoretically about distances from one point to another. At SOMAFCO, they had to measure such distances practically.

It is then not surprising when interviewees say that most students tended to choose science-related courses. This can be explained by the fact that over the years the school became increasingly well resourced both in terms of facilities, and in terms of specialists like the volunteer teachers from various countries. The ANC, as has been seen, was also involved in training its own teachers, of whom Mzwandile Kibi is a good example. Another is Mirriam Saohatse. She was an active student, becoming secretary of the Student Union. After Form 5 she went on a scholarship for six years to Bulgaria, came back to teach science at SOMAFCO, and subsequently did an MA at the Institute of Education, London University. The approach of the ANC was favourable towards the study of science, and the movement made a conscious attempt to counteract the effects of the contemporary South African policy of channelling black youth into non-scientific and non-technical areas. However, that students were doing mathematics and science does not mean that there were no problems in these areas. SOMAFCO continued throughout its existence to receive students from South Africa with a Bantu Education background, and it is not to be expected that such an inheritance could be easily counteracted, even with good teachers and excellent facilities.

Other courses offered at SOMAFCO, as mentioned earlier, included development of societies and history of the struggle. Clearly, these were overtly ideological courses intended to orient pupils towards the ANC view of the world, or at least towards one amongst the various ANC views. Kibi says students saw development of societies, which inculcated a Soviet-style analysis of world history, as a difficult course to handle and preferred history of the struggle, which concerned the freedom struggle in South Africa over the years, which was said to be 'close to their hearts'. This course dealt with the history of resistance against oppression going back as far as Dutch expansion in earlier centuries, but stressing the history of the ANC and milestones in its development such as the Freedom Charter. The roles of the other liberation movements like the PAC and the BCM were also mentioned, but emphasis was always placed on the ANC. The part that all political parties might play in the transformation of South Africa also formed part of this course, including the role of the right-wing parties. History of the struggle overlapped with history, taught by John Pampallis, and ideas and reading material, Patrick Mtshaulana says, were often interchangeable between the two.

The Marxist-orientated development of societies seems generally to have been unpopular amongst students. One student, Rafube, feels that the course was forced on them, and that there ought to have been the alternative of religious education for those who had interests in this area. But Rafube also claims a positive side for development of societies. It moved people from the idea that everything comes from God and stressed that humanity's future is in its own hands. Though development of societies seems to have been generally an unpopular course, it may be, as Kibi says, that it 'taught students to be analytical'.

Like development of societies, agriculture was also not favored by most students. On the whole, South African-born students, who, it should be remembered, were largely from urban backgrounds, tended to have a negative attitude towards this subject that was, it seems, seen as rural and therefore backward. For example, Tladi Ditsego, an ex-SOMAFCO student and then teacher, argues that it was associated with backbreaking and mindless manual labour, and hardly at all with the application of scientific methods to cultivation and the raising of stock. This of course is an aspect of the particular trajectory of South African agrarian history, where black communities have been confined to marginal areas of the country, and where land holding has been kept for the most part within artificially preserved communal systems out of line with modern agricultural development.

However, there were some students who became interested in agriculture, not least because the presence of the modern farm at SOMAFCO opened their eyes to what could be achieved in this area. As well as providing a constant

8. Inside the library at SOMAFCO

reminder of the nature of modern agriculture, the farm was also used for practical demonstrations in agriculture lessons. However, there were very few students who did agriculture at SOMAFCO, and even fewer who did it at tertiary level.

What type of literature was available at SOMAFCO to teach courses like history? This of course varied over time, and there is no doubt that the library, supported by Finnish resources and personnel, was a major achievement and became over the years the intellectual hub of the school. The books available, and utilised, contrasted greatly with those used in South Africa itself at the time, and indeed many of them were banned within the country and would have been completely unavailable to township pupils or even university students. They included, to mention a few, *The Revolutionary* and *The Rise of the South African Reich* by Brian Bunting, *The Struggle is my Life* by Nelson Mandela, *South Africa: The Peasants' Revolt* by Govan Mbeki, *Freedom for my People* by ZK Mathews, *A History of the African People of South Africa* by Paul Maylam, *Forced Removals* by Elaine Unterhalter, and, between literature and history, *Emperor Shaka* by Mazisi Kunene. John Pampallis, who was a teacher at SOMAFCO, also made a contribution. He wrote *National Struggle, Class Struggle: South Africa Since 1870*, used as a textbook at the school, and published later with an additional final chapter as *The Foundations of the New South Africa.*

Literature ranged from Shakespeare and the other standard authors of the established English canon to works of the most notable contemporary African writers. These included works by Chinua Achebe, Ngugi wa Thiong'o, Wole Soyinka and the other major authors writing in English, or those like Sembene Ousmane whose works had been translated into English. South African works included *Mhudi* by Sol Plaatje, *The Unbroken Song* and *The Wanderers* by Es'kia Mphahlele, *In the Fog of the Season's End* by Alex la Guma and *The Children of Soweto* by Mbulelo Mzamane.

While the smuggling of banned books into South Africa is familiar, in the case of SOMAFCO there was a need to smuggle books published within South Africa to those in exile. People leaving South Africa brought reading material they thought might be useful. John Carneson describes the circuitous but more reliable route developed from the early 1980s to acquire books from South Africa. Because they could not be ordered direct from South Africa, they were bought first by a company in Botswana, and in turn, SOMAFCO bought the books from the company.

Tensions at SOMAFCO

Interviews with some pupils and teachers who were at SOMAFCO in the school's later years give a picture of an institution that, though certainly better equipped and more professional than it had been, had to some extent lost its way. Though accounts differ, some feel that for reasons ranging from failure to deal adequately with the traumatised youth who left South Africa during the fierce conflicts of the mid-1980s and thereafter, to an officious security department which did not answer to the school authorities, disillusionment increased. Tensions at SOMAFCO were analysed in a report compiled by Jack Simons after a visit by members of Neduc in September 1986.

Students told Simons that they were unhappy with the alleged failure of the school authorities to solve problems presented to them. They complained that leadership and guidance was absent, and that teachers were remote and unable to socialise with students. The vice-principal was singled out 'for his apolitical stance and malice to students … [they] proposed that he be relieved of his duties as vice-principal and be asked to make the teaching of English his full-time occupation'. The students also complained that their political upbringing was not being seen to, and that as a result attendance at school was poor and participation in political gatherings low. A Student Representative Council member spoke at length about the inadequacies of staff and administration. Simons concluded, 'the spirit of adventure and excitement that stimulated the first intakes of students has dwindled, leaving only apathy, despair and symptoms of withdrawal.'

Simons' next meeting was with 28 teachers. They agreed that they did not serve pupils to the extent that they should, that they did not form a collective and that leadership was lacking. Some expressed resentment of volunteer teachers, who though they did not belong to the ANC, were alleged to receive preferential treatment, for instance in the allocation of houses. One teacher complained of being grossly overworked. Though they agreed that they had failed to interact socially with students, they pointed to the lack of time, which made them unable to provide remedial classes to students handicapped by their poor background for the work they were called upon to do. The teachers also complained that they were cut off from the administration, which was generally viewed as an autocratic bureaucracy.

When Simons met with nine members of the administration there were several overall conclusions that he presented to them. In a surprising change of tone which, however, was very much part of the discourse of the ANC in exile at the time, he argued that there was an urgent need to look into the operation of subversive forces, as well as into weaknesses in the administrative structure. He also alluded to the negative attitude of the students and their refusal to co-operate.

There were also general meetings with other residents of the Mazimbu complex. One of the more unsettling complaints, also made by the students, was about the activities of a secretive group calling itself the Social Order Committee (SOC), also known as the Law Enforcement Group. This body was accused of creating an atmosphere of terror by arbitrarily arresting suspects and removing them at night to Dakawa. This undercurrent was not new; in a letter of resignation to the principal, Tim Maseko, on 23 March 1982, Terry and Barbara Bell expressed their indignation about assaults meted out to people who were accused of dagga smoking, even though their cases were before the disciplinary committee. These people, like the victims of the SOC, were roused from their beds in the early hours of the morning. The perpetrators, the Bells argued, were still trapped in the mindset of apartheid dawn raids.

The ANC was in armed conflict with a ruthless regime, which could breed corresponding ruthlessness in the movement. This resulted in human rights abuses, at their worst in some of the military camps in Angola. Neither Mazimbu nor even Dakawa were military establishments, yet there was every reason to suppose that they might become targets of South African military action. Attempts would certainly be made to insinuate spies and saboteurs. Vigilant security was, therefore, an obvious necessity. However, while bearing in mind the neuroses, enmities and exaggerations that were inevitable in a tightly-knit but threatened community like Mazimbu, there is no doubt that vigilance and unavoidable secrecy spilled over into paranoia and brutality that at times completely overstepped the bounds of duty.

The SOMAFCO community manifested all the problems that can be expected with compound existence. However, they did not stop the daily routine. Projects were developed which, it was hoped, would make Mazimbu a better place. Classes were held. Teachers came and went. Students continued to strive for scholarships.

CHAPTER 7

Curriculum and pedagogy at SOMAFCO

The question of what curriculum and pedagogy to use forcefully raised the relationship between the political and educational aspects of the school. Theoretically, there need be no conflict between the two. In practice, there was constant tension between SOMAFCO as a revolutionary academy, raising the political and social consciousness of its students, and SOMAFCO as a semi-conventional school, preparing a cohort of young South Africans who would one day return to their country equipped with a variety of skills. Clearly, the contrast is not absolute. Those stressing a revolutionary role also wished for good general education, and those wishing for a comprehensive scientific and humanistic education certainly saw this in the context of building political activists. Curriculum as an area is a wide topic, which can be defined as the entire learning experience of a person – both what is formally taught and other informal learning. This whole study deals, in a sense, with curriculum. In this chapter, the formal curriculum in the secondary school, education with production, and political education, are the central issues.

Pedagogy at SOMAFCO

Pedagogy, or teaching methodology, was extremely varied at SOMAFCO. This represented the varied backgrounds of teachers, some of whom, in the early days, were untrained and tended to teach as they had themselves been taught. Teachers came to SOMAFCO from the fractured educational system of South Africa itself, and from many parts of the world, with numerous educational traditions.

The predominant educational tradition in South Africa under apartheid was that of fundamental pedagogics, a highly conservative reading of certain German and Dutch educational traditions, adapted to the racially divided and authoritarian South African environment and integrated with the system of Bantu Education. This overlaid the earlier Christian mission educational tradition, which could be more liberal and inquiring, but could also bring with it some of the conservative and authoritarian traditions of the European education of the time, embedded particularly in the religiously-oriented sector of British education. Black South African teachers came to SOMAFCO from both traditions, the younger teachers in revolt against Bantu Education, yet themselves inevitably influenced by it. Older teachers came with a background from the mission schools destroyed by the South African regime. At their best these had been high-minded institutions that took black education seriously and regarded their pupils as equal in potential to pupils anywhere. At worst, they could be paternalistic and authoritarian.

In one of the many ironies generated by apartheid, English-speaking white education in South Africa, though set within the context of racial privilege and injustice, did sometimes provide niches where a relatively liberal education could exist – at least in pedagogy if not in curricular content. Such education related in some cases more to contemporary British education than to the fundamental pedagogics preached by the state. The origins of this no doubt derived from differences between the Afrikaner and English traditions in the white population. Some key teachers at SOMAFCO came from this more liberal background.

Superimposed on this South African background were the cosmopolitan educational influences of the time. In general, these can be called 'progressive', but this encompassed numerous tendencies. These ranged from the educational thinking of the Soviet Union – which, though posited on an allegedly egalitarian philosophy, was in fact highly structured, with detailed and prescriptive syllabi which teachers were obliged to teach in a precise manner – to the variations of more libertarian educational thought, which tended to stress individual pupil initiative, and to regard the teacher as a facilitator rather than as the fount of knowledge.

These cosmopolitan influences were not merely an indirect influence on South African teachers, but were present physically in the form of colleagues from the Eastern Bloc, and from supporting countries and unofficial organisations in Western Europe and elsewhere. East Germans, often experienced senior teachers at home, rubbed shoulders with radical young volunteers from Sweden, Britain and Holland. South African teachers, trained in the context of the Christian ethos of the mission schools and of the University of Fort Hare before the government takeover of 1960, and those whose experience was the township schools of the Department of Bantu Education, worked with those whose background was the schools of the white suburbs of Cape Town, Johannesburg and elsewhere, and liberal South African universities such as those of the Witwatersrand and Cape Town. It was a stimulating mixture, and students at SOMAFCO experienced a remarkable range of teaching styles and philosophies.

Curriculum in the secondary school

From the first meeting of the Joint Committees – later named Neduc – held in Mazimbu in October 1978, there were moves to develop a curriculum matching the aspirations of the ANC. This first meeting drafted the conceptual framework of the Education Department, which was to be closely followed by a curriculum in line with it. At the end of this first Joint Committees meeting, each regional education committee was allocated syllabi to prepare within a specific time, to be presented at the next meeting in April 1979. The drafts were given to the members and they quickly produced a survey of the priority areas that had been worked upon so far. The curriculum would be structured around ten subjects: mathematics; general science; biology; geography; agricultural science; history; history of the struggle; development of societies; literature and English. It was felt that South African indigenous languages should be 'taught mainly to acquaint the students with the similarities of the various languages … by this, it is hoped, the divisive attitudes that have been inculcated in the minds of our people will be greatly reduced.' Other subjects mentioned were performing arts, arts and crafts, and languages used as the means of communication over wide areas of Africa, like French and Portuguese. The ANC Health Department submitted a draft syllabus on personal hygiene and public health, food and nutrition, and first aid. From the London Committee came a draft syllabus on journalism. It was hoped that, later on when people undergoing training had returned, dressmaking and design, carpentry, plumbing, building and building maintenance, would be introduced as subjects at the school.

At the third Neduc meeting in August 1980 it was proposed that the planned entry of South African students for Tanzanian examinations for 1980 should be abandoned and candidates withdrawn. Instead, from June 1981 Form 5 would be entered for London GCE O-level examinations. Candidates would be examined in English language, mathematics, physics, chemistry, biology and geography. The ANC would conduct its own examinations in history, development of societies and literature, and set up its own examinations board for this purpose in conjunction with the University of Zambia. Geography, which was originally to be included, was ultimately examined through the London examinations board. The main reason for abandoning the Tanzanian examinations was language. In Tanzania Swahili is an official language in which much teaching is done, and is compulsory for promotion from one school level to the next. Thus, though the movement kept some of the more ideologically sensitive areas of the curriculum under its wing, to a considerable extent the ANC chose to align itself with the British-centred, though cosmopolitan, examination system as utilised at the time in many ex-British territories such as Zambia and Malaysia.

Emanating from a recommendation of the third Neduc meeting, a Curriculum Development and Planning Unit (CDP) was set up. Its aim was to develop 'a genuine curriculum programme for liberation so that the present demands our people are able to confront the enemy with, must be in line with the thinking of our organisation and the experiences it is gaining at SOMAFCO'. The experience of the Zimbabwe African People's Union (Zapu) and Swapo in designing and implementing a primary school syllabus should form, it was said, the core around which ANC education for liberation would be built. Further, these concepts would be filtered back into South Africa to contribute to the debate on curriculum development amongst relevant structures. The CDP saw itself as co-ordinator of curriculum development and of the design of curricular material. The teacher, it was argued, would always be central in the process. Following panels and seminars on these issues conducted with teachers and other stakeholders, CDP would systematise and compile the outcome. Thus there would always be ongoing innovation at SOMAFCO 'or any of our ... schools which we hope will come into existence in future'.

By 1988, as well as the original core syllabus, there was more specialisation in the sciences. In addition, typing, technical drawing and art had been added. However, though some technical subjects were by then taught at Dakawa, other languages had not been introduced. The campus was a cauldron of African *lingua franca*, like French, Portuguese and Swahili, that were not taught at the secondary school. Neither were South African indigenous languages. English was the language of instruction, though especially in the primary school, indigenous languages, or a mixture described by one teacher as 'kiSwazulu', were in fact often used for communication. At this level conversational use of some indigenous South African languages was taught.

However, the lack of concentration on indigenous languages was one reason for the suggestions, which came to nothing, that SOMAFCO should be transferred in its entirety to South Africa in the early 1990s, rather than incorporating its returning students into South African schools. SOMAFCO students, speaking them only out-of-school, had no academic familiarity with the indigenous South African languages, which were routinely taught in black schools in South Africa. Apart from the anxiety of the ANC to stifle any 'tribalistic' tendencies in its ranks, the lack of competent language teachers, the congestion of the syllabus and the dilemma of deciding on which language or languages to choose, caused difficulties in teaching indigenous languages.

A problem that constantly faced SOMAFCO was the lack of textbooks in line with ANC educational policy. In some cases, particularly in history, it was considered necessary to have texts specially written, such as the text by John Pampallis. John Carneson also wrote a book for use in teaching history. In the meantime, teachers improvised in all humanities subjects, sometimes using local Tanzanian materials, and also using material such as the *ANC News Briefings*, extracts mainly from the South African press compiled in London by Gill Marcus and her team and distributed throughout the movement. It was easier with the sciences, as donor agencies from Britain and the Scandinavian countries kept a regular supply flowing. The excellent school library, built and supplied with Scandinavian – especially Finnish – support, played a crucial role in supplementing classroom texts, and in opening doors to the wider physical and intellectual world.

Some of the most useful teaching materials came from the South African Committee for Higher Education (Sached), which published alternative educational matter within the country. In 1984, following contacts at a conference in Botswana the previous year, Sheila Sisulu, who worked for Sached, brought books with her to Swaziland – especially those produced by radical publishers such as Ravan Press – from where they were sent to SOMAFCO. From then, regular supplies were ordered through Botswana, where South African publications could also be obtained. As well as supplying high-quality material, this arrangement also, as John Carneson put it, provided 'a window back to South Africa,' and helped reduce the isolation from thinking at home that was always a danger in the exile community. South African newspapers, such as the *Weekly Mail* and *New Nation*, also made their way to readers at the school. Nevertheless, contacts with South Africa were difficult and dangerous, and one consequence was the tenuous relationship between radical educational thinking and practice within the country and in exile in the 1980s. The two streams developed largely independently of each other.

Curriculum development was always a contentious matter at SOMAFCO. As Patrick Mtshaulana puts it, 'there were meetings day in and day out, [and they] changed the curriculum time and again.' He adds that the timetable, the framework for the formal curriculum, also 'changed all the time'. Nevertheless, progress was made. For example, work on curriculum development came to a standstill when the ANC Education Policy Document was questioned in the 1982 Curriculum Development Workshop held at SOMAFCO, only for the issue to be resolved at the August 1983 Neduc meeting. Development work from this stage onwards was more clearly organised. It consisted of recruiting more members into the curriculum committees, constituting groups of specialists in various curricular fields, recruiting and recommending for training personnel who would specialise in particular areas of curriculum development, planning for comprehensive research on problems at SOMAFCO, evaluating the school's achievements in its first five years, and, finally, producing a second edition of the SOMAFCO syllabus handbook.

These were the organisational issues. What is more interesting are the ways in which the ANC tried to give educational reality to its aims and ideology, with particular attention given to how to deal with 'revolution within education'.

Neduc declared that there must be a separate subject, history of the struggle, compulsory for all students, dealing with the movement for South African liberation. It dealt with the ANC and other movements and political parties, and formations like the Afrikaner Broederbond. It examined the relationship between the political and armed struggles and the role therein of the students of SOMAFCO. The underlying theme was that the armed struggle was central to the revolution, but could not advance without the political struggle.

The history of the struggle was taught at the secondary school. However, pre-primary children were also taught revolutionary songs, and were familiarised with leading figures in the ANC and with the ANC flag and emblems. Primary school children were taught history, with the emphasis on the injustices experienced by the mass of the South African population and the fight against them. Out of formal school hours, an ANC-oriented view of history was also inculcated in the Pioneers, an organisation for primary school students.

The motivation behind learning the history of the struggle is clear. As a school operating in the abnormal conditions of armed conflict, morale needed to be boosted and students had to be oriented towards the ANC's agenda. Wintshi Njobe makes this a point of pride: 'I must really say that the History of the Struggle was very biased because it followed the ANC struggle.' Though it was unashamedly intended to indoctrinate students with ANC ideology, it must be remembered that since in South Africa access to information about the freedom struggle was prohibited or presented in a skewed manner, the ANC had to take bold steps to remedy this through education. Indeed, even in learning the history of the struggle there was room for debate and disagreement.

SOMAFCO students who were interviewed generally feel that their education allowed them to develop a strong sense of individuality. Vigorous class discussion was encouraged, and through this they gained personal confidence and, in spite of the geographical isolation of the school, a keen sense of their significance in regional and international developments. They also feel that the school helped them to mature quickly and not to be overwhelmed by the usual teenage preoccupations. Though this is problematic, in that such preoccupations are a normal part of growing up, what cannot be ignored is that these students were markedly better off than their contemporaries in South Africa. The ANC was involved in a life-and-death struggle, and it would be unrealistic to expect that its school would completely adhere to the liberal educational ideas of more settled and peaceful communities. Bearing the context in mind, accounts of students and teachers indicate that education at SOMAFCO showed a remarkable level of intellectual openness and tolerance.

Another educational area deemed crucial was literature. The school authorities felt that what was available needed broadening, and that all 'acceptable' books, from whatever culture, could be used so long as they were available in English translation. From Forms 1 to 5 themes were developed which overtly served a political agenda. These, in the words of a 1980 Neduc document, were 'disintegration of traditional society, the emergence of political sufferings, from defensive to offensive – challenging – appeals to demands, and finally confrontation.' Books highlighting such messages were used, most by African authors and some by revolutionary writers from other parts of the world like Chile, Cuba, Palestine and the Soviet Union. The great writers of the English language were largely ignored. When it is considered that just about every theme – from pacifism to war, puritanism to eroticism, oppression to revolution – is dealt with in this literature, it seems that this approach was to a certain extent blinkered and geared towards a narrowly interpreted socialist agenda. However, once again, the context within which the school operated to some extent explains this approach. The Soviet Bloc and the Scandinavian countries were the main supporters of the school until late in its history. Most scholarships were in countries like the Soviet Union, East Germany, Bulgaria and Cuba. The West, with the exception of the Scandinavians whose largely social-democratic governments of the time sometimes flirted mildly with the Marxist left, not only ignored the school and offered no scholarships, they still supported apartheid South Africa and branded the ANC a 'terrorist' organisation. It is thus not surprising that the school leaned towards a Marxist-oriented outlook.

The school's curriculum gave priority to three areas, natural sciences, social sciences, and communication and culture. There was an emphasis on science, which was in line with attempts to create complete beings who would regard the sciences as crucial, in contrast with the wilful downgrading of this area in contemporary education for black South Africans.

The earliest plans for the school and the complex as a whole were ambitious and creative considering that funds were not yet readily available and that in 1978 the overriding requirement was simply to build a secondary school to absorb the influx of youngsters from South Africa. Only later, when numbers swelled and SOMAFCO became the ANC's central educational institution, did divisions like the nursery, kindergarten, primary school and maternity section come into existence. The movement found itself with a facility at which all their children could be gathered and looked after in an environment whose political orientation it controlled. This enabled it to exploit the growing guilt of the world recently dismayed by media images of South African state brutality, and shocked by the police slaying of Black Consciousness leader Steve Biko. This was the time to show the world that the ANC was not merely a warlike structure fighting apartheid, but a 'broad church' with a first-class civilian educational establishment. With this image in place, they could proceed to garner more support, even from those who had previously felt uncomfortable supporting a liberation organisation involved in military struggle. Thus the curriculum was based on the recognition that the ANC had multiple tasks at hand that needed to be reflected in the school project.

These tasks also involved finding gainful employment through vocational training for the *mgwenyas*, some of whom were located in Kongwe, Tanzania, with no clear prospects for the future. Most of them had been in Nelson Mandela's Luthuli Detachment of 1962, which formed the core of MK. Vocational training would also assist younger MK veterans who had sustained either physical or psychological scars and were not fit to return to the army. Additionally, and conveniently, the camp-like structure of the complex at Mazimbu, and later Dakawa, made them both ideal places to oversee social misfits and others who had somehow come into disfavour with the organisation, thus keeping them away from the centres of real power. However, whatever the sometimes mixed motives for such training, the contents envisaged for the vocational training programme were ambitious, and included agriculture, sewing and tailoring, woodwork and carpentry, metal work, building, electrical repairs, printing, motor mechanics, and catering. This was to be linked to an adult education structure that would offer lifelong skills that could be taken back to a free South Africa.

If curriculum means the entire learning experience, then the classroom is not the only, and perhaps not the most important place where learning takes place. SOMAFCO students, as will be seen, had a vigorous social life: boxing matches, fashion parades, conjuring, ballroom dancing, music and a multitude of other activities were as much a part of learning at the school as daily classes. The musician Ndiko Xaba, for instance, who became heavily involved in extra-curricular musical activities, was as crucial to the education of some SOMAFCO students as the teachers themselves.

Education with production

Education with production, often referred to as 'bridging the gap' between mental and manual labour by the Mazimbu community, was aimed at combining academic activity with physical work, producing, in the words of an ANC document, 'such cadres as will be able to serve the society in all spheres'. The implication is that education is not just a classroom matter but can take place on the farm and other workplaces. Thus even a person who drops out of school will possess manual and mental skills with which they can try to make a living.

Though the concept of education with production emerged firmly in the twentieth century, its origins can be traced back to the mission schools established in the previous one. In various forms according to their particular approaches and backgrounds, missionaries sought to combine mental and manual labour in an effort to produce Africans whom they considered appropriately educated for their environments. This was an ambiguous process, frequently resented by pupils who felt patronised by being given what they often considered a second-rate education; perhaps some of these ambiguities persisted in the secular context of SOMAFCO and other revolutionary institutions.

There is a sense in which Bantu Education, also, emphasised the relationship between classroom education and production. It was a norm for black students at school to do sewing, bricklaying, gardening and home economics for their alleged benefit. This adulterated form of education with production was not put in place to benefit the whole society, but rather to perpetuate a master-servant relationship. Arguably this background created difficulties in popularising the concept in the different context of Mazimbu.

However, one significant version of the idea of education with production is associated with socialist or other politically radical ideas. Socialist countries like Cuba attempt to bridge the gap between mental and manual labour, and Cuban university students, for example, are expected to help with the harvest and other agricultural tasks on the farms in rural areas during vacations. Another variation is the polytechnic approach promulgated in the GDR, which, however, assumed an essentially urban and industrial form of social organisation.

The educationist, Patrick van Rensburg, a South African exile who implemented his educational ideas in neighbouring Botswana after having started Swaneng Hill School in 1974 and the Foundation for Education with Production (FEP) in 1981, was a leading proponent of education with production. Van Rensburg envisaged the 'brigades' system, providing alternative education for the numerous primary school leavers who could not be absorbed into the secondary school system. These brigades were to operate in impoverished rural areas, pointing the way to economic self-sufficiency, and inculcating such skills as weaving, carpentry, building, horticulture and mechanics. He argued that there was a need for a mass-based pedagogy that would raise the cultural level of the whole population and give them the tools to understand and control the political, economic and social forces determining their lives. This pedagogy would depart from the often elitist forms and authoritarian methods of conventional schooling and redefine the relationship between teachers and learners, and school and society.

The ANC took the idea of education with production from socialist and quasi-socialist approaches, particularly that of Van Rensburg, who visited SOMAFCO in its early days and attended some of the earlier Neduc conferences where he argued for his ideas. He brought some people to Botswana, and a few went to Zimbabwe for similar training. The ANC also drew on the experience of other liberation movements. Countries like Namibia, Zambia, Zimbabwe and Guinea-Bissau – especially in their early and idealistic days of independence – attempted to implement similar concepts. Zimbabwe's Zanu-PF took the approach to government from the bush war, and its liberation schools in refugee camps in Mozambique, Zambia and Botswana laid the foundation for pilot schools under the new Zimbabwe Foundation for Education with Production (Zimfep). In the case of Tanzania, FEP was instrumental in persuading the country to continue with its 'Education for Self-Reliance', which was associated with Julius Nyerere's *Ujaama* policies.

Other South African liberation movements also attempted to implement similar concepts. For instance, the PAC did so at their settlement near Bagamoyo, and the Black Consciousness Movement of Azania at the Duku settlement in Botswana, which housed freedom fighters from a number of liberation movements, including Swapo.

The ANC, therefore, was reacting to an idea with a long history and a widespread contemporary appeal when it decided to implement this concept at SOMAFCO. It was attempting to put into place a system thought to be diametrically opposed to Bantu Education. Summarising briefly what the ANC aimed at through education with production, Patrick Mtshaulana, a former SOMAFCO teacher, says:

> What was clear was that the ANC favoured, broadly ... a less strait-jacketed approach to education so that you shouldn't have academics on this one hand and stupid people ... on the other side ... the education given to people must be all round, giving and recognising the talents and capabilities of those that were not necessarily academics and yet enriching those that were going to go academic by giving them access to practical things like electric workshops so that they should know more or less when they have a house what happens if a plug explodes.

This is close to what Mzwandile Kibi says about the aim of making sure that every young person in South Africa 'is able to see the link between the hands and the mind'. The two had to be combined to produce a balanced person. SOMAFCO provided a context where this experiment could be tried.

There was, however, some ambivalence about education with production from the beginning, with the abiding tension between political and more purely academic views of the school surfacing in this sphere as in others. As early as the second Neduc conference in April 1979 it was reported that 'the students are reluctant to co-operate either on the farm or at the building site.'

In *Problems of balancing work and study at the Mazimbu ANC School Project*, a document circulated early in 1981 in response to dilemmas that had surfaced in the implementation of the production side of education with production, the uneasiness is palpable. The school, it said, must:

> rectify this situation as one of its priorities. This means in its teaching it must draw on the most advanced scientific knowledge, that is, teaching science in depth with thoroughness. Increasing teaching time to effect this emphasis reduces time available for food production and extensive involvement of students into vocational skill production of a level that could make the project 100% self-sufficient in most areas of its material needs.

To implement education with production, students were grouped into units called brigades using Van Rensburg's model – there were Tambo, Luthuli and other brigades. A brigade would spend a certain time in a particular place, for example the farm, and then move to another. Andrew Mohammed, a student in the school's early stage who later worked in the school's photographic laboratory, recollects that teachers also took part in education with production, working with the students in the maize fields at Mazimbu, and undoubtedly becoming closer to them as a result. However, the whole process of education with production did not go according to plan. It changed form over time, and in the end, it can be argued, it collapsed.

There are various reasons for this. According to Barney Mogane, an ex-SOMAFCO student, there was a lack of co-ordination between the departments and the school. For example, students would be sent to the engineering department where the workers were repairing vehicles. Far from assisting the workers, the presence of students would often irritate and distract them, and as a result students were habitually given menial tasks such as washing cars that had nothing to do with motor mechanics. Even in carpentry, where it might seem that there was an urgent need for assistance with the building programme, the students tended to get in the way of the regular workers and slow down production. The effect of this, according to Mtshaulana, was to demotivate students, who felt they were learning nothing. He adds that the problem was compounded by the lack of trained teachers at the workshops. In other words, there was tension between the training needs of the students and the immediate imperative to proceed speedily and efficiently with construction. In this situation training often suffered.

From the students' point of view, it was not just the ignominy of being in the way that made them lukewarm about this sort of on-the-job experience. There was also a lack of incentives, and, above all, diligent students tended to resent time taken away from their studies. Especially where they had problems, as they frequently did, with courses like mathematics and science, it is hardly surprising that they found the demands of education with production irritating. Many teachers sympathised with this view. According to Dominic Tweedie, one of the people in charge of the furniture factory, students were more interested in acquiring academic skills than in doing manual labour. Kibi adds that it was not easy to change mindsets that had been formed in South Africa and that were often hostile to manual labour, which for many was associated with exploitative racial definitions of work allegedly appropriate for black people. Such attitudes led to resentments as some brigades slouched through certain activities while others had to do the hard work. All this came on top of the fact that conditions in the fields and elsewhere could be extremely hot and unpleasant, to the point that some of the students – mostly, it should be remembered, urban youth unused to both the climate and the work – became seriously ill.

Manual labour did not only have a bad reputation, but often when students did something wrong they would be punished through being given manual tasks to perform – often identical to those undertaken in education with production sessions. Tweedie, for instance, remembers three students punished by being sent to the furniture factory. Instead of working, he found them sleeping on the floor. He concludes, as did many, that production should never be used as a form of punishment, but should rather be seen as a dignified contribution to the welfare of the community, or even as a pleasure.

In the face of this passive resistance, education with production did not come to a standstill, but rather changed its form. Mogane says that even though organised work-groups stopped, students who had developed an interest in certain activities, for instance, engineering, continued to go to those departments in their spare time, only now on a voluntary basis. Phumeza Ngxale feels that the authorities realised that they were not going to win this struggle and simply got tired of meting out ineffective punishments. Students were now asked what their fields of interest were, and an attempt was made to allocate them appropriate work. For instance, as someone interested in librarianship, Phumeza helped in the library and later went on to study the subject at tertiary level.

The question that loomed behind the concept of education with production was that of what sort of school and, beyond that, what sort of future South Africa the ANC envisaged. The vision tended to stress a simplistic form of social and political egalitarianism, arguably most appropriate for societies at a low level of economic development, utilising masses of unskilled labour. However, as has been seen, SOMAFCO was based on suppositions that underlie most modern secondary schools, with a stress on academic subjects and success in examinations, and the assumption that ideally its graduates would proceed to third-level education. The two visions are in essence incompatible.

It is perhaps this incompatibility that underpins Kibi's belief that it was the growing centrality of academic teaching – producing well-qualified and technically competent graduates for the 'New South Africa' – that led to the end of education with production at SOMAFCO, at least as ideologically motivated mass labour. Other sectors at Mazimbu, like the farm, ceased to be treated as arenas for politically motivated educational labour, and were directed above all to support the school in its activities.

However, the move away from education with production was not a principled decision. The institution was, after all, trying to appeal to various constituencies, and the emotional resonance of the apparently egalitarian policy was considerable, however much it may have interfered with the work of the school in practice. The concept was used for propaganda purposes, so that, as André Proctor put it, when donor delegations came to the school 'suddenly everybody would flood out into the fields and pretend to dig, put on this wonderful apparent show of self-reliance'. The policy continued rhetorically, and the school continued to make efforts to incorporate it in the timetable. Mtshaulana's conclusion that there 'wasn't a coherent theory' about the relationship between education with production and academic schooling seems correct. The move away from it occurred in an ad hoc way.

The change in policy also mirrors the evolution of SOMAFCO from the early days of impoverished struggle in an unyielding environment. In the initial stages of construction there was real need for much unskilled labour, but as the complex became more mature, and as subsequent construction became

9. Working in the vegetable gardens

10. Education with production – a group of students

more sophisticated in design and building technique, the mass of unskilled labour represented by education with production was no longer required. In addition, a large number of Tanzanians began to be employed and for this reason it was no longer crucial to also tap the students for unskilled labour. All this gave students more time to focus on their academic studies.

Thus education with production was not abolished, but rather changed form gradually. It was incorporated in *letsema*, communal days involving the whole Mazimbu community on which the grounds of the complex would be cleaned, a beast would be killed, and there would be a feast. *Letsema* had always been practised at SOMAFCO, and should not be seen precisely as replacing education with production. However, it increasingly displaced work which aspired to be productive in a fuller sense, and later students like Vuyani Mlati, who joined SOMAFCO in 1984, experienced education with production as tidying the secondary school gardens, and working jointly with the wider Mazimbu community on the grounds of the campus as a whole on weekends and commemoration days. This is borne out in a 1990 Unesco Consultancy Mission Report. The section on School Production Units simply says, 'students are not yet practically involved in Education with Production. The farm runs on paid labour.'

Students and politics

SOMAFCO was an educational institution run by a movement for political liberation. Therefore the way in which the political sphere was dealt with at the school is of particular interest, and in keeping with the broad definition of curriculum as an individual's total learning experience, the students' political organisations as well as what was formally taught will be discussed. There was structural tension between the students' position as first and foremost members of the liberation movement, which implied equality, and their position as students, which could be taken to imply a degree of subordination. This was shown at the time of the ANC Kabwe Conference in 1985, when the students pressed hard, and in the end successfully, for representation, arguing that as members of the movement they must participate in shaping its policies.

The SOMAFCO Student Union consisted of the chairpersons and secretaries of the following committees: Political; News and Information; the Editorial Board; Cultural; Commanders' Council; Hostel; Health; Sport and Entertainment; Class Leaders' Council; Catering, and Student Disciplinary. The Executive Committee of seven of the student body was elected from this council. It was the task of the Executive Committee to form a link between the students and the administration.

Before anything that affected the students could be brought to the attention of the school management, it had first to be debated by the Student Union. The Union would then decide whether to pass the issue to the administration or to try to solve it itself. SOMAFCO students had certain grievances relating to schooling. The course on development of societies, based on a broadly Marxist ideology, became increasingly unpopular as the 1980s proceeded and it appeared more and more out of tune with changing world politics. Some also objected to mathematics being compulsory when they planned to follow careers where the subject did not feature, or because they were simply handicapped by the lack of mathematical training in the South African schools from which they came.

It was the students' view, as expressed through the Student Union, that development of societies should be removed from the curriculum, and mathematics be made optional. The authorities responded by making development of societies optional in Forms 4 and 5, but maintained it as a compulsory subject from Forms 1 to 3. However, with the profound changes in the Soviet Union around 1989, this course was withdrawn. The school authorities said that the reason for this was that the textbook had to be revised. However, it may be that this was a pretext for eliminating a course that no longer appeared opportune, given the disappearance of the state – a major supporter of the ANC – that had backed it. The students did not succeed in having mathematics made optional. This is hardly surprising, since one motivation for the foundation of SOMAFCO was to reject the Bantu Education system that had systematically disadvantaged black students in the fields of mathematics and science.

Apart from representing the students to the management, the Student Union also organised functions on campus. These included commemorations on 21 March, the anniversary of the Sharpeville massacre; 6 April, the day on which Solomon Mahlangu was executed, and 16 June, the anniversary of the Soweto uprising. The Political Committee organised these gatherings with the assistance of the Zonal and Regional Political Committees. On such occasions, when classes were normally suspended, students would wake up early to begin celebration of the day. They would parade through the campus singing revolutionary songs and chanting in memory of fallen heroes. Sometimes, a 'coffin' containing an effigy of PW Botha would be made, and usually burned, with students chanting and singing around the pyre. The raising of the ANC flag would follow. All this usually took place in the morning. Subsequently, students would divide into groups and clean the classrooms, plant trees and cut grass, then returning to their rooms to prepare for the main ceremony in one of the school halls around 19h00.

Students were an integral part of such ceremonies, which included plays and other cultural activities. Even the very young Pioneers, primary school children whose ages ranged from 6 to 13 years, participated. Usually, the plays would reflect the South African political situation, emphasising the regime's misdeeds. Through such performances, the collective memory of a South Africa receding into the past was boosted, and the commitment to the struggle, the outcome of which must often have seemed uncertain, was affirmed.

Leaders of the ANC, including Oliver Tambo, often attended these gatherings. The atmosphere is reflected in the address of Stanley Mabizela, the ANC Chief Representative in East Africa, during the ANC Youth Seminar at SOMAFCO on 17 November 1984. He said, 'It is in this society that we need the so-called radical – the liberator,' and, he continued, 'there will be no neutrality in the future South Africa, for neutrality is a … cowardly and immoral position to take in life.' In the context of SOMAFCO, the role of youth was emphasised of course, as in Tambo's speech at the opening of the second National Youth Conference of the ANC at SOMAFCO on 14 August 1987, when he said that, 'In saluting you, we are saluting the cross-section of South African youth who are today locked in decisive battles … to rid our country of the scourge of colonial and racist domination.'

Political activities were not limited to the campus. Students went to other countries, and interacted with their Tanzanian peers. One student, Qapane, wrote of his 1986 trip to Italy in the *Student Journal.* He not only met Italian students, but also trade union leaders, and even Pope John Paul II, and former Italian President Sandro Petini. Through such trips, SOMAFCO students played their part in ANC campaigns to inform the world about South Africa, broadened their experience and refined their political ideas.

Journeys abroad by SOMAFCO students reflected different aspects of ANC international relations. On the one hand, countries like Italy were visited, with an emphasis on fraternal relations with trade unions and other bodies on the left. On the other hand, students visited congresses and other gatherings in the socialist bloc, reflecting the support that the ANC received from this source. Attendance at such events continued to the time when these regimes were forced, or retreated, into an impoverished and embattled isolation. For instance, the 1989 World Festival of Youth and Students in North Korea was among the international gatherings that SOMAFCO students attended. The festival was attended by President Kim il Sung of North Korea and President Robert Mugabe of Zimbabwe. North Korea, a country ruled by one of the most secretive and totalitarian regimes in the world, was where the SOMAFCO students shared their experiences about the South African government and its repressive system. The Pioneers also took part in these international visits. For example, in 1989, they were invited to attend 'international summer camps' in Cuba and Bulgaria.

SOMAFCO students played a role in the maintenance of Tanzania's image as a supporter of southern African liberation movements, from debates with students from local Tanzanian schools to participation in national events. This was seen, for instance, when they were invited to the official celebration of Tanzania's twenty-first year of independence in 1982. The SOMAFCO student representative said that 'the people and government of Tanzania have made us feel at home,' adding that 'today armed cadres of the ANC are dealing blow after blow with the enemy in widespread areas throughout South Africa.' Though subtleties are not to be expected from such set-piece speeches, there is no doubt that these were extraordinary events in the lives of students, who would never have been invited to express themselves at such venues in apartheid South Africa.

SOMAFCO students also participated in the Zonal Youth Committee (ZYC), a local ANC political structure intended to mobilise young people, whether students or workers, and bridge any gap there might be between these groups. Mazimbu itself was regarded as a zone, and the ZYC consisted of all the youth on the Mazimbu campus aged between 18 and 35. The ZYC was, in turn, linked to the Regional Youth Committee (RYC), and both of these bodies were represented on the National Youth Committee (NYC), the highest organ amongst the youth structures.

Meetings of the Mazimbu ZYC took place at SOMAFCO. Before any discussion, *Nkosi Sikelel' iAfrica* was sung. In these meetings, students could raise problems with which they felt the ZYC could deal. These included delays in student scholarships, and lack of good teachers, which resulted in poor student performance. Such problems would then be handled by the ZYC or taken to

11. Seminar on the Freedom Charter in the Hector Petersen Hall

other structures of the ANC, depending on how serious the matter was. Through this route, problems could reach the National Executive Committee of the ANC, where students had a representative.

Another representative structure, the Zonal Political Committee (ZPC), also existed on campus. Every South African, regardless of age and including teachers, workers and students, was represented on this committee. In this forum everything, not only politics, was open to discussion, and, where appropriate, student concerns could be raised in the context of the activities of Mazimbu as a whole.

Students had their own newspaper on campus, the *Student Journal*. This was an important medium for the expression of student views on politics, on SOMAFCO itself, and on a whole range of concerns from the trivial to the profound. Students of all ages and academic levels often expressed themselves in verse, some of it printed in the *Student Journal* and some surviving in class projects and the like. They wrote about oppression, exploitation, poverty and pain, white privilege and black suffering. They praised freedom fighters and attacked apartheid leaders. They wrote about exile and about Mazimbu. Sometimes, a more personal note appears, as in Sunya Lai-Thorn's 'For Babu', a tribute to the principal of the primary school:

> To a person who has
> conquered weakness
> to a person who has

delayed old age
to a person who has
educated the young

The flowers of life
you have left behind
the buds of your efforts
will bloom in your absence
ensure that you
core of the fruit
shall pick the results
in all its fullness.

In 'Peace', 17-year-old Molly Khanyile linked Mazimbu with the wider struggle for peace and freedom:

Let's build a wall of peace.
I'm not satisfied with this little peace of Mazimbu
We need peace in our own country
We will never be satisfied by the peace of exile.

We will be satisfied when freedom comes
When we will be finding ourselves in our own country

On the day that South Africa will be finding only
peace

Freedom is needed
Peace is needed
Peace high and low
Freedom day and night.

Occasionally a poem reminds us that many SOMAFCO students were adults with extraordinary and complex experiences upon which to draw, such as in Musa Ngwenya's 'Letter To', which ends:

Broer! I'm missing you
missing that calm reassurance
of your little body
generating the quiet hope
of simmering South Africa's future

Remember our last chat on them
you said
'Ek moet haar nooit los'
but like a calabash
from hand to hand

the nurtured rose flicked
past my life
its petals gradually reddening
the future we are fighting for

Broer – only you 'n I
know the therapy of these lines
think of our lasting comradeship
for real

Nkomati serpent-like
still hisses
maar jy moet kom
front

Na Front ons moet weer gaan.

It was crucial in isolated Mazimbu to keep informed about the wider world, and especially about news from South Africa. The News and Information Committee, a substructure of the Student Union, collected news from the radio, listening in to stations such as the BBC World Service, Radio Moscow, and Radio Tanzania and other African broadcasters, and presenting the main issues as a written summary. Radios were scarce at SOMAFCO. Only a few students had sets, and there was no Tanzanian television service. There was, however, a video machine which students usually watched at weekends. Some video cassettes shown to students had been smuggled out of South Africa and showed political events in the country from the perspective of the internal forces opposed to the government. Added to the constant stream of information coming with new arrivals at the school, students were well briefed on contemporary events and debates in South Africa.

The collection of news helped to update students about what was happening around the world, and especially in South Africa. News summaries were read by one of the News Committee members to the students in one of the college halls, usually at 21h00, after evening study. Then, as Vuyani Mlati says, 'there were those students who were very politically minded who would argue about what they have heard from the news.' Typically discussion would last for about half an hour, and would be followed, on some days of the week, by 'jazz hour', when students would sing revolutionary songs.

At leisure in their rooms and elsewhere, students still engaged in political discussion and also debated current issues at SOMAFCO. With the collapse of the Eastern Bloc and the disintegration of the Soviet Union, students asked themselves how they would survive, since the Soviet Union and its allies had played such a crucial role in support of the ANC, including SOMAFCO. Some ex-students were studying in countries like Czechoslovakia, East Germany and

Bulgaria. With the fall of communism, students like Lungi Mankazana, who was studying in Czechoslovakia, had to leave the country as their funding dried up, often in the middle of their academic programmes. The fears of these SOMAFCO students were well founded.

Anxious debate swirled amongst the students, above all about what their future would be now that return to South Africa really seemed to be at hand. At a school where Oliver Tambo had been a constant support, the release of Nelson Mandela generated joy, but also speculation as to the future leadership of the movement. Mlati says that students wondered how Mandela and Tambo, both giants in the struggle for liberation and commanding so much respect worldwide, would work together in the final phases of that struggle. In the event, this issue never arose because of Oliver Tambo's illness and subsequent death.

Clearly, political education at SOMAFCO was focused on perceived imperatives of the struggle. However, the often traumatic context of exile made it necessary that students be enabled to think for themselves and understand their own, their country's and their continent's situation in more subtle ways than through mere slogans. Manala Manzini, the ANC political officer at SOMAFCO and chief representative of the ANC in Tanzania from 1987 until the end of the school, notes, for instance, the need to help young people understand the often disturbing conditions in some African countries. At the time, in a country like Nigeria a corpse could lie unattended for days in the street, a profound shock to young people who had left South Africa idealising independent Africa. Manzini says that political education was stressed 'because if you had your people understanding what was happening, half of the job was done … Political education was the arming of those individuals to be able to stand on their own, to understand and analyse the situation and be able to understand why certain things were happening in certain ways. Outside of that, I think it could have been very difficult.'

[illegible]

CHAPTER 8

The social life of students

SOMAFCO students, most of them young urban people, were far from home and from the township life with which they were familiar. Isolated as they were, the students had to create much of their own entertainment and social life. At the core of student life from pre-primary to secondary levels were their living quarters, the dormitories. Here they slept, ate, gossiped, flirted, quarrelled and enjoyed themselves.

The dormitories

As well as spending their days at the Charlotte Maxeke Children's Centre, the pre-primary children of the campus also resided there. The matrons were responsible for their well-being, providing for their daily needs like food, and washing their clothes. Caregivers like MaSkosana told stories to the children, helped them with their homework and resolved any problems there might be between them.

The primary school children also had their own accommodation, which was more closely associated with the older students, though separate from them. Primary school children occupied Unit One, for girls, and Two, for boys. The living arrangements of the pupils were in the hands of the matrons. But, as with the primary school in general, it seems that they were not as well cared for as the pre-primary children who were the responsibility of professionally expert and temperamentally affectionate people like Farida Mussagy.

Why were primary school children not better cared for? Barney Mogane thinks that lack of formal training in childcare amongst the matrons, who were often ANC veterans, contributed to this. Sherry Maclean, an Irish social worker stationed at SOMAFCO, says that because of the lack of such training children were often deprived of individual attention. There was little attempt to simulate family conditions. In particular, the children of parents who were studying abroad and who were unable to keep closely in touch tended to lack care and individual attention. But despite this, she says, efforts were made to integrate these children into other families on campus in a type of fostering relationship, and those in a position to do so advised boarding staff on child development and on how to respond to children's problems.

During the evenings, primary school children would play cards, draughts and other indoor games. At weekends, the children would watch videos, as did the secondary school students. During the day, the primary school children could cycle around the campus on the bicycles that had been donated to the school.

The secondary students, while they had their problems, were naturally more mature and independent than the younger children. They lived in four of the six units, each of which was built in a u-shape. Each room could accommodate about 8 students and a single unit had 144 students. Every unit had its own dining hall, laundry, store room, toilets and showers and a house attached for the boarding teacher, whose responsibility it was to monitor his or her unit. The teachers' cottages were close by. Before students went to bed at 23h00, it was the boarding teacher's responsibility to make sure, through a roll call, that all of them were in their rooms. The boarding teacher worked hand-in-hand with the room commanders, who were students elected in each room to monitor others and help with the daily running of the hostels. The Boarding Master, Jimmy Phambo, managed the difficult task of running the crowded and potentially explosive world of the dormitories with a light but capable hand. There were no mixed residences at SOMAFCO, and female and male students were housed in separate units.

In the residences, students were responsible for good order in their rooms and the well-being of their inhabitants. Students made their own arrangements about cleaning. There was no specific time as to when this had to take place and students simply cleaned when they found time to do so. The school's records give glimpses of this aspect of everyday life, as when 'Sonwabo Gaika rushed to his room after school to clean as it was his turn.' To motivate the students, rewards were offered, usually once a year, to those whose rooms were the cleanest.

Students spent most of their time in their rooms, where they chatted with their roommates. Much was discussed in those rooms, including politics and the social life of the campus. On weekends, and sometimes during the week when students were not busy, they would visit each other. There were no rules restricting male students from visiting female students in their rooms, or vice versa. Most of the younger students were at SOMAFCO without their parents, and they tended to seek the company and protection of older students. Some of these older students were males and were often referred to by their young protegés as *malume*, a Zulu and Xhosa word for uncle.

Most SOMAFCO students had to spend almost all their time on campus. In this sense, the place was even more all-enveloping than a normal boarding school where pupils get away at holidays. However, those born in exile were lucky enough to have the occasional opportunity to visit their parents in whatever country they were deployed by the ANC. The authorities made the necessary arrangements for this. One can envisage the excitement of Lilian Dinumo, for example, a daycare centre pupil, who was flown to visit her parents in Zambia late in 1989.

Sometimes, people who lived on campus fostered children whose parents were not living at SOMAFCO or who had died in exile. John and Xoliswa Bolton, for example, applied for the adoption of Lebohang, a child residing at the Children's Centre. In the letter, the couple promise to raise the child as their own. They also promise to hand Lebohang back to the daycare centre should a relative or parent of the child ask that she be returned.

Cases of fostering at SOMAFCO also took place across racial lines. A white couple fostered Sasa Zikalala, who attended pre-primary and primary school at SOMAFCO. This could not have taken place at the time in South Africa where there was legislation outlawing interracial contact, and is another example of how Mazimbu can be seen as a microcosm of a future non-racial South Africa. This applies also to the interracial marriages that took place at SOMAFCO.

Apart from actual visits, which were of necessity widely spaced, parents abroad also tried to keep alive the bonds between themselves and their children. Writing from Sweden to Jane Dumasi, a teacher at the pre-primary school, Mbali Ndlovu asked her to pass her love and concern to her child Max. She sent him sweets and a present for his birthday, and requested that certain people in Mazimbu, including her husband, Lizwi Zondo, should be permitted to visit Max in the Children's Centre, and take him for weekend visits to their homes.

During the early days of SOMAFCO, students were not allowed to drink alcohol. Only workers, whose tuckshop sold liquor, were allowed to do so. However, students often went to Morogoro to drink, sometimes buying alcohol there and bringing it back to campus to drink in their rooms. They would hide it in their bags and the guards at the gate would generally not bother to check. Even if they did check, they would be bribed by the students to allow them through. By 1985, older students were permitted to buy liquor at the campus stores that stocked it, probably so as to limit movement to town.

Radios were scarce at SOMAFCO, and those who were lucky enough to have them played them to pass time. This was the case with Mohale, a male student, who was reported to be sitting outside Room 12 with Hilda, a female student, at three in the morning, playing a transistor radio. That students could sit outside their rooms at such a time indicates that although there was a roll call every night before the students went to bed, they either did not always adhere to it or the boarding teachers did not enforce it. This was so much so that cases arose like one in 1985 when a female student was found guilty by the school authorities of sleeping with her boyfriend in her room.

Students also held parties, or what they called discos. A soccer team would sometimes decide to celebrate, with music and dancing, in one of the dining halls. Friends would be invited. Those who had no interest in parties or were otherwise at leisure would watch the videos that were usually organised for weekends and holidays.

Occasionally fights broke out in the hostels. For instance, on the afternoon of 5 March 1985, two male students had an argument resulting in a fight in which one stabbed the other 'in the forehead and cut three of his fingers' In December 1984, at about 03h45, unidentified students entered Moeketsi's room through the window and stabbed him with a screwdriver. This prompted Jimmy Phambo to suggest that burglar bars be installed in students' rooms. These were not part of the original plans because the architect, Spencer Hodgson, thought that there would be few robberies. However, when the local people realised that the ANC residents were not armed as they had at first assumed, burglary became a constant problem.

Recreation

Sport was one way in which SOMAFCO students spent their free time. After afternoon classes, which ended at 16h00 to 16h30, many would go to the sports fields. There were many types of sport at SOMAFCO, including tennis, boxing, football, netball and karate. There were also activities like the aerobics group formed by female students in the late 1980s, which differed somewhat from the conventional sports. Following afternoon sports, students returned to their rooms at 18h00 hours to prepare for supper.

Sport was played and followed avidly at SOMAFCO. The passion for football in Soweto and other townships, the personal commitment of Dennis September, the primary school principal, the presence of physical education in the syllabus, and perhaps also the Soviet Union's emphasis on sport, all contributed to this enthusiasm. Also, many came to the school with high levels of skill in various sporting codes. Sport played the ambiguous role both of providing healthy and enjoyable recreation, and of diverting students' attention from the problems and tensions of life at Mazimbu. However, this stress on sport was similar to that in schools in South Africa, and in this respect SOMAFCO was not very different from schools back home. During the weekend, students grouped themselves into teams to play soccer and other games, both amongst themselves and, in the case of soccer, sometimes against local teams or staff teams.

Student leisure time was not always dominated by sport. SOMAFCO students did not abandon the varied cultural life of South Africa. This was shown through their participation in activities organised by the Cultural Committee. The five sections of this committee were music, drama, poetry, art and dance.

12. Students playing scrabble outside their dormitories

Dance included styles from different parts of South Africa, as well as gumboot dancing, an art generated by migrant labour and mine compounds.

The cultural groups held concerts on campus to entertain their fellow students. Observers agree that the standard in drama, dance and music was high. Some students went on to join the Amandla Ensemble, the ANC cultural group that performed internationally in support of the fight against apartheid. Entertainment spilled over into other spheres: the News Committee, as has been seen, was a prominent institution at the school, with its daily summaries of the current news.

As well as performing on campus, SOMAFCO cultural groups also performed for Tanzanian audiences and abroad, acting as ambassadors and propagandists for the school and the ANC. In December 1983, for instance, the drama group visited the Netherlands and Sweden, where they socialised and debated with local students and shared the stage with renowned performers like the exiled jazz musician Hugh Masekela. The other dimension of such trips was that SOMAFCO students were given opportunities that they would never have had in South Africa to travel and expand their mental horizons.

Religious activities

In many boarding schools in South Africa there is a church or chapel. There was no church at SOMAFCO, and no formal religious activities took place. This was because the school, especially in its early days, was influenced by a Soviet style of Marxist ideology in which religion had no place. So, for example, there were no prayers at morning assemblies. Students sang '*Nkosi Sikelel' iAfrica*' (God Bless Africa), which is indeed a hymn, but was sung as a national anthem. The singing was followed directly by announcements, usually by the school principal. Unlike what was common in South Africa, meetings were not preceded by a prayer. Even at funerals only revolutionary songs would be sung, as well as the national anthem. The tenor of parts of the curriculum, and in particular the course on development of societies, was materialist and in essence incompatible with the religious point of view.

The absence of churches in Mazimbu does not mean that people were refused freedom of religion. People were allowed to visit local churches for worship. It is then not so surprising that the ANC sent staff members for courses to Mindolo Ecumenical Centre in Ndola, Zambia, a church-affiliated institution that offered religious education as part of its curriculum. After all, in a phrase frequently used to describe the political position of the ANC, the organisation was a 'broad church' accommodating divergent groups, including religious organisations, and individuals like Frank Chikane and Allan Boesak who were leaders in the struggle against apartheid within the country during the turbulent 1980s. Nevertheless, religion was tolerated rather than encouraged in the school's early days.

However, some SOMAFCO residents, like many South Africans, felt the need for spiritual support, especially when there were deaths or other crises. There was a corresponding tendency for religion to take on a more prominent role as the years went by, to the extent that in 1989 to 1990 a clergyman by the name of Sasha was assigned to Mazimbu, though this does not seem to have led to any large-scale religious revival. He began his ministry using one of the classrooms for worship. Though the Reverend Sasha was later discovered to be an imposter, he played his pastoral role well. It is interesting that the increase in visible religious observance at SOMAFCO coincides with the disintegration of the Eastern Bloc and its generally atheistic ideology. Remote though it was, SOMAFCO was not divorced from the impact of political change in the world at large.

Dealing with prejudice

On occasion various forms of sectionalism manifested themselves at SOMAFCO. Nana Masusu, a student of mixed South African and Tanzanian origins, says that the relationship between students was generally good but that at times there were tensions amongst some of them. Students born in South Africa tended to refer to those born in exile as *makwerekwere*, a derogatory term used in South Africa to refer to other black Africans, whilst those born in exile called those who fled the regime *wakimbizi*, a Swahili word for refugees. This tension was most intense in the early days of SOMAFCO, leading sometimes to physical clashes. However, this did not go unchallenged by the authorities, who explained to students the importance of living together as South Africans. According to Mercedes Seete, an ex-SOMAFCO student, as time went on people learnt to live together in harmony. The administration also used other methods to unite the students. For example, they would periodically be shifted around in their dormitories, generally every six months, to avoid the formation of cliques as far as possible. The attempt was also made to avoid possible sectionalism at staff level. Nevertheless, it may sometimes have been a factor: it is said, for instance, that the reason for the departure of one prominent official is that he was alleged to favour Transkeians.

There were also some divisions between the students who came from South Africa. Tladi Ditshego says that in his days as a student in the early 1980s, it was not easy, for example, for a young Sotho man to go out with a Xhosa girl. He attributed this not to ethnic feeling as such, but rather to the fact that Sotho students might not have gone through initiation, and could be seen as *amakhwenkwe*, 'boys' – as males who have not yet undergone initiation are referred to in Xhosa society.

The attempt to maintain local traditions did not, of course, necessarily imply conflict. There were attempts to hold on to South African customs in the very different context of exile life in Tanzania. For those who wished for it, circumcision was performed in a traditional way with *ingcibis* like Tatu' Mgabelo and Mr Maluti in charge. But as Dr Siphokazi Sokupha, a medical practitioner at SOMAFCO, says, the peculiar conditions of exile did have an impact, and boys were not taken to live in the bush for some time, as the tradition requires. It was feared that in tropical surroundings so different from the veld of the Eastern Cape, students would develop diseases like malaria.

Sectionalism revived as SOMAFCO experienced a further influx of youth from South Africa in the troubled years around 1988 to 1989. The student refugees of the late 1980s were the products of the shattered educational system of those years, moulded more by the almost anarchic violence of the time than by the educational and political concerns typical of 1976. They grouped themselves into Xhosas, Zulus (usually referred to as *inkatha* because of their Natal origins, a nickname that itself indicates the confused political consciousness of many of these young people), and Sowetans (those coming from Johannesburg). SOMAFCO students of an earlier generation were often shocked by the violence displayed by some of the new arrivals. Cases of stabbing were one result. A curfew was declared on campus, and the Tanzanian Defence Force tightened security. Those responsible for the death of a student who had been stabbed in one incident were arrested, handed over to the Tanzanian police, and ultimately imprisoned. It was a frightening indication of the extent of social disintegration in parts of South Africa.

The group that appeared most threatening was that from KwaZulu-Natal, an area wracked by factional violence. In the context of SOMAFCO, however, a kind of Zulu identity seems to have predominated over tensions existing within the region, and their attitude towards their fellow students and others in the complex was totally different to the behaviour expected at SOMAFCO. They tended to form themselves into consciously Zulu groups and harass non-Zulus. Portia Fritz, a student at the time, asserts that a person could not even pass them by without being teased about his or her ethnic affiliation. As a result, she says, the character of SOMAFCO, which had become home to those who had been there for some time, changed decisively. The attitude of these students of course also reflects the increased use of an ethnic divide and rule strategy by the South African government through, for example, the homelands policy.

Dealing with offences

In addition to stealing and fighting, there were other acts committed by the students which the college authorities regarded as offences, including dagga smoking and becoming pregnant. These were dealt with harshly by the authorities and sometimes by the students themselves.

The students had their own disciplinary committee, which prosecuted and convicted students for minor offences such as stealing clothes from another person. The most common punishment for those found guilty was to be made to cut grass, thus making sure that the offender paid for his wrongdoing while, at the same time, keeping the school premises tidy. If a student ignored the decision of the disciplinary committee, he or she would be denied the normal stipend until punishment had been served. Otherwise he or she would be reported to the school authorities that would take tougher measures. Cases which students felt they could not handle were referred to the school disciplinary committee. An example is that of one female student who slept with her boyfriend in her room. When the school disciplinary committee met on 22 May 1985, a decision was taken to punish her: it was decided that 'she must clean the laundry and the dining hall for seven weeks'.

Justice was not always done impartially. According to some ex-students, the student disciplinary committee could be slow to punish certain offenders. This was because some of them were protected by their friends on the committee. At times the offender himself might have been on the disciplinary committee and thus would not be punished.

Cases of rape and attempted rape were rare at SOMAFCO. However, they did occur occasionally, as when an attempted rape was reported on 2 January 1983. The disciplinary committee convicted the student accused of the crime, and sent him to the Rehabilitation Centre at Dakawa Development Centre, 55 kilometres north of Mazimbu, for two years.

Love affairs between students sometimes resulted in pregnancy, in spite of the family planning advice that was meant to be available to all campus residents including students. This was a constant worry to the authorities, which were divided on how to respond – caught as they could be between revolutionary puritanism, sometimes strangely allied with religious and social conservatism, and open-minded tolerance. Many of the students of SOMAFCO were, after all, adults in their late teens and twenties, ages at which people would normally be expected to take responsibility for the results of their actions. This clashed with the assumption that the students were children who had not reached the stage when they were entitled to both the pleasures and responsibilities of sex and pregnancy. While steady relationships were not opposed, there was no attempt to encourage couples to establish a family unit and care jointly for the infants that they brought into the world. The argument was that unplanned pregnancies diverted the couple from their mission of acquiring education and training, and the authorities therefore responded harshly to such cases.

An attempt was made to equalise treatment of men and women, but on the basis of punishment rather than the encouragement of family responsibility. As seen in Chapter 4, male students who impregnated their female partners were suspended from school for two years and sent to work at the Rehabilitation Centre at Dakawa or elsewhere. The woman was also suspended from classes for two years.

In spite of these tensions, the high rate of pregnancy amongst SOMAFCO students and others did lead to the adoption of a proactive approach to family planning. In May 1984 a committee was appointed to draw up a programme for youth and students, and to compile teaching material on family planning, graded according to age. Later in the same year a survey was carried out to get the views of the Mazimbu community on unplanned pregnancies and abortions and how they might be minimised. In November 1985 a working document, *Taking Care of Yourself*, spelt out an educational programme that dealt with areas like substance abuse, stress, exercise, sexuality, health and fertility, birth control and sexually transmitted diseases. However, this issue, sometimes controversial in the most placid of societies, was never addressed in a wholly satisfactory way at Mazimbu. Oral accounts give contradictory versions of the amount of advice and support available, no doubt mirroring the differing experience of individuals in relation to health professionals with a range of attitudes.

Dagga smoking was one of the problems encountered by the SOMAFCO authorities. They regarded this as a serious offence, and the college disciplinary committee prosecuted anyone apprehended. Punishment normally consisted of manual labour; for instance, in April 1984, one student found guilty was given the task of uprooting a number of trees. Dr Wintshi Njobe reports that sometimes dagga smokers would be arrested by the ANC security branch and taken to the school farm where they would be kept for about two weeks in what students knew as 'Alcatraz', an isolation centre away from other students. However, the possible repercussions on a student's future career were more serious than such punishments. The student who lost his scholarship to study in the Soviet Union in 1980 is an example of this. As an internal memorandum put it, 'this student is addicted to dagga and continues to behave dishonourably … we propose to replace him with Jimmy Mohohlo.'

Sometimes the disciplinary committee would feel compelled to expel students from school. When it met on 12 April 1981 to consider the case of three male students who were reported to have stolen clothes to sell in Morogoro, all three were convicted. Their punishment was to 'empty all the dustbins around the school and the kitchens daily for a period of three weeks'. They were also confined to Mazimbu for two weeks. But when one of them refused to take his punishment, the school authorities decided to expel him. The expulsion, however, was from the school, not the organisation. According to Njobe, this student went to Angola to join MK. Expulsions, however, were rare, and sometimes the school resorted to the less extreme method of suspension, which did not remove the student permanently from the campus.

Students smoked dagga and drank liquor, often in the neighbouring settlement of Dark City where alcohol and other pleasures were widely available. Did they do so in large part because of the exceptional frustrations and difficulties of life in exile? They were young people. At home they would have had the support of families and others who might have known how to respond to their problems. At Mazimbu they experienced nostalgia and homesickness that could lead to anti-social behaviour. They knew very well that going back home would mean arrest by the South African security police and possibly torture or death. However, there were no doubt also students at SOMAFCO who engaged in smoking dagga or drinking liquor simply from a sense of adventure.

Many students seem to have found the physical surroundings of Mazimbu depressing. Vuyani Mlati remembers that 'there was a mountain this side ... and a mountain that side ... you'll never know where South Africa was.' Dr Njobe tells the tragic story of a student who had performed very well in a play staged at the school one evening. The next morning he committed suicide by throwing himself in front of a train. He feels that suppressed homesickness could lead to some students becoming psychologically disturbed. In a place like Mazimbu, where students were far from their parents, it was not easy to recover from depression. The refugee situation with its uncertainty, restlessness and deprivation of family relations could generate strains that were hard to bear, in spite of strenuous efforts to build a community. There were no relatives to comfort students with mental problems. Everyone had to nurse his or her own frustrations.

But the problems of some disturbed students went beyond conditions at Mazimbu. Dr Sokupha says that some of the students who were psychologically disturbed had earlier been detained, tortured and maimed by the police in South Africa, and denied treatment for injuries so sustained. There was thus a high incidence of physiological and psychological post-traumatic disorders. Some could not even tolerate the singing of freedom songs, at the sound of which they would break down and scream. Others had unexplained headaches, or signs and symptoms of peptic ulcers that apparently had no real physical cause. Some had 'unexplained skin rashes which were not biological', while others experienced chronic insomnia. Dr Sokupha attributes this to stress and anxiety. Freddy Reddy, a medical practitioner and psychologist who visited the school each year to treat cases within his speciality, adds that the change of environment often upset the young people who were mostly from urban areas. He takes Dakawa as an example, where new arrivals faced the tropical climate, where the water was not good, and where city and township life was absent. Many caught malaria and some succumbed to the virulent cerebral variety which, if they survived, could effect their mental stability. Those not affected would watch with anguish as their comrades became ill.

Dr Sokupha also suggests other reasons why the youth became frustrated in exile. According to her some of them had no political motivation. She says that:

> People would go to exile because the boyfriend is going to exile … and the police are going to seek some information … around that person and somebody will decide to leave. Other people believed that going to exile was going abroad where things are happening and once you're out there …[you] … suddenly discovered that life was not what you thought it to be.

Dr Reddy says that criminals from South Africa escaping prosecution were amongst those who lacked political motivation. Another factor that contributed to the psychological breakdown of students, according to both Dr Sokupha and Dr Marco Mkya, a Tanzanian medical practitioner at SOMAFCO in 1992, was the abuse of drugs, particularly alcohol and dagga.

CHAPTER 9

South Africans and Tanzanians

The story of the ANC in exile can be told on various levels. On the one hand, it is a story of the geopolitics of liberation. African states, committed with greater or lesser enthusiasm to South Africa's freedom according to geographical proximity and ideological orientation, interacted with the South African liberation movements and were subjected to complex and changing pressures from both sides in the bipolar Cold War world. Such pressures further complicated the already intricate course of national and social liberation. On the other hand, it is a story of individual South Africans wrenched from their homes and scattered over the globe, especially over the continent of Africa.

In both spheres, the ANC and its members were thrown into close relationships with the governments and people of African countries. There were ironies in these relationships. Those who hoped to return one day to South Africa, the most powerful and populous state in the region, were at the mercy of policy changes over which they had no control in states, many of which were struggling economically and some of which were highly unstable politically. However, the exiles, though politically dependent, after an initial period of real deprivation, gained access to substantial resources. They were able to tap into generous donations, especially from Scandinavian countries and the Eastern Bloc, and this made the complex at Mazimbu, and to a lesser extent Dakawa, a centre of remarkable modern development in the context of the Morogoro District. They became large employers of Tanzanian labour, creating a perhaps unanticipated dynamic within the relationship between South Africans and Tanzanians. The intersection of Tanzanian poverty, but also ultimate political control, with relative South African wealth, and ultimate political dependence, was a complex situation with many social and psychic dimensions, and it is remarkable that neither side allowed it to become more tense and problematic than it did.

SOMAFCO, the Tanzanian government and security

The environment provided by Tanzania was crucial to the foundation and survival of SOMAFCO. The danger from South Africa was very real, and the political decision to host the school was backed by the Tanzanian security apparatus. ANC security also played a role in safeguarding the campus and its inhabitants – at times over-zealously, some felt.

Tanzania under President Julius Nyerere had a long history of support for the South African liberation struggle. Morogoro – where the ANC had its first headquarters in exile and where a crucial conference of the organisation had taken place in 1969 soon after the Wankie campaign, when ANC and Zapu forces entered Rhodesia from the north – was symbolically and practically an ideal venue for the new school. As Brigadier Hashim Mbita, the Executive Secretary of the Organisation of African Unity (OAU) Liberation Committee and a Tanzanian, says, SOMAFCO was 'a late child' of the relationship between the Tanzanians and the South Africans.

The OAU Liberation Committee was the key body liaising between the ANC and the government of Tanzania in finding a location for the new school. Brigadier Mbita was the crucial figure. There were squatters on the abandoned sisal estate which composed the bulk of the land handed to the ANC, and others lived under customary tenure in the north of the area made over to the organisation. However, discontent at the ceding of the land was not publicly aired. In interviews with local people, their resentment at their removal by the Tanzanian authorities is clear, and stories are told of police action to remove those who resisted.

Once Mazimbu had been handed to the ANC the question arose as to how relations between the newcomers and the Tanzanian authorities should be structured. The settlement benefited from the fact that Mama Anna Abdallah, the Regional Commissioner or Governor for Morogoro Region in the key years from the foundation of the school to 1983, sympathised strongly with the project, and gave it constant support. Every Monday she chaired a Security Committee meeting which dealt with relations with the ANC settlements, but which went well beyond security to explore ways in which bonds between the South Africans and the local community could be strengthened. Even after her departure for an equivalent post at Dodoma she continued to take an active interest in the school.

Another key Tanzanian figure was Alex Francis, the official appointed to liaise between the Liberation Committee of the OAU, the liberation movements and the Tanzanian government. Francis acted in this capacity to the ANC, the PAC and Swapo, the three recognised liberation organisations from South Africa and South African-occupied Namibia. He was based in Dar es Salaam, but paid frequent visits to Mazimbu and, later, Dakawa, and worked closely with the ANC chief representative in Tanzania. He facilitated the issue of travel documents and other bureaucratic matters, dealt with the aftermath of the many motor accidents in which the South Africans were involved, and with the quarrels that occasionally arose between them and their Tanzanian neighbours, and put the South Africans in touch with whatever government department was appropriate to particular needs. As Francis says, his office was a 'clearing-house' for the many issues that arose involving the South Africans and the host government and community.

The Tanzanian official who liaised with the settlement on the ground was the camp commandant, assigned by the Ministry of Home Affairs. While major security matters, such as the possibility of an attack from South Africa, were the responsibility of the armed forces, the commandant dealt with daily relations between the settlement and the Tanzanian authorities. Neither Mazimbu nor Dakawa had the extra-territorial status of an embassy, and the state's jurisdiction covered the settlements. As Francis puts it, 'You wouldn't commit an offence outside SOMAFCO and think that you can hibernate inside SOMAFCO, and you'll not be picked up.' However, whenever possible the Tanzanians left internal security to the ANC, and in practice there were grey areas in which the ANC carried out security functions not normally permitted to non-governmental organs.

Such grey areas were the inevitable product of the ambiguous situation of exile. The ANC asserted, and the Tanzanian government agreed, that the South Africans were not refugees, but rather political exiles. The settlement had a sort of *de facto* autonomy, yet when at one point the national authorities insisted that passes be shown at the gate to the complex, the Mazimbu authorities had a distinct feeling that the South Africans were being hemmed in. On the other hand, at times the Tanzanians did not merely assent to, but positively insisted upon the ANC signing agreements with other states, thus implicitly acknowledging the autonomy of the organization *vis-à-vis* themselves. Essentially, the twilight world of political exile and insurgency cannot be pinned down to precise constitutional and administrative formulae.

Tanzanian support of SOMAFCO, as of the South African liberation movements in general, was generous and sustained. The country did benefit to some extent from the presence of bases and settlements such as SOMAFCO that were funded from elsewhere. SOMAFCO became an important employer of local people in Morogoro. However, before the changes of the early 1990s, this was in the broader context of a lukewarm or even hostile reaction from Western countries, and of the ever-present danger of attack by South African government forces. The South African liberation movements have every reason to be grateful to the Tanzanian people and government of the time, and their leader, Julius Nyerere, for their unstinting support.

The Tanzanian authorities were aware that the South African government could attack SOMAFCO at any time, as they had attacked the ANC in other countries. The 1982 raid on Maseru, Lesotho, for instance, in which civilians including women and children were murdered, indicated that the population of Mazimbu could also be in danger. The possibility of such attacks made the security of the South Africans a national issue also for Tanzanians.

A Tanzanian voice on this matter is that of Mama Anna Abdallah. She puts the ANC and PAC presence and attendant threats from South Africa in the context of the long history of Tanzanian support for African liberation movements, including those from Mozambique, Zimbabwe and Angola as well as South Africa. 'Once you embark on such things,' she says, 'you have to expect all the problems that go with accommodating them.' Brigadier Mbita shared these concerns.

The sense of threat from the South African regime was also noticeable at Mazimbu itself. Tladi Ditshego says that the school authorities continually emphasised that being outside South Africa did not mean that they were safe, and that vigilance was essential. In the early 1980s there were rumours that the regime was going to attack SOMAFCO, and that South African forces would use Malawi as a staging post to fly to Mazimbu. It was said that the official opening of the school in 1985 was to be targeted. It appears that there may indeed have been some substance to this rumour, as subsequently emerged at the hearings of the Truth and Reconciliation Commission. As a result of such fears trenches were dug all over the Mazimbu campus. Alex Francis recalls the wariness and suspicion that necessarily characterised attitudes to potential visitors: anyone who wanted to visit SOMAFCO or make contact with the school authorities first had to receive clearance from his office. Usually visitors were only allowed to enter the campus after the SOMAFCO authorities had responded through this office.

As the Tanzanian government had accepted the responsibility for the safety of Mazimbu, it provided soldiers from the Tanzanian Defence Force (TDF) to ensure security and monitor the movement of Mazimbu's inhabitants in and out of the school. This was the main reason why students and staff had to get permission before leaving the campus. As Brigadier Mbita puts it, SOMAFCO was provided with enough soldiers to patrol the complex but not so many as to militarise it. However, the threat from South Africa was not the only reason for the presence of Tanzanian forces. Students from SOMAFCO sometimes misbehaved in town, brawling in discos and taverns, and this was another reason for attempting to limit and control the movement of people to and from the complex. In this, the ANC agreed with the Tanzanian authorities.

An army that had been instrumental in the overthrow of Idi Amin in Uganda in 1978 was not to be underestimated, even in a possible clash with the sophisticated forces of the South African regime. On the other hand, the cell system in Tanzania also contributed to ensuring the safety of the South Africans. Every ten houses in Tanzania were organised into a cell, which were intended to be the eyes and ears of the Tanzanian security forces. The arrest of some alleged South African security agents in Morogoro, there to bomb the complex or to spy on it, was the result of this system. However, in spite of such co-operation, the government did not really encourage contact between the local people and the inhabitants of Mazimbu. As Patrick Mtshaulana puts it:

> The situation in Mazimbu was very complex. The leadership of the complex and of the ANC was under considerable pressure from the Tanzanians … that we should not expose their people to dangers and therefore less contact with their own people. And this … in a way contributes to the attitude that our people have … because they have no understanding of the Tanzanians. They only see and meet Tanzanians who are doing manual work and look down upon them.

The fear of attack grew when SOMAFCO and Dakawa received ANC cadres from the frontline states after the Nkomati Accord of 1984. The regime could easily have used the presence of these militants as an excuse to attack Mazimbu.

Apart from security provided by the Tanzanian government, the ANC also had its own personnel, who worked closely with ANC security in other countries like Zambia, as well as, at times, with the Tanzanian authorities. Many SOMAFCO students regarded ANC security with ambivalence. Apart from ensuring the safety of the complex, it was responsible for screening people who had left South Africa for exile. It was crucial to establish whether they had left the country for political reasons, or whether they had been sent to spy for the regime. Manala Manzini, the ANC Political Officer at SOMAFCO in 1985 and Chief Representative of the ANC in Tanzania from 1987 until the end of the school, says that by the time people had been allocated to the school or to MK, much would have been already done to investigate their backgrounds. In that way, infiltration to the ANC camps was avoided. But, Manzini says, 'there are those who slipped the net.'

Mary Thuse, who was first at Mazimbu and then became the Director of Dakawa, says that both Dakawa and SOMAFCO were victims of infiltration. Some infiltrators, she says, worked to turn the inhabitants against the authorities. Some were allegedly sent on assassination missions, while others poisoned food. Some appeared conspicuously loyal and were promoted to positions where they could get information about the ANC's activities and plans; a good example is a political commissar at SOMAFCO found to be a collaborator in 1983.

In one incident, the water supply from the nearby Ngerengere River was poisoned. Luckily, local people noticed that fish were dying in the river, and they notified the SOMAFCO authorities. The reservoir supplying Mazimbu was cut off for a time, and it was discovered that the water contained a poisonous substance. It was never proven who was responsible. This sort of incident goes some way to explain the near-paranoia that the very real threat from the South African regime inevitably generated. In another case, some people who were arrested agreed they had been sent to sabotage the ANC. As Siphiwe Xaba, a security operative, says, they had been trained to make poison. After demonstrating how the poison was made, the substance was given to a dog that died instantly.

Those who confessed to spying were usually rehabilitated and reintegrated into the community after some time. But first, Xaba says, they were sent to Lusaka to extract information from them. Others would confess to spying even before they were arrested. As Mary Thuse says, the reality of life at Mazimbu could lead some spies to abandon their covert activities. Colleagues who had already been arrested exposed others. 'Difficult people,' as Xaba calls them, would be taken to ANC holding camps in Tanzania, and then sent to Quatro, the detention camp in Angola identified by the Motsuenyane Commission of Enquiry in 1993 with the abuse of ANC prisoners. SOMAFCO itself had a prison, known as 'Alcatraz', next to the farm, where those suspected of espionage were initially interrogated after being picked up by ANC security, usually at night.

Sometimes security made mistakes, and innocent people would be accused of spying. Joe Mukwalo remembers a student who was held. Security was suspicious of him because of his smart clothes, which they suspected were paid for by the regime in return for information. It was later discovered that a girlfriend working in Botswana had sent them to him. It was realised that a mistake had been made and the student was returned to Mazimbu society. But Mukwalo says that even after such a return, the stigma of having been a suspected spy remained.

The mutiny that shook the ANC in Angola in 1983, and its suppression, had echoes at Dakawa and Mazimbu. In 1988 the imprisoned mutineers were transferred to Dakawa, and during the following year they played an active and critical role in the political life of the centre. They believed that there was a lack of democracy at the centre and in the ANC more generally, and they confronted the authorities, including Andrew Masondo, the SOMAFCO principal, who had been one of the leading figures taking a hard line in the suppression of the mutiny.

In the chaotic late 1980s and early 1990s, young people flooded into SOMAFCO, mainly from Natal. It was feared that many of these were infiltrators, though probably most were in fact simply desperate refugees from this disturbed and divided region rather than actual government agents. George Mwali, a student at the time, notes how these incomers broke the school code of conduct and brought drugs onto campus. They were involved in stabbings, resulting in the tightening of security and the declaration of a campus curfew. Again, the line between conscious subversion – to which some of the alleged infiltrators were said to have confessed – and the disruption born of poverty and despair, is a fine one.

It is difficult to balance the methods arguably necessitated by security in a perilous situation, against the danger that those methods would subvert the very justice and human rights for which the ANC was fighting. There is no doubt, however, that an atmosphere of fear prevailed in relation to the security apparatus, where, if people were perceived as differing from the organisation, they could be seen as enemy agents and treated accordingly, without the protection of an established judicial system.

The politics of food

The origins of the productive modern farm at Mazimbu have been described. This example of relative South African wealth, contrasting with Tanzanian poverty and even hunger, led to debate within the ANC about the selling of surplus agricultural production. The farm was intended to be a training institution as well as a source of food, as emphasised in late 1983 in a report by H Tudor-Evans, in which he said that:

> The primary aim of the food project at SOMAFCO is to obtain self-sufficiency in foodstuffs, generate collective employment and increase and diversify production. It is also intended to extend the concept and practice of education and training with production, the aim of the training is, of course, to feed members with skills for similar rural food processing projects and not to train people for formal sector industry or employment. Each unit would be run on an autonomous commercial basis and although the main market outlet would be within the college, to generate additional income from neighbouring communities would be of mutual benefit to both parties.

It could be argued that there is a touch of romantic rural communalism in the insistence that training was 'of course' not for formal sector employment. Nonetheless, this was the first time that commercialisation was mentioned in conjunction with self-sufficiency. The realisation of such possibilities was triggered by the disastrous failure of Tanzanian agriculture to meet the food needs of the country. Thus, there were several requests to buy the more than 50 tons of surplus maize produced by the settlement. In 1985 Likobe Primary School in Morogoro asked to buy 20 bags of maize. Mchikichini Hostel, which housed 250 students, made the same request, adding that the National Milling Corporation in Morogoro had no maize. Such requests were not limited to neighbouring Morogoro. For instance, the Coastal Salt Works Company in Dar es Salaam wrote bemoaning the shortage of food for its workers and asking for 200 bags. The Ardhi Institute, a parastatal organisation that carried out soil surveys and related work, requested 300 bags. Commercialisation was not necessarily planned, but conditions presented the farm with the opportunity to think seriously about the matter and refocus their vision to incorporate a market-oriented outlook.

To test the Tanzanian government's feelings about this new venture, Director Mohammed Tikly wrote to the regional commissioner for Dodoma on 27 July 1985, offering to sell the regional government maize flour, which was evidently in short supply, as attested by the requests from institutions. He said that Mazimbu had a surplus of 50 tons and that they were willing to sell this to the government at the market price plus the transport charges. On 6 September, the regional commissioner's office responded that 'currently the maize situation in this region is somehow healthy promising [*sic*]'. This official rebuff, however, did not stop requests from individual agencies that wanted maize, and illustrates the government's unwillingness to admit to the very real food security problems in the area.

The situation led the Farm Committee to formulate an agricultural produce sales policy. They decided that they would only sell maize to the National Milling Corporation and to Tanzanian nationals working at Mazimbu. This decision was calculated to ensure good relations with the government and, in the context of food shortages in the region, hopefully to guarantee favorable treatment in the future if ever insufficient production at Mazimbu led to a need to purchase food supplies. Nevertheless, the entrepreneurial spirit remained, with, for instance, the farm manager writing to Tikly to say that the farm was willing to hire out a tractor, disk-plough and driver at 250 shillings per hour.

The farm was an unusual phenomenon in Tanzania. It was probably the most modern and mechanised agricultural establishment in the country, operating on the basis of large sums of money from Scandinavian countries and elsewhere, yet was seen as representing the ideology of self-reliance. It was founded on principles of socialist egalitarianism, yet probed towards a more commercial and entrepreneurial mode of operation. It was a South African enterprise supported by Sweden, yet the farm labourers were Tanzanians. Few South Africans actually worked on the farm, and those who did were mostly in managerial positions. It represented a level of technology, expertise and investment that proved impossible to maintain once the ANC withdrew from Mazimbu, and today it is a sad relic, barely functioning as a productive enterprise.

SOMAFCO in its local context

The South African inhabitants of Mazimbu were a diverse group, united by their political loyalty to the ANC. Amongst the staff were some who had arrived recently from South Africa and others who had spent many years in exile in different parts of the world. Although there were many students born of exiled South Africans, or of marriages between exiles and Tanzanians, Zambians or others, the core student body was composed of those who had fled in the aftermath of the Soweto uprising of 1976 and subsequently.

Most SOMAFCO students were from an urban background. As well as a tradition of political militancy, they also brought with them the atmosphere of the township youth culture of the day. This is not easy to summarise, but includes sharp dressing, personal bravado, colourful slang, familiarity and sometimes involvement with the criminal world, and a certain contempt for the country bumpkin. It is a world that had been described, and perhaps romanticised, by the talented writers of *Drum* magazine in what retrospectively may seem the halcyon days of the 1950s. This world persisted recognisably into the 1970s and 1980s, though it was given a bitter and confrontational edge, and at the same time isolated and confined, by the intense repression that began in the 1960s.

This township world was almost as different as it could be from that of rural Tanzania. The Morogoro area was essentially one of peasant agriculture and herding, with a few sisal estates, the remnants of an industry in decline. For the most part, the people of the area endured a grinding rural poverty that followed the rhythms of the agricultural year, with its bare sufficiency and occasional famine. The newcomers, however, emerged from a poverty measured in monetary resources, or the lack of them, with a capricious quality derived from the occasional sudden opportunities offered by the urban economy. These two worlds met surprisingly, and battled to understand each other at Mazimbu.

Though the Mazimbu complex, with SOMAFCO at its heart, aimed to some extent at self-sufficiency, it was not an island. The population was, in fact, in constant contact with the local people, linked to them in various ways from educational activities to sport. Mazimbu also deliberately served the local population, notably by providing medical services. The hospital at the settlement treated 2 500 to 3 000 patients per month, with about 75 per cent of these from the local Tanzanian population. The hospital could accommodate 20 in-patients and a similar number of 'in-out' patients who stayed in bed at home and were brought to the hospital for observation and medication every 24 hours. Apart from such services, there were also many other, less formal contacts between South Africans and Tanzanians.

13. Building SOMAFCO: Tanzanian workers such as these were essential to the school

Though the various schools that made up SOMAFCO operated independently from the Tanzanian educational system, there were some links of an informal and extracurricular kind. For example, children from the pre-school were brought on visits to Tanzanian pre-schools in Morogoro and Dar es Salaam, with the aim, according to Farida Mussagy, of helping the children to relate to and co-operate with those from other backgrounds, and of promoting the exchange of ideas between teachers. This school also donated surplus toys to local crèches, a gesture which was intended to demonstrate the gratitude of the South Africans for Tanzanian hospitality, but which also emphasised the differences in the resources available to the two systems. In a similar spirit, SOMAFCO primary school was linked to the local primary schools, for example assisting Lukobe Primary to prepare its gardens for cultivation every year. Given the highly mechanised nature of the Mazimbu farm, unique at the time in the Morogoro area and perhaps in Tanzania as a whole, it could be asked if a gesture such as this, digging with hoes while tractors ploughed Mazimbu's extensive fields, did much more than highlight the disparity between the two systems.

Sports and culture

As everywhere, the ambiguous battleground of sport was one arena for interaction. During weekends students would group themselves into teams to play soccer and other games with each other. The school, in turn, had teams that competed with those from the locality. For example, SOMAFCO students had a football team called *Chiawelo*, named after one of the zones in Soweto, which competed in the local league. There were no league teams in the immediate vicinity of the school, and good players from Mazimbu, Darajani, Dark City, and other villages, would sometimes be drafted into the SOMAFCO team.

Apart from sports like football, which can engender a cosmopolitan consciousness of a sort – though sometimes as much the reinforcement of stereotypes as a genuine internationalism – South Africans and Tanzanians probed each other's cultures in other ways. One can sense the excitement of Nkosana Sithole as he describes what were to him the exotic leaping dances of the Maasai people. SOMAFCO was very open to such interchange, and local Tanzanian schools were often invited to participate in concerts at Mazimbu. In turn, cultural groups from SOMAFCO would be invited to perform in places like Morogoro stadium and the University of Dar es Salaam, where, no doubt, cultural exchange took place, but where solidarity between the Tanzanian regime and the forces of South African liberation was also displayed publicly.

The transition to Tanzania for South African students, introduced for the first time to a non-South African culture, could be a difficult yet exciting one. Even on first arrival at Dar es Salaam, students were, for instance, often confused by the long black outfit worn by some Tanzanian Muslim women, resembling that worn for about a year after the death of their husbands by widows in black South African communities as a sign of mourning. Black children in South Africa, locked in the townships as a result of apartheid laws like the *Group Areas Act*, were deprived of opportunities to familiarise themselves with other races and their cultures. Bantu Education was meant to confine children in all spheres including the religious. For example, until she went to Tanzania, Helen Radebe thought that Christianity was the only religion in the world. For her, the move to Tanzania was a real psychological liberation. This liberation worked both ways: Jabu Mahlangu recalls that the South Africans were thought to be cannibals by the village children, who would run away, thinking that they would be seized and eaten by these strangers. But, he says, eventually the villagers began to see that they were like them and the idea that they were cannibals disappeared.

Yet similarities between the Tanzanian and South African ways of life are as striking as the differences. The question of indigenous healing is particularly interesting. Take for instance the case of a female ANC cadre who had psychiatric problems and needed treatment. In a letter of May 1982 to Stan Mabizela from Joe Nhlanhla, the Administrative Secretary of the ANC in Lusaka, it was suggested that this person had to undergo 'the normal treatment there at the hospital' (in Tanzania) and in addition 'black psychiatric treatment [from] the local black traditional psychiatrists (*amagqira*)'. The South Africans had come to trust the traditional healing methods of the local people, and the use of the Xhosa word *amagqira* indicates that the Tanzanian healers were seen as using virtually the same craft as those from South Africa.

Another case of what science in the Western tradition would describe as psychiatric illness was that of two SOMAFCO students, a man and a woman, who had recently left Mozambique for Tanzania in the wake of the Nkomati Accord, and whose case was taken up by the Women's Section in Mazimbu in July 1984. A letter about the case from the Mazimbu branch to the head of the organization in Lusaka was written in Sotho:

> *Bothata ba bana ba ke gore ba na le badimo. Ba tlogile Maputo ele gore ba tshwanetse go direlwa moletlo wa Badimo, ba be ba tshepiswa (ke ofisi-Maputo) gore ba tla lokesetswa go busetswa gae go yo phetisa morero. Tshepiso eo ga e kebe ya phetiswa. Botlhoko ke gore ga janong bana ba ba gateletwse … Ophela ka tlhogo e remang le mokwatla o pang mo gare ga magetla, ositwa go robala gontle le gore a tshegetswe a robale a ntse mo bolaong. Ere go ntse jalo o na le go lora a tsamaya a ya bodibeng. Bolwetse bo bo mo tshwenya le mo thutong tsa gagwe ga a sa tswella sentle … le yena o phela ka bothata boo. O phela ka tlhogo e remang e mo direlang le sedidi abe a ifale matlho.*
>
> [The problem with these children is that they are filled with ancestral spirits. A cultural ritual was supposed to be done for them before they left Maputo and they were promised (by the office in Maputo) that they would be sent back home for this ritual. However, the promise was not kept. The problem is that their ancestors are unhappy … (she) has a headache all the time, and cannot sleep at night. Sometimes she dreams about visiting her ancestors at the valley. Due to her sickness, she is no longer doing well at school. (He) … has the same problems also. He has a severe headache that causes dizziness.]

This letter indicates the persistence in political exile of belief in the spiritual world of the ancestors. It also, incidentally, illustrates the use of South African languages in this context; it is probably not coincidental that one such language should have been used when dealing with an issue so involved with the fabric of African life.

As well as utilising what could be called indigenous psychiatry, ANC cadres also used Tanzanian herbal treatment. Jane Dumasi describes the medical help she received when her daughter, a SOMAFCO student, had persistent sores and treatment at the hospital was ineffective. After speaking to a Maasai about the problem, he picked some leaves from a tree in her yard, warmed them for some time, and applied them, with butter, to the sores, which soon healed. He made no charge, regarding medicine as something that should not be sold.

These examples show that at least in some cases the ANC, a nationalist organisation that identified itself as modern and scientific, was not averse to making use of indigenous medicine. Indeed, according to Joe Kabetso, if a person wanted to go to one of these healers, the ANC would pay for the treatment. However, there was uneasiness in the minds of some ANC officials about this pan-African approach to indigenous healing. For instance, in 1985 the residential commissar at Lilian Ngoyi Residence at Dakawa noted what he saw as 'a serious problem': 'Cdes [*sic*] are frequenting the witch doctors in the villages and this [*sic*] finally come to our residence to do their work to their customers.' The commissar instructed that such visits to the residences should stop immediately.

There was also constant interaction between the formal medical sector at Mazimbu and the Tanzanian system as a whole. The medical resources of Mazimbu, notably the hospital, served the local population as well as the South Africans. When, on the other hand, cases arose beyond its capabilities, they were referred to the regional hospital in Morogoro, or to Dar es Salaam. The Mazimbu medical department was generally well stocked with drugs and other medical supplies, and when any medicine was approaching expiry, it would be transferred to the Tanzanian system, which had many shortages, where it could be used speedily.

Language is both the vehicle for and part of culture. Familiarity with another language certainly does not guarantee sympathy with the culture expressed through it, and of course a single language will always be the medium for many 'cultures'. However, the command of another's language is, if not a precondition, at least a potent enabling factor for such sympathy. How did Jane Dumasi explain to the Maasai that her daughter had sores that needed to be cured? How did the Tanzanians employed in the complex, and the South Africans who went to enjoy themselves in town, communicate? The answer to this is the acquisition of new languages by both parties.

The language in which the ANC operated educationally and administratively was English. Mama Abdallah believes that the South African presence greatly boosted competence in English amongst the people of the area. However, the linguistic influence went far beyond this. It is possible to hear people today in the heart of Dark City speaking excellent Zulu. For instance, Kaburu, also known as Khasimbazi, or Javas, a dealer in stolen goods who was always in the company of SOMAFCO students and who resided in Dark City, is fluent not only in Zulu but also in tsotsi taal, the vernacular of black South African township youth. Yet Khasimbazi has never been outside Tanzania. Amongst the South Africans, many of the students and others at Mazimbu and Dakawa became proficient in Swahili, the *lingua franca* of East Africa. The intensity of the relationship between the South African and Tanzanian cultures is well illustrated by the interpenetration of their respective languages.

Social relations between South Africans and Tanzanians were embedded in language. Intermarriages took place between some adults from the two communities, and male students tended to have less-permanent relations with local girls that did not result in marriage but did sometimes result in pregnancies. Adult men of the older generation of exiles had often settled with their wives in the neighbouring villages. Many of this group had spent much of their lives in exile and when the complexes were closing they were sometimes unsure about resettling in South Africa. EM Siyo married a Tanzanian woman and became exposed to Swahili, while his wife learnt Zulu. Monica Mathe, who lived in Dark City at the time of the research and had married one of the South African veterans, speaks Zulu, as do her children who attended SOMAFCO. Palmiro Coedoe, whose father was a South African and mother a Tanzanian, was familiar with various South African and Tanzanian languages as well as English. He was also exposed to the Christianity of his father and the Islam of his mother. This sometimes led to family conflict on dietary matters, such as the eating of pork, forbidden to Muslims.

Students and Morogoro

At Mazimbu, Tanzanian soldiers were stationed at the SOMAFCO entrance at the bridge leading to Morogoro over the Ngerengere River, which demarcated the boundary between the settlement and the populated area towards Morogoro. Before going to town, students had to show the guards written permission endorsed by the school authorities. If they wanted to leave the campus without permits, they would, as ex-Mazimbu resident Lungi Mankazana says, 'have to bribe the guards because they were corrupt'. A cheaper but more risky alternative was to swim the Ngerengere in one of its more secluded reaches. The boundaries of the ANC settlements were in fact highly porous.

Mazimbu and Dakawa were in many ways demonetarised welfare societies. The basic requirements of food and clothing were provided by the ANC through the *umphando* system. In addition, every month students received a small amount of pocket-money from the school authorities, which few, if any, regarded as sufficient for entertainment and other indulgences like cigarettes and liquor, or for necessities like soap and toothpaste that were not provided by the organisation. Though the pocket-money was meagre, it did rise somewhat in real value with the decline of the Tanzanian shilling. The school arranged transport for students to travel the five kilometres to and from Morogoro, where they could buy what they needed with their stipend.

Frequently, local people would come on campus, usually late in the afternoon, to sell peanuts and other snacks to students. When, as often happened, students did not have the necessary money, they 'fried' with the local people. 'Frying' involved students exchanging goods with the neighbouring inhabitants for whatever was for sale, for example clothing that came as gifts from donor organisations overseas. One result was theft on the campus, which could involve students stealing clothes from each other, or stealing food or other items from the school. The stolen goods would be sold at Morogoro or sometimes in the villages. Though students were supposed to get written permission to leave the campus, as has been seen, they had, when necessary, surreptitious means of going to Morogoro to sell what they had stolen.

There are many examples of students who stole from others to sell in Morogoro. In March 1981, three friends were reported to have stolen clothing that they sold there. They had not been granted permission to go to the town, and they were missing from their rooms for three consecutive nights. In another incident on 5 January 1985, after a trip to Dar es Salaam, two students, said to have been drunk during the trip, were reported to have 'got off the bus at Morogoro round about 10 pm and disappeared into town'. Next day they came back on campus, stole Christopher Morgan's clothes and sold them in Morogoro.

But most stealing seems to have been done by local people. Those working at the complex were familiar with the campus and some had keys of departments in which they were working, which made access easy. Alex Francis says that there was also co-operation in crime between the South Africans and the Tanzanians. While South Africans knew the campus well, the locals knew where stolen goods could be sold. Stealing, he says, grew worse during the last years of SOMAFCO. This was because the South Africans knew very well that they were to leave Tanzania, and under cover of the excitement and dislocation they resorted to stealing campus property in collaboration with the local people.

Though to some extent it could be a co-operative enterprise, theft also created tensions between the campus and the surrounding population. Grace Mbigwa, a Tanzanian worker at Mazimbu in most respects well-disposed towards the South Africans, says that thieving by locals created problems for the honest majority of Tanzanian workers at Mazimbu with the office of Home Affairs, which had a sub-branch at Mazimbu. In one case some South Africans came to the officials and accused Tanzanian workers of collaborating with people outside the fence in stealing campus property. Wilfred Mgina, a local leader in Dark City who worked closely with the ANC, reports regular meetings between himself and the ANC authorities. These concerned the security of the complex, and also about how to deal with theft by the locals. Crime against property was a very real concern.

To the impoverished villagers around SOMAFCO, the ANC seemed wealthy. They wanted to benefit from this even if it meant doing so in unacceptable ways. There might have been a feeling, justified or not, that their government must have contributed a lot to building Mazimbu while they, the locals, had nothing. The South Africans, on the other hand, could not ignore such theft since they had worked hard to build up the complex. In addition, those from the complex could not always relate to the conditions, often of outright hunger, that could lead to stealing by their neighbours. It is easy to see why tensions arose as SOMAFCO grew in the midst of a village environment.

Apart from selling *umphando*, or buying necessities, there were other activities that students undertook in town. They could go dancing. Some of the men would spend time with their girlfriends. Male ex-students stress that, even aside from the stern official disapproval, it was not easy to bring a girl on campus because there were eight students to a room. Students from mixed South African and Tanzanian backgrounds could spend time in Morogoro simply by claiming that they were visiting their parents or relatives. Three girls, Mlati says, were discovered to be doing this, when in fact they were visiting their boyfriends. When questioned, their defiant response was that 'the campus was lousy and *nabafana balousy* [the boys were lousy as well]'.

Such intimate relationships between South African women and Tanzanian men were, however, looked down upon by their fellow students. Such girls, Huddleston Pompi says, earned themselves names like 'second-hand'. Nomagqabi Sokupha says it was more acceptable for South African men to go out with Tanzanian girls than vice versa, though there were a few South African girls who reversed this pattern. According to Daniel Rafube 'we were regarded as *abelungu* (whites), the way we dressed, the way we talked, the way we did things. We did things different from them'. Pompi, amongst other ex-students, feels that the trappings of relative prosperity, and the air of urban sophistication clinging to the South Africans were too much for many young Tanzanian women to resist. Not surprisingly, Tanzanian men resented this, especially when added to the spirit of superiority that he says characterised the attitudes of most South African students towards the Tanzanians.

The question of why South Africans sometimes looked down upon the Tanzanians, in spite of the official ideology of fraternity and the reality of Tanzanian assistance, is a complex one. Patrick Mtshaulana argues that differences in access to goods were important, saying that because of the relative plenty at the complex, a tendency developed for some of the cadres to look down upon the locals. Phumeza Ngxala stresses failure to understand circumstances forced on people by near-absolute poverty, as when a Tanzanian using a dish for both washing and cooking might be accused of slovenliness. No doubt these urban people often had the city's sometimes patronising attitudes towards the countryside. Contempt for Tanzanians sometimes went to the extent of referring to them as 'peasants' or 'stupids', or, as Khasimbazi says, reporting a South African opinion expressed in tsotsi taal (slang), '*Ama-Tanzanians amabhari,*' meaning that Tanzanians are foolish and slow-witted. That this undercurrent of xenophobia, or at least of unreflective arrogance, could be disturbingly prevalent, is indicated also by the Afrikaans term *moegoes* (stupid) with which some ANC cadres in Cuba referred to their hosts. At Mazimbu, John Carneson recalls, some South Africans could even be heard referring to Tanzanians as 'foreigners'. He emphasises, however, that this attitude was strenuously opposed by the leadership and by the more politically and socially conscious, who were often, as he puts it, 'Swahiliphiles'.

The inhabitants of Mazimbu and Dakawa came from a technologically relatively advanced country. Certainly, the trappings of urban life were lacking in the Morogoro area and throughout most of Tanzania. Though black South Africans were the downtrodden in South Africa, they were living a materially better life than most Tanzanians. It remains an irony that while whites at home oppressed and looked down upon blacks, many of these blacks in turn despised the Tanzanians.

Though Tanzanians often referred to the South Africans as '*wakimbizi*' or 'refugees' instead of 'revolutionaries' as the South Africans preferred, Nomagqabi Sokupha asserts that this did not imply animosity. Joe Kabetso adds that though at first the term was rejected, South Africans became used to it, with some proudly referring to themselves in Swahili as '*Wakimbizi wa Africa Kusini*,' meaning 'Refugees from South Africa'.

Dark City

Between SOMAFCO and Morogoro there was a small village originally called Mazimbu Darajani, but which students called 'Dark City', a name that has persisted until today. It is difficult to provide a precise etymology for this evocative name. Some say it was so called because of the lack of electricity. It is worth recalling that Alexandra, a Johannesburg township with a reputation for violence and criminality, and similarly without electricity, was also known colloquially as Dark City. In some instances, indeed, people from Dark City would waylay SOMAFCO students to rob them of whatever they had. To travel at night in this area, especially without informing the college authorities, could be dangerous.

But Dark City was not as dark as the name suggests: it can be seen as a frontier, a place of contact and exuberant creativity. Some of its inhabitants were Nyamwezi from western Tanzania, and others were from Burundi and Rwanda. Yet others were people who had been living in the houses on the abandoned and derelict Mazimbu sisal estate where they had once worked. On the arrival of the South Africans, these people had been obliged to leave the estate, crossing the Ngerengere River to join local people living in Mazimbu Darajani. Wilfred Mgina, a local village leader, says these first inhabitants of Dark City were the people who had worked on the estate until the departure of the previous owner following the land nationalisation decreed by the Arusha Declaration in 1969.

That Mazimbu was in some ways associated with loss of livelihood and housing might have given local people reasons to hold grudges against the newcomers. However, it seems that this was more than compensated for by new opportunities, and the relationship between the campus and Dark City soon went from strength to strength. A unifying event was the floods that swept across Tanzania in 1980 and 1981. Although the complex lost the wooden bridge connecting it to Dark City and the outside world, the villagers faced a more extreme situation, losing their belongings, in some instances including even their shelter. SOMAFCO provided accommodation and clothing and this may have helped reconcile the people to the presence of their new neighbours.

Students went to Dark City for various reasons, including buying and drinking liquor. Often, when they had money, students would drink beer. But when funds were low, they resorted to locally distilled spirits known as *gongo*, sold by people like Mama Wakchaka and Mama Chuma. Local women also made *umqombothi*, the traditional beer much loved by South Africans, in the South African style. It was also in Dark City that students bought dagga from a person called Niza, though this was also sold at other villages further away, like Jamina. As well as students and the working youth, visitors to Dark City included the *umgwenya*, the ANC veterans who had left the country in the 1960s to join the ANC, especially MK. These adults often went to Dark City after work and at weekends, where they enjoyed beer and *gongo* with the local people.

It was also in Dark City that intimate relationships took place. As Khasimbazi says, the children of South Africans still live in Dark City. Some were left behind even after repatriation. These were the children of married couples and from informal relationships between South African men and local women. Families like that of Monica Mathe, already mentioned, are examples. Two children who presently live in Dark City resulted from her marriage to one of the *umgwenya*. Her husband died in South Africa soon after repatriation and thus their plan to bring the whole family to South Africa came to nothing. The question of the children of relationships between South African fathers and Tanzanian mothers came to media attention in 1998, and it remains a difficult legacy of the South African presence.

Economically and socially, Dark City benefited considerably from the complex as compared to more distant villages. As Wilfred Mgina puts it, 'we got a lot of things for free.' Though the Tanzanian authorities facilitated infrastructural improvements at Mazimbu and Dakawa, it was the many donors who assisted the ANC that actually paid for them, and not the Tanzanian government. For example, when in 1988 SOMAFCO, with French assistance, began to receive water from pipes that ran through Dark City from Morogoro, thus ending dependence on water from the Ngerengere River, the request by the village authorities to be allowed access to this water was approved. Connecting SOMAFCO to the national grid made it possible to electrify villages which otherwise could never have hoped for this, and improvements such as the bridge over the Ngerengere were of considerable benefit to local communities. It was also the Dark City inhabitants who benefited most from the 'trade', or 'frying' system, and who were in a position to take advantage most easily of employment opportunities offered by the complex.

Composed of mud-huts on the arrival of the South Africans during the 1980s, Dark City developed into a village of brick houses. Some attribute this to 'trickle-down', seeing the complex as having provided a developmental model that Tanzanians were able to imitate. Joe Kabetso, for instance, believes that the skills the local people acquired in building SOMAFCO enabled them to develop the physical fabric of Dark City. The Tanzanian politician, Mama Abdallah, believes that the South African example led to an increase locally in the growing of fruit and vegetables, and to modern methods of pig keeping. She argues also that the ANC practice of hiring out tractors to local people underlined the benefits of mechanisation in farming. Many South African observers make similar comments.

It seems undeniable that agricultural and technical practices at Mazimbu influenced the local economy and technology. However, arguably the main influence of the complex was to inject substantial resources into these spheres. The local people were then able to utilise these resources in ways with which they were already familiar, but for which they had previously had insufficient capital to exploit to the full, such as building brick houses and using more fertiliser on their crops.

CHAPTER 10

Women at SOMAFCO

As early as 1918, the Bantu Women's League was formed as part of the ANC. In 1943 the Women's League came into being. Disrupted by the banning of the movement, the Women's Section (WS), which later reverted to its earlier title, was formed in exile. As throughout the ANC, women at SOMAFCO were formally represented by this movement. However, important though this organisation was, there were aspects of female experience, particularly that of female students, that were not fully reflected by such official structures. We will pay most attention to the WS, relating it to the personal as well as the public lives of women. Our discussion of personal relationships is not intended to imply that these are more significant for women than men, but rather that the consequences in societies where women are often at a disadvantage can be particularly momentous for them.

Women were considered equal to men in the eyes of the ANC. This applied also to SOMAFCO, where there was no formal or intentional discrimination against female students, or against women in general. A few women rose to important positions in the ANC, the most outstanding example in the case of the settlements in Tanzania being Mary Ngozi (later Mary Thuse), the first Director of Dakawa Development Centre. There was a real, and often successful, attempt to bring issues of women's equality into the open, and to insist, for example, that all forms of labour should be done equally by both sexes. This attitude was not merely rhetorical, and at Mazimbu women could be found doing jobs such as electrical maintenance that were, and sometimes still are, considered 'male'. Nevertheless, sexism is deeply engrained in South African communities, and it did not always prove easy to shrug off this heritage, even in a school committed to ideals that prominently included equality of the sexes.

'Our women'

Ideas of a proprietary male right to women within some national, racial, class or other context – 'our women' – are familiar all over the world. Mazimbu was no exception. Sexism was not confined to people of a particular age or standing. Amongst the students, the xenophobic disdain that was shown by some South Africans for Tanzanians could incorporate the idea that the South African women of the settlement were in a sense the preserve of the South

African males. Such conceptions did not appear to operate in reverse, and as has been seen, there were numerous relationships ranging from lasting marriages to casual affairs between South African men and Tanzanian women. Sexual politics were complicated by the fact that some students at SOMAFCO were themselves the children of South Africans and Tanzanian, Zambian or other mothers, and young women from this category seem to have been more open to relationships outside the settlement's fence.

There appear also to have been occasional sexual liaisons between some female students in the secondary school and a few men in official structures. Though these students were adults, the school situation raises questions about the propriety of such relationships. One female staff member in close touch with the students feels that the wish to bring this issue into the open conflicted with a feeling that to do so might provide ammunition to attack the school and the ANC. As a result it 'was not dealt with very well at all, and it was hidden'.

On the whole, the proprietary male attitudes towards South African women on the campus seem to have been tacitly accepted by most of them. Nevertheless, within this world, many of the assumptions of female inferiority in the classroom or male resentments against women who excelled academically seem to have been challenged, and in many cases overcome, at SOMAFCO. However, though in many ways the students were treated as the adults they often were, the school did not show a sure touch in its approach to sexuality and pregnancy amongst students.

As has been seen, young women who fell pregnant were removed with their babies from school for up to two years and sent to the Charlotte Maxeke Mother and Child Centre. Though it was not precisely a punishment, time in the Charlottes was regarded by the authorities as a way of isolating those who had behaved in an unacceptable way, while continuing to care for them and their babies. To some, this was a just and even-handed policy, while others considered it a virtual criminalisation of procreation and shattering of potential family groups. Some felt that official attitudes, in the words of Rica Hodgson, a respected and longstanding member of the Communist Party who worked at SOMAFCO from 1981 to 1986, were 'terribly old-fashioned – conservative ... holier-than-thou'. The sensitivity of the issue, which touched on attitudes towards age, gender and 'culture', is shown by differing responses to the elderly African women whose prerogative it was assumed to be to advise and chaperone those who became pregnant. To Alpheus Mangezi such women were dependable stalwarts; to someone like Rica Hodgson 'they were the worst,' embodying harsh, backward-looking, social attitudes. Such multiple voices are to be expected in a community as diverse as Mazimbu.

The Women's Section at Mazimbu

As far back as the 1950s, the ANC saw itself as according women their rightful place in the struggle against oppression in South Africa. A key event was the march of women of all colours and backgrounds to the Union Buildings in Pretoria on 9 August 1956, protesting against the extension of pass laws to African women. On 9 August 1986, at a commemoration at SOMAFCO, Mendi Msimang expressed the way in which this event had entered the ANC's political and historical consciousness:

> The great surge in women's participation from the 1956 Women's March ... resulted in the advent of new stalwarts in the struggle against apartheid. Women like Lillian Ngoyi, Helen Joseph, Lily Diedricks, Rahima Moosa and Sophie Williams emerged as new role models for those females long starved of pacesetters ... [T]he ANC recognized this as a new era of united mass action by the women and as part and parcel of the forces struggling ... for freedom and justice.

The 1960s saw the intensification of attempts by the apartheid state to stamp out opposition to its policies of separate development. After the banning of the ANC and PAC in 1960, the Women's League entered a period of relative quiescence as the ANC moved its operations outside South Africa, only re-emerging as a formally structured organ of the movement in the early 1970s. On 3 September 1971 the reorganised secretariat of what was now called the WS met for the first time, in Lusaka. Its members were Florence Mophosho, Magdalene Resha, Edna Mgabaza, Kate Molale and Theresa Maimane.

The WS in East Africa followed existing patterns of ANC organisation. Areas with settled ANC communities were formed into units, each consisting of about 20 members. These elected the usual office bearers, who then met to elect a Branch Committee Executive. This form of organisation was meant to facilitate discussions on contentious issues from the units up. For example, a report from the Charlottes Unit in March 1983 on young mothers who were said not to observe the rules of the local unit, moved via the branch and the ZPC, to the Directorate of the complex. Amongst other things, these women were accused of bringing boyfriends into the Centre, refusing to carry out their duties and disregarding rules on cleanliness. The intention was that such local issues would be considered and solved before they became the basis for wider grievances and discontent.

Thus it was intended that the units should collectively set the tone and the formal agenda for the whole branch, and be effective in addressing the specific problems of members. In the case of Mazimbu, units were drawn from different sectors of the community, such as teachers, students, and residents of a certain area, all of these finally coming together to form the Mazimbu branch of the WS.

Above the Branch Committee was the Regional Committee, whose executive was elected at a Regional General Meeting. A representative of the National Scholarship Committee (NSC) and the chairperson and secretary of each branch sat on the Regional Committee. The insistence on a representative of the NSC was because the WS as a body was actively involved, through its linkages with other women's organisations, in lobbying for scholarships, sometimes specifically for females, but more usually as part of the general effort to broaden the pool of opportunities, within which women competed on an equal basis. The inclusion of branch office bearers was to make sure that processes and decisions were as inclusive as possible. The East Africa Region comprised the Mazimbu, Dakawa and Dar es Salaam branches. The Regional Women's Committee (RWC) was answerable to the Regional ANC office and the Regional Political Committee. The RWC was thus responsible for the co-ordination of the political work of the branches, and from time to time was called upon to resolve problems and disputes at branch level. It also approved all policy documents in the region, and was expected to raise funds for the WS and submit quarterly reports to the Women's Secretariat.

The question of language was of particular concern to the WS, though it affected all ANC structures to some extent. The women of Mazimbu came from a great variety of linguistic backgrounds, reflecting the many countries in which the ANC operated. This reflects the fact that, for the most part, it was women who followed men rather than the reverse. Zulu and English were dominant, but, though women from other backgrounds did learn such languages so as to communicate with their husbands and children, many were initially more at home in, for instance, Swahili or Portuguese. The WS was sensitive to the possibility of exclusion by language, and an effort was made to have translation where needed. The corollary was that meetings tended to last a very long time.

One of the first matters that the revived WS considered was education. The first meeting of the secretariat urged that, 'the NEC should be approached on the question of a school for ANC children. Preliminary discussions have already started ... preferably the school should be in Tanzania or Zambia.' This concern was an aspect of what can be interpreted as the maternal or nurturing role that characterised the WS in ANC missions all over the world, including Mazimbu. This was not problematic up to a point. However, there was continuing tension between the tendency to confine ANC women, or for ANC women to confine themselves, to issues that were perceived as characteristically female, and to limit their participation in the full range of questions that faced the organisation. This was one of the basic dilemmas that faced the WS.

The 1971 reinvention of the Women's League as the WS was followed by its emergence as an active participant in various political debates within the movement. For instance, on 18 October 1971, the WS issued an open letter congratulating the women of China on the admission of the People's Republic of China to the United Nations, denouncing 'imperialists' as stooges and enemies of peace, applauding the expulsion of Taiwan, and stating that the WS was confident that 'the progressive women of China, with the rich experience of a revolution, and in the struggle for the rights of women, will play their part in the international scene, by contributing to peace in the world'. The language was the declamatory revolutionary jargon of the time. However, behind the rhetoric was an eagerness to engage with issues of general concern to the ANC from which women had hitherto been marginalised, and not in such a way as to place them in a female ghetto.

It might be expected that the WS would have taken a similarly all-embracing activist line on the SOMAFCO campus. However, though the WS certainly played a role in determining overall policy on the campus, it tended to focus in particular on inducting female students into the uncertainties of political exile and in fighting for the interests of the younger children. There were tensions in this area.

Amongst the earliest WS contributions in relation to SOMAFCO was its participation in the ANC delegation to an Inter-Agency Consultation in Dar es Salaam in November 1979. The delegation proposed to develop and cultivate links with two UN agencies, UNDP and Unesco, outlining in the process how the organisation conceived of the Mazimbu complex. As the agencies that they were addressing were there to help with funding, the statement focused on educational needs, construction, equipment and furnishing, and the development of the production units.

Such initiatives stemmed not from women at Mazimbu, but rather from the regional structures of the WS. Now that there was an ANC community growing at Mazimbu, the WS began to expand amongst the women of the settlement. A pattern soon began to emerge in its activities. One aspect was the attempt to provide what was considered a proper political grounding to women students. Characteristically however, the efforts of women in Mazimbu came to be geared in large part towards the welfare of the many children of the complex. As the settlement grew from a secondary school to a large institution with many branches, and as Dakawa Development Centre (55 kilometres to the north) was added, the expanding population meant that inevitably there would be infants and children in the community. Various facilities, already described, were needed, including a crèche, pre-school and primary school. The responsibility for developing these sectors was to a considerable extent handed over to the women. Such initiatives were workshopped by the WS. Then units responsible for fundraising within the WS went into action, passing on their requests to sister organisations all over the world, though they were clear that they were not fundraising for the WS as such, but rather for the ANC.

Thus the WS played a prominent role in the education of the younger children, in keeping with the maternal role that it had been tacitly assigned and had adopted. This maternal status was emphasised by Dennis September in February 1985 in a paper entitled *Our Children's Welfare*. He said that the welfare of the primary school children at Mazimbu was a question 'that involves much responsibility on the part of the Women's Section ... we want you to help in getting a fair deal for all the children when clothing and shoes are handed out. Children who have parents to fight for them are favoured over the others.' September also complained about the inadequacy and irregularity of meals for the children. In effect this paper implored the WS to extend the traditional role of women from their homes to the whole complex, saying that mothers were best suited to deal with domestic issues like clothing and food, as their male counterparts dealt with other issues. This request was criticised and contested by those who had a broader view of women's role. However, it does indicate that there were tendencies at Mazimbu towards the reinforcing of the hierarchical gender relations considered normal in many societies. This raises questions about the coherence of the ANC policy of non-sexism and gender equality at the time. The ANC did indeed urge women to be more active at all levels, thus, it was hoped, making their emancipation more concrete, and ending the exploitation of women by men. However, perhaps women themselves were not always proactive in charting their future, and did not always directly confront the dilemma as to whether they should embark on protest against their own oppression where the overall struggle against national and racial injustice might seem to have priority.

Another area in the sphere of gender relations in which the WS played a valuable role was in relation to domestic violence. Though the number of incidents should not be exaggerated, some men, amongst them those who had been in the military camps for a long time, took out their frustrations in violence against their partners. The WS took the issue of domestic violence to the level of the director, and the organisation's suggestion that offending men should be locked up for two weeks, whether or not this was requested by their partners, was adopted. This was based on the idea that such violence was not just an offence against the woman, but against the community as a whole.

At some stages there were attempts to take the gender debate forward. In a paper presented at a seminar on 20 June 1982 in Mazimbu on 'The political

14. Female students participating in construction at SOMAFCO

participation of women', several ways were proposed by which women might assert themselves. It was suggested that all SOMAFCO committees should have equal numbers of males and females, and that the 'traditional division of labour between men and women should be consciously avoided at SOMAFCO. It should be obligatory for students to do all kinds of work, regardless of sex. For example, women should be involved in cement unloading and men in cooking and vice versa.' Women were also implored not to neglect their political responsibilities because of their social activities. Men and women were to assist with childcare so as to allow mothers to attend meetings or fulfil political tasks.

In effect these recommendations meant that domestic work would affect men and women equally. The ANC's Eastern Bloc orientation may have contributed to this approach, as suggested by the recommendation that women from socialist countries should be invited to address the WS on the way in which, allegedly, 'women have overcome inferiority in those countries,' though other streams of feminist thought also influenced the ANC. Whatever the origins, this approach certainly defied many typical male attitudes to relations between the sexes in South Africa at the time, amongst whatever racial group.

If this was what women set out to achieve as emancipation, why then was it that the welfare of children should be the particular domain of the WS? September's paper appealed for the intervention of women in ways characteristic of role divisions in paternalistic societies, reaffirming the old division of labour where women looked after children's well-being. The question thus arises, in this context as in others, as to how much political theory actually affected day-to-day activities in the complex.

Questions such as these dogged the ANC more generally. For instance, in an interview in Hilda Bernstein's *The Rift*, Frene Ginwala reflects on her feelings about the ANC's perception of women. She states that:

> Working as a woman in the ANC is difficult on two counts. As a woman people don't take you seriously politically. They see you as a technician ... if a committee was set up, they'd look around and say that so-and-so, a man, would be the chair, and you, the woman, would be the secretary to take the notes. In fact, for many years I used to make an absolute point of refusing to take the notes ... It takes a lot out of you ... It makes you aggressive, it makes you prickly when it's not necessary.

The WS was uncomfortably aware that the ANC dealt with women simply as another sector to be mobilised for the struggle against apartheid, rather than for women's liberation. Arguably, this mobilisation reinforced rather than challenged patriarchy. Arguably also, the popular ANC formulation recognising women as facing the triple oppression of class, race and sex was not fully acted upon, since dealing with the latter seemed likely to have to wait until the first two had been resolved by the dissolution of apartheid.

A contentious and important issue with which the WS became involved, which simultaneously points to the way in which certain spheres were considered characteristically female, is that of pregnancy and abortion. The WS organised a seminar on the topic on 22 December 1982. The reason put forward for the seminar was that most of the staff were not entirely satisfied with Neduc's policy on pregnancies. The WS therefore felt that it was necessary to discuss these matters and forward any resulting recommendations. The third Neduc meeting recommended that when a student became pregnant, the man and woman concerned should be suspended for two years after the birth of the child. This policy did not specify whether those suspended could write examinations, and neither did it take any specific position on abortions. So far the administration of the complex had implemented the policy by suspending both students in a pregnancy case immediately, sending the male student to work at the construction site and the female to the Charlottes. There was no consistency on whether suspended students should be allowed to write examinations, and young women who had abortions were suspended for one year. In the end, unsatisfactory though many considered this to be, policy on pregnancies remained the same until the complex was wound up in 1992.

Very young students sometimes became pregnant, as with a 13-year-old primary school pupil in 1986. It was felt that while she was pregnant she had to be separated from the other youngsters who lived in the same unit, but she was so young that she could not be sent to the Kate Molale Mothers' Centre where the residents largely looked after themselves. One of the matrons was asked to care for her until she gave birth, and the WS arranged for another matron to look after the child once it was born. The girl was to be allowed to go back to school as soon as possible, meaning also that the 16-year-old boy responsible for the pregnancy was also to remain in school. Such ambiguities led to accusations of inconsistency by some students. Another result of this pregnancy was that the head of the boarding section immediately called for a pregnancy test for all the girls at Mazimbu. This was not implemented, but had it been, it would undoubtedly have been traumatic for the children, especially for those still too young to comprehend what was happening.

It could be argued that a more forthright policy on contraception would have been a better response. Interviews with ex-students and teachers suggest that such advice could have been taken more proactively to the students. While contraceptive advice was freely available from the clinic, and while individual teachers and others did what they could to offer advice and support, there was no overall programme attempting to integrate the medical, social and individual aspects of the question. As everywhere, for many the subject was embarrassing and was avoided rather than confronted. The isolation of Mazimbu meant also that there was a lack of the information that might have filtered in through the media.

An issue that greatly concerned the WS was the accusation that a matron had severely beaten a child in her care whose mother was away on a scholarship. The beating was so severe that subsequently the child could neither sit down nor walk properly. While an extreme case, untypical in the extent of the violence, it did raise the question of the rights of adults *vis-à-vis* children. The WS tried to take the background of the matron concerned into account in dealing with the case. She was elderly, and it emerged in the inquiry that she was not malicious but rather stuck in outmoded disciplinary methods, convinced that beating was the only way to make children obey rules. The WS called her to a meeting, and lectured her on the shortcomings of physical assault as a form of discipline. She was told of the psychological scarring that might result from such beatings, and that her conduct meant that young mothers would in future be reluctant to trust the ANC with their children when they were awarded scholarships to study abroad.

Women's concerns overlapped with those of young people. In a youth conference earlier in 1982, the students pressed for the inclusion of sex education in the school curriculum. They also called on the authorities to allow everybody to use contraceptives, and urged that the campus medical facility play an active role in advising students on the best methods in individual cases. They said that the option of abortion should be made available to students in the case of failed contraception. They also urged that all students involved in pregnancies should be allowed to write their examinations.

Positions taken by the WS were similar to some of the Youth Conference recommendations. The organisation resolved that the administration should introduce sex education, which would neither encourage nor discourage sexual relations. Its main purpose would be to discourage and prevent pregnancies. It was suggested that an informal lecture be given to the whole student body one evening a month, allowing time for questions and answers. The more mature members of the Mazimbu community would lead the discussions, and would then summarise the proceedings. From time to time experts would be called in to give talks from a medical perspective.

It is clear that the ANC needed to tackle vigorously the issue of relations between the sexes at SOMAFCO, and indeed all the social issues that such a varied school presented. Students at SOMAFCO tended to be older than the usual schoolchildren, as in many cases their education had been stalled, sometimes by several years, by the uprising of 1976 and subsequent upheavals. The normal rules governing pupils in residence would not always make sense to people in their twenties. A case in point, recounted by Mrs Makho Njobe, is that of two students, man and wife, who decided to resume their studies at SOMAFCO. The rules governing the campus meant that they had to live separately. Indeed, a number of women decided to leave their husbands temporarily and live in the hostels for the sake of education. For example, Joyce, the Mozambican wife of Johannes Phungula, known as 'Pass Four', went to study and live in the school hostels with the support of her otherwise quite traditional husband. Conversely, there were much younger students who were not used to being away from strict family controls and who found their relative independence a novelty to exploit to the full.

CHAPTER 11

Dakawa Development Centre

From its educational origins, the ANC's settlements in Tanzania grew to include many different activities. At Mazimbu the school came to be supported by a range of institutions catering for the welfare of students and a number of productive enterprises, such as the furniture factory and the farm, the original rationales of which were to provide furniture for the schools and dwellings and food for the community.

Education was, however, at the heart of the Mazimbu project. When it became clear that there were needs that could not be answered at Mazimbu, and that there were certain ancillary functions that SOMAFCO itself required, it was decided in 1982 to accept the Tanzanian government's offer of a 2 800 hectare tract of land 55 kilometres north of Morogoro, at Dakawa. It had become clear that a place was needed where young people newly arrived from the south might stay until they could be received at SOMAFCO in an orderly way. Here, the academic level of young people and their security status would be checked, they would receive basic education in subjects such as mathematics and English, be given political instruction and be taught about the history of South Africa and the ANC. In addition, Mazimbu was beginning to be overcrowded in terms of available facilities, and Dakawa provided an outlet for the growing population.

Dakawa, however, was not just an adjunct to SOMAFCO. It was also intended to play a developmental role, where adults would learn skills that they could put to use in the service of the ANC, and in a liberated South Africa. Thus the settlement was named the Dakawa Development Centre. This dimension was given even more urgency with the signing of the Nkomati Accord between Mozambique and South Africa in 1984. Dakawa acted as a reception camp for ANC cadres expelled from Mozambique and neighbouring Swaziland under the terms of the agreement. Education and development now had to take place within the context of the occasionally tense atmosphere generated through the presence of these doubly displaced and sometimes frustrated people, amongst them, from 1988, alleged spies who had been pardoned.

Dakawa was undeveloped, isolated, without electricity or access to clean water and sources of building stone, malarial, flat, and was therefore a difficult site on which to install piped water and a waterborne sewerage system. During the rains the place turned into a sea of mud. The pastoral Maasai moved through the area with their stock, damaging the crops that the ANC settlers attempted to grow. Having no natural immunity, the South Africans were badly affected by malaria, particularly in the mosquito-ridden rainy season, and indeed tropical diseases of all kinds took their toll. Isolated from Morogoro and Mazimbu, it was not possible to make frequent trips to these centres. The inhabitants of Dakawa were therefore thrown on their own resources, and, apart from the occasional video or film and a small library, they had little with which to entertain themselves. It is, therefore, not surprising that there was a considerable amount of drinking, dagga smoking and, perhaps partly as a result, petty and sometimes more serious crime. As Spenser Hodgson, the ANC architect, says of the physical and social conditions, 'Dakawa was a very difficult area'.

The first ANC personnel at Dakawa, in place on 3 March 1982, were drawn from the old comrades, the *umgwenya*, some of whom had been in exile since the early 1960s, amongst them veterans of the joint campaign with Zapu in Rhodesia in 1967. The experience of extended exile had, however, taken its toll, and many sought comfort from displacement and isolation in alcohol and drug abuse. An investigation in May 1982 found that, '[s]ome comrades smoked dagga and the Administration could not do anything much since it was itself completely soaked with the local brew ... [t]he whole Administration is not sure when they went to Dakawa and remembers rather hazily what its terms of references [*sic*] were or what it was supposed to do.' The first few months of the Dakawa administration were thus not a success, with poorly housed and badly-fed youths under the control of an often unreliable and capricious leadership, 'overwhelmed with the responsibility and authority'. The picture rapidly became clear to the leadership in Lusaka and Mazimbu. After dealing with the immediate situation, meetings were called to discuss the long-term future of Dakawa.

The first Dakawa Seminar, in July and August 1982, laid down policy for the rest of the institution's existence. Dakawa was to become a centre for the orientation of youth from South Africa, who in many cases would proceed to SOMAFCO, and a new community would be built free from the racialism and inequalities disfiguring South Africa. The pressing requirements of newly-arrived exiles, and the need to wage a liberation war, had somehow to be accommodated with the need to build, in a foreign country, a living community that would provide a model for a new South Africa. It followed that Dakawa would have to go well beyond what might be expected of a camp for exiles, and would require development in many dimensions. As Mendi Msimang, chairing the seminar, put it, '[it] is essential for the Movement to strike a balance between the prosecution of the armed struggle and the implementation of projects of a developmental nature.'

It was estimated that the population of Dakawa could rise to as many as 5 000. The foundations of the centre would be education, agriculture and small-scale industry. Medical, social, transport and cultural facilities would also be necessary, and a department to build the infrastructure. The question of whether Dakawa should be autonomous from SOMAFCO, which was to be a continuing debate, was raised but not resolved. With the assistance of the Norwegian consultancy, Norplan, plans were further refined the following year at the second Dakawa Seminar, which resulted in the 1984 Development Plan, a comprehensive and ambitious document.

The settlement did not grow to the dimensions envisaged. Not all of the projects outlined were actually undertaken, and planners admit that mistakes were made during construction. However, much was done, and the building of a functioning settlement in this very difficult environment was a remarkable achievement. The effort involved may very well have hastened the death of the Project Manager, Oswald Dennis. Though the original plans were based on a projected population of around 5 000, by 1990 there was in fact a South African population of approximately 1 200. The largest group amongst these, 704, worked in construction. There were 221 in the Education Orientation Centre (EOC), 76 in the Vocational Training Centre (VTC), 76 in the leather factory, and smaller numbers elsewhere.

Orientation and rehabilitation

The immediate need in the early 1980s, which remained to the end, was to cater for new arrivals from South Africa. Thus, the Student Orientation Centre, later called the Ruth First EOC was established. Since its foundation, SOMAFCO had tried to deal with a continuous trickle, and sometimes a flood, of exiled youth. This was disruptive educationally, in that it was difficult to assess the academic level of newcomers in the context of the ongoing school programme. Few arrived with certificates, and it was common for pupils to inflate their achievements, dislocating the educational programme considerably. The worth of genuine qualifications, even at third level, was sometimes suspect. Hintsa Tshume, the author of a 1984 report, was convinced 'that even those comrades who have been in the "bush" universities do not come to standard' when exposed to education elsewhere. It was inconvenient to slot newcomers into their classes at various stages during the school year, and he felt that some might be better placed in MK or elsewhere, rather than at SOMAFCO.

It was also necessary to screen new arrivals, since there were undoubtedly spies and *agents provocateurs* for Pretoria amongst those arriving in Tanzania. This could lead to a kind of paranoia. Educationalists like Wintshi Njobe, the VTC principal, while recognising the need to screen new arrivals, were uncomfortable with the extent of control by security personnel. 'Security men are the authority at EOC,' he wrote in 1988, '[t]his situation and much else that goes on there disturbs many residents of Dakawa.' He thought that even where there was reason to suspect a security risk, this suspicion should not be revealed until there was definite proof. He argued that the specifically educational character of the EOC should be emphasised, and that new students should be separated from disciplinary cases. Mature teachers and boarding staff should be appointed to run the Centre, rather than the 'four energetic youth [who] run the place'. The headquarters of Dakawa security, he said, should be removed from the EOC.

The role of the EOC was in some ways ambiguous. On the one hand, classes were held in basic subjects, and in the history of the liberation movement, and at the beginning of the school year, and of the second term, groups of students considered ready were sent to SOMAFCO. On the other hand, it tended to become a 'place of punishment' for malefactors from SOMAFCO, to which students who were temporarily expelled would be sent for 'reorientation'. One aspect was the sending of male partners of young women who fell pregnant at school to the EOC. There were sometimes even more serious problems perceived as requiring imprisonment. In this way the widespread perception by ANC cadres of Dakawa as 'a dumping ground' was enhanced, and the developmental and formative purpose of the centre was undermined. As Simon Mohale, who was involved in developing the VTC says, 'It was reputed, especially from SOMAFCO, if you are undisciplined, or you don't cope up in your studies, then they send you to Dakawa.' The Dakawa authorities complained frequently about this policy and people like Mohale tried to change the image through their work. In Siphiwe Xaba's words, 'Everything that a person does wrong: Dakawa.'

Similar ambiguities surrounded the Raymond Mhlaba Rehabilitation Centre. This part of Dakawa had two sections. One was devoted to those who were mentally ill, and the other to those who were considered to need political or social rehabilitation. It was clearly difficult to deal with the mentally disturbed – the tragic products of South African exile, warfare and torture – in a remote area of a very poor country. There were attempts to institute community-based care, and to utilise the meagre resources of the Tanzanian system, but there were too few people available skilled in psychiatry, and, though intentions were good, this group was fated to neglect and further degeneration. As Jackie Morake put it in 1985, '[t]hey spend most of their time sitting or sleeping at the residence with nothing to do.'

The section of the Rehabilitation Centre devoted to social and political rehabilitation was bound, by its nature, to be controversial. Officially, in the words of a 1983 document, its intention was to house and rehabilitate 'socially, politically and otherwise':

> [m]embers of the organisation who, after being assigned by the movement on missions, failed to fulfil their tasks for one reason or the other; people who committed crimes against the movement, crimes against the countries and governments to which they were sent on missions; students expelled from Europe or withdrawn from their studies for various other reasons.

To some, the Rehabilitation Centre represented another aspect of Dakawa's reputation as 'a dumping ground'. Certainly, a report prepared in 1986 by Mary Ngozi (later Mary Thuse), the Administrator of Dakawa, referred to 'sentences' of two or even three years served by expelled SOMAFCO students at the Rehabilitation Centre. There were also at the centre 'comrades who might have offended the movement', who were drawn from amongst 'students, working youth and adults'. Though they would rather not have had them at all, the Dakawa authorities urged that students expelled from SOMAFCO should at least be sent to the EOC where there was some kind of student life, rather than to the Rehabilitation Centre which was 'not capable of maintaining the student life desired by SOMAFCO'. The impression cannot be avoided that the Rehabilitation Centre was virtually a penal settlement, with the local leadership noting on one occasion that they must be prepared for physical confrontation with the inmates.

ANC members who had been sent to study in countries in Europe or elsewhere, and who, through ill discipline or lack of academic success did not complete their courses, were generally sent to the Rehabilitation Centre. Given the stresses of studying in an unfamiliar environment, often in languages like Bulgarian or Russian, it is not surprising that there was a considerable 'failure' rate. Some students believed that the way such returnees were treated was insufficiently supportive.

Land and industry at Dakawa

These, however, were not the only aspects of early Dakawa. From the beginning there were attempts to develop the farm so as to provide useful work for the cadres and promote self-sufficiency in food. There were also efforts to develop small industry and the social infrastructure.

Though the land at Dakawa was potentially fertile, it was heavily overgrown with bush and required enormous effort to clear for cultivation, and, being flat, there were drainage and irrigation problems. Because it was remote, and because donors often provided machines that were not in common use in Tanzania, there were continuous problems with maintaining farm machinery and acquiring spare parts. Tractors and other implements often lay unusable for long periods for want of an oil seal or other simple component. The

15. The first residents of Dakawa lived in tents

hazards of tropical agriculture also hit the farm, as in 1988 and 1989, when rats ate three-quarters of the sunflower crop. Maasai stock devastated crops grown with such effort. At times, wild pigs, and even, on one occasion, elephants from the Mikumi Game Reserve, wreaked havoc. Nevertheless, though never on the scale of Mazimbu, crops were grown and the settlement became partly self-sufficient. Starting with 30 hectares cleared painfully by hand, by 1987 250 hectares were under crops such as maize, sorghum, beans and sunflower, and by 1990, about 400 hectares. To the chagrin of the ANC leadership, much of this labour was carried out by Tanzanians as was also the case with building Dakawa's infrastructure, though never as much as at Mazimbu.

As is to be expected amongst a displaced population from a traumatised country, there was often social dislocation and personal maladjustment, leading at times to criminality and violence amongst the inhabitants of Dakawa. As in Mazimbu, there was a centre at Dakawa to care for infants. Its staff perceived, from their perspective, some of the tensions that beset the exile community. Violence, even among the very young, was a problem: '[t]hey beat and kick each other, the same way adults do, eg., a husband beating his wife or two comrades fighting each other. Children learn through copying ... The staff cannot undo what has been copied from home.' On another level, the effects of trauma could turn inwards and take the form of addiction to alcohol and dagga. As at Mazimbu, theft by both South Africans and Tanzanians was a problem. Conditions such as these led to the creation of the Social Order Unit. This was not a police force since the ANC was on the soil of Tanzania, a sovereign state. However, it did act in a semi-policing role, resented by some of the Dakawa population.

Some problems of criminality and labour relations may have stemmed from the way in which Dakawa was organised. Blurring of student and worker roles could lead to difficulties. As at SOMAFCO, trainees tended to see themselves as learners rather than workers, whatever the theory might be, and when confronted with work that did not contribute obviously to their training, they were often reluctant to participate. This is particularly so as the *umphando* system supplied residents with clothing, and other basic necessities of life. Supplies were generally distributed irrespective of whether people worked or not, and for many the preferred option, as Wintshi Njobe said in 1988, was to 'just sit day in day out watching out for the supply lorry coming round to distribute something', and then to 'dice' or 'fry' some of these supplies with local people for cash. There were financial 'incentives', but they were small, and only slightly graded between different levels of work. There was thus little motivation to work hard for extra money. In addition, a proportion of the other workers at Dakawa were likely to have a tepid approach to their duties as some had been sent there because of academic or disciplinary shortcomings at SOMAFCO or overseas. The problem was clearly stated in the minutes of a Dakawa administrative meeting in April 1988. The authorities felt that Mazimbu was faced with 'a problem of loafers', and that they simply unloaded it on Dakawa. They resolved 'that Dakawa should not be used as a dumping place for people who were problematic in their places, e.g. Mazimbu.'

As the settlement grew it became necessary to boost the service departments. Health, transport, educational and construction facilities were expanded, in line with the crucial 1984 Development Plan. As the 1980s progressed, there was also steady expansion in other areas. Amongst the most important was the VTC that operated in areas such as carpentry, brick-laying and electrical installation. The idea of a VTC had been mooted at the very beginning, and there was a certain amount of vocational training from an early stage. Indeed, the concept had an ANC pedigree that long predates the foundation of Dakawa. However, though rough-and-ready training began early as part of the construction programme, the VTC did not come into full existence until 1988. Indeed, when the Development Centre closed in 1992 not all the planned buildings were complete.

The VTC encapsulated a dilemma, which was never resolved, between the needs of the individuals who were being trained, and the needs of Dakawa as an institution. Various reports, including an incisive survey by MH Manyanga, the Director of Tanzanian National Vocational Training, make clear that trainees were used for the immediate purposes of the construction programme, with little attention given to the creation of a satisfactory training curriculum. If this had been part of well-structured and monitored work experience, it could not have been criticised, but this was not the case, and it amounted to cheap labour for the building programme. This resulted in dissatisfaction amongst trainees, who were aware that their experience would not be of much use in the world outside – in South Africa or elsewhere. There were never sufficient well-qualified instructors, and satisfactory certification, which would have validated the course and qualified the trainees for employment elsewhere, was never achieved, though at the end of the centre's existence there were moves to acquire Tanzanian certification. Thus absenteeism was high, and completion rates low. In April/May of 1991, there were 49 students at the VTC, only one of whom was in the second year of the two-year course.

The attempt was also made to create a centre of small industrial production. The building programme in itself encouraged this, with a workshop being established for prefabricated components. There was a leather factory making shoes, belts, bags and the like, and a garment factory. The garment factory was first mooted in 1976, and Dutch sympathisers raised money for the venture in 1982. The factory was established at Mazimbu soon after, using cloth from the GDR, moving in 1988 and 1989 to Dakawa. Three Finnish experts assisted the 25 garment workers. In 1989 the factory produced, amongst other items, 1 550 SOMAFCO school uniforms, 700 curtains, 100 nursery uniforms and bed sheets for the whole community. Such institutions did not always run smoothly. Labour discontent stemming from petty nepotism and a lack of effective stocktaking, bookkeeping and training plagued the leather factory.

Authority and democracy

In the midst of this complex process of development, the ANC had a real dilemma in balancing humanitarian considerations with political imperatives. One example is that of a young man who returned from the Soviet Union in 1982 because he was missing his pregnant girlfriend. The political commissar thought that he was an excellent person, but 'we are in a liberation movement and one wonders how on earth shall such cases be treated. We have tried our best to persuade this man to change, but strange to say, he is not prepared to effect even a semblance of change in his attitudes.' Indeed, some leaders felt that in the context of the struggle, personal liberty would have to take second place to discipline and authority. This was apparent at the second Dakawa Seminar in November 1983, when the ANC Treasurer-General, Thomas Nkobi, claimed that '[t]he ANC suffers from democracy', castigating those who had been trained but, instead of contributing to the struggle, 'are in Morogoro drinking'. Andrew Masondo added, '[w]e have Dakawa because some returnees have been refused jobs because they are uncontrollable ... We need to exercise authority.' When mixed with the grievances of those alienated from one or other aspect of ANC politics who also tended to be sent to the

Rehabilitation Centre, it can be seen that there was a potentially rich brew of disaffection.

One result of these difficult physical, social and political conditions was frequent complaints about morale. Writing to the secretary-general of the ANC, the Education Secretary, Henry Makgothi, reported on a visit to Dakawa in May 1985: 'The living conditions', he said, 'are grim', and he proceeded to describe atrocious accommodation, food and hygiene. He went on:

> The inhabitants of the camp appear completely listless and indifferent. Some of them appear not to have had a wash for several months. There were sullen looks and ominous comment, but there was also doggedness and courage. But generally speaking the morale is low.

He urged the sending of 'committed comrades' to assist the Dakawa administration, and indeed around this time the pace of development began to accelerate. However, complaints about apathy and low morale never ceased, reaching one of a number of peaks in late 1986. The zonal commissar stated that there were secretive moves to oust the acting co-ordinator of Dakawa, and that '[t]he general political situation remains as before – dormant political life, malfunctioning of political structures and low level of political consciousness of the members of the community'. In October the political commissar reported 'apathy in the community ... Political life is limited to celebrations and marking of certain days in our revolutionary diary.' At this point the situation degenerated into virtual revolt, with the zonal commissar and acting co-ordinator hauled before a meeting that they deemed irregular. The dissidents accused the administration of 'creating conditions for mutiny', of torture, misuse of transport, favouritism and other abuses. The Dakawa leaders accused their opponents of 'organised anarchy' and 'mafia-type activities', and hinted that 'the movement was and is being attacked'. 'In a way', the zonal commissar and the acting co-ordinator said, 'we are reaping the "fruits" from our Dakawa that has a high concentration of anarchists, disgruttled [*sic*] elements and even a few non-members who manage to remain and participate in our activities.' In the end, the alleged ringleader was, as the co-ordinator put it, 'chucked out'.

In 1989, disenchantment with the Dakawa administration gathered around the Zonal Youth Section, though now within the framework of accepted procedures rather than open defiance as in 1986. Preparatory meetings for the third Dakawa Seminar were used to voice various grievances. Healthcare, physical infrastructure, facilities for welfare, youth, education and food were all criticised. The old accusation that Dakawa was 'a dumping ground' was made once more. The authorities were accused of mismanagement, and of wilfully ignoring warnings about problems with labour relations and construction. The demand was made that democratically elected bodies should run Dakawa, rather than what they called 'militarist-type of structures', and that the dominance of the co-ordinator's office over 'the people's structures' should be ended. 'We demand', they said, 'that the Freedom Charter be immediately implemented in Dakawa so that our place should serve as a model for a future democratic and nonracial South Africa.'

There was a range of reactions amongst the Dakawa and Lusaka leadership to this sort of discontent. Oswald Dennis, labouring unceasingly to finance and develop the complex, strongly criticised the approach of the Youth Section and other political organs. To Dennis, 'instead of consistent hard work to raise the morale and contribution of the community, the political organs have come to see their role almost exclusively as the spokesmen for every demand or grievance – justified or unjustified.' Reg September was more sympathetic, recognising that though circumstances had often obliged the ANC to adopt a centralising and even commandist approach at times, this was not fundamentally desirable. He believed that Dakawa was faced 'with the challenge of laying the foundation of a democratically governed area, which will be a picture of what we hope to be able to build in South Africa, a MODEL TOWN.' A compromise was suggested at the third Dakawa Seminar in April 1989. The tensions between the administrative and political elements at Dakawa were aired, and a partially-elected Dakawa Municipal Council was recommended, with the chairman or mayor to be appointed by the elected members.

However, though some steps were taken to deal with the causes of the discontent, there were also disciplinary moves to eliminate the protests. There was a crackdown on the youth column in *Dakawa News and Views*, alleged to have published 'harmful articles against administrative structures'. The paper was said to be 'in the process of re-organisation assisted by the administration'. The ZYC, influenced, it was claimed, by dissident elements from Angola, was accused of attempting to undermine authority, with political structures vulnerable to occupation by people with a suspect security background harbouring grudges against the movement. In what the Administrative Co-ordinator called '[t]his loophole', that is, the electoral system of choosing office bearers, 'our own democratic procedures' were blamed for the discontent, or at least for enabling it to be articulated.

Some complex issues arise from this episode. Wintshi Njobe, the principal of the VTC, raised some of them when he described the '*Mphando* mentality'. Free distribution of necessities could result in 'apparent rejection of self-reliance', Njobe thought. However, though the demands of the Youth Section may indeed have ignored many of the real problems of constructing and administering Dakawa, and may to some extent have been based on a 'culture of entitlement', the agitation for a more democratic dispensation was not confined to such bodies. Njobe himself, for instance, in a paper delivered to an ANC internal conference in Lusaka in mid-1988, wrote that there was a need 'urgently to re-organise management structures for Dakawa and introduce more democratic procedures in the management of life of people living there'. He regarded these authoritarian structures as the main source of the 'open defiance of authority and non co-operation', which he said characterised Dakawa at this time. He advocated democratic local government for Dakawa, and the abolition of the system symbolised by *umphando*, which he said should be replaced by a purposeful life of self-reliance. In this way, he argued, Dakawa could become a worthwhile model for a future South Africa. He went on to say that in the uprooted and isolated situation in which young people found themselves at Dakawa, there was a tendency to daydream about study overseas. Some were not really qualified to go abroad; others might qualify, but were unlikely to find places quickly. This could lead to grudges against those who were supposedly delaying applications. While the ANC attempted to present more realistic options, such as VTC courses, to such people, Dakawa, Njobe said, was 'a society whose day to day hopes and future plans tend to be dominated by illusions that will probably never materialise'.

Making daily life liveable

With the need to serve the growing population of Dakawa, the provision of social facilities improved markedly over the decade. The hospital at Mazimbu, and beyond that the resources of the Tanzanian medical system, were available for serious cases. However, a clinic at Dakawa, which had its own problems and inefficiencies, dealt with immediate needs. There was a primary school, a nursery, and a daycare centre for toddlers and babies. A visiting group of educationists from South Africa in April/May 1991, impressed with what they had seen, considered that '[t]he Dakawa primary complex should be used as a model for similar establishments in South Africa'. They feared that the children would return to much less well-equipped and organised South African schools.

Because Dakawa was primarily intended for adults, many of whom had received little or low-quality education in South Africa, there was a need for adult education facilities. The Adult Education Division provided these. However, attendance at these classes was low, and the division suffered a particular loss of interest during the political changes of the early 1990s, with attendance becoming erratic and the consequent need to go over lessons repeatedly. The South African Extension Unit, supported by the Commonwealth, South African liberation movements, the UNHCR and the Tanzanian government, provided materials for use in adult education. There was also a library, at first in a tent, then in a temporary building. In 1986 readers could choose from a limited selection of books such as RL Stevenson's *Treasure Island*, stories by Enid Blyton and works by Shakespeare, Gorky, Arthur Hailey and Frederick Forsyth, as well as technical manuals and textbooks. Plans were made to erect a purpose-built library, with assistance from Finland, in the early 1990s. Overtaken by events, this new library was never built. In this latest phase, there were also plans to build many other facilities, such as a social centre. As with the library, these plans were forestalled by the momentous political changes of the time.

Plans for a cultural centre were also caught up in the events of the early 1990s. It had long been realised that the struggle against apartheid could not be defined in narrowly political terms, and that it was necessary to contest its dominance on many levels, including the cultural. There were plans for such a centre from the foundation of Dakawa, though the first discussions on the topic did not give a particularly prominent place to textile printing, which as it turned out became the first, and only, aspect to be implemented. Thus, when a group of Swedish anti-apartheid activists secured the support of the Swedish overseas funding agency, Sida, for a textile-printing workshop, this was adopted as a first step in the foundation of a cultural centre not just for Dakawa, but for the movement as a whole.

The projected centre, in the words of a 1989 report, 'was intended to answer the pressing need for an ANC Cultural Centre, as well as to serve as a community cultural centre for the ever-growing Dakawa settlement'. It was intended that *Amandla*, the ANC performance troupe, should move to Dakawa, and that a wide range of cultural expression should find a home there, including film, fine art, graphic art, photography, theatre, music, and all the training, organisational, library and other activities needed to support this ambitious programme. When Dakawa was about to be abandoned, plans had already been drawn up for a centre that would include a theatre, pottery, graphic design facility, weaving looms, the already existing textile-printing workshop, and many other facilities. None of these were built, and the textile-printing workshop alone made the transition to the new dispensation, as will be described in the final chapter. Officially opened on 18 July 1988, though in operation before this, the centre began to function in a small building with the assistance of a Swedish consultant, Malin Sellmann, who had previously worked at the Rorke's Drift Arts Centre in Natal. The next stage was intended to be the building of weaving and dyeing and graphics workshops, but the political changes of 1990 and thereafter put these plans on hold. Looms had indeed been bought in Sweden to start weaving at Dakawa, but they were ultimately sent to South Africa rather than Tanzania. It was, therefore, Swedish assistance that enabled textile printing to transfer to South Africa, as it had enabled it to start in the first place.

16. At the textile-printing workshop in Dakawa

The early days of the textile-printing workshop were difficult, with breaks in the electricity supply frequently interrupting work, and with various personal and professional problems that made it impossible for some of the trainees to continue with the programme. Nevertheless, the centre produced sufficient work of quality to be shown at exhibitions in Scandinavia and the Netherlands. It was made clear – and in this it differentiated itself from the approach taken at the VTC – that the task of the centre was essentially educational, training artists in this medium over a period of five years. The aim was not to mass-produce goods, though the centre was willing to comply when called upon to print designs on cloth or T-shirts for political purposes.

An educational partnership

Dakawa was only beginning to get into its stride when it closed. It played a number of roles, amongst others that of a laboratory for social and economic development, and a staging point for ANC cadres expelled from countries under pressure from the South African regime. However, it also had its own educational institutions such as the excellent primary school and daycare centre, and bodies like the EOC acted as adjuncts to SOMAFCO itself. In addition, Dakawa operated in educational spheres not handled at Mazimbu, such as certain kinds of technical and artistic training. Dakawa was essentially Mazimbu's educational partner.

CHAPTER 12

Funding SOMAFCO

After initial hardships, SOMAFCO, though never an easy environment, became an island of exceptional educational and infrastructural development in the sea of Tanzanian poverty. This required considerable resources that the ANC sought all over the world, persistently and ingeniously, particularly through the efforts of Thomas Nkobi, 'a magician', as John Pampallis refers to him. Indeed, the funding drive in itself became part of the ANC's search for international recognition and support.

One aim of the educational project was to foster international appreciation of the aims and activities of the ANC. Indeed, the picture eventually presented to the world ensured that many of even the most parsimonious and suspicious countries in Europe and elsewhere were finally persuaded to assist. The school was packaged so as to highlight the beneficiaries of the institution and their planned contribution to a free South Africa. This explains the priority given to the constant stream of visitors, from official and unofficial organisations, to whom administrators like Mohammed Tikly devoted so much time. Prospective helpers and donors were made to feel that they were helping shape a future South Africa. The result was that the school developed an exceptionally wide support base, which in turn promoted the image and assisted the funding of the movement as a whole. The ANC cast its bread upon the waters: it came back a hundred-fold.

The commemorative brochure produced for the formal handing over of the Mazimbu and Dakawa facilities to the Tanzanian government in July 1992 indicates the extent of the physical infrastructure developed by the ANC. There is too much to itemise here: the list for the 1 000 hectare settlement at Mazimbu alone includes the secondary school, with 6 fully-equipped classroom blocks, 2 science blocks, an art and technical block, 6 dormitory units, 24 staff houses, the library and multi-purpose hall, and the covered main square with stage. There was also the primary school, the daycare centre and nursery, the administration block, hospital, farm, maintenance department, transport office and petrol station, stores, furniture factory, government representative's office and gate house, the numerous residential and community facilities, and the well-developed road, electrical, water and sewage systems. There was development on a similar scale on the 2 800 hectare Dakawa settlement. This had all been made possible through the assistance of governments, non-governmental and solidarity organisations, schools and individuals, from all over the world. Apart from physical infrastructure, solidarity workers came from Australia, Cuba, Denmark, Finland, the GDR, Great Britain, Guyana, Ireland, the Netherlands, Nigeria, Norway, Poland, Sweden, Tanzania, Tonga, the United States and Zambia. All this could be the subject of a lengthy separate study; an outline of the main sources of assistance must suffice here.

Mazimbu was a large complex with many activities taking place at the same time. Donors were encouraged therefore to concentrate their efforts on specific sub-projects. This also helped to give donors a sense of identification with particular aspects of the work. However, before donor assistance was possible, there had to be a site. The school was on Tanzanian soil and could not have flourished without Tanzanian support. Since the early 1960s Tanzania had maintained a close relationship with liberation movements from southern Africa, and played a significant role in the struggle for independence of most nations of the region. SOMAFCO, in fact, was a relative latecomer in the country's dealings with South African liberation movements.

Though it did assign technical experts and teachers to the school, Tanzania, being a desperately poor country, could not be expected to give direct financial support. That is why it became so important to activate the foreign donor community. Help was needed for the building of the physical structure of the school, for feeding the students and the Mazimbu community, and for developing other sectors such as the farm, furniture factory and transport section. Initial support came from several UN agencies, from Scandinavia, from the Netherlands and from many Eastern Bloc countries that gave scholarships and on occasion actual goods, like the shipload of Siberian timber that kept the Mazimbu furniture factory in operation for several years. Eventually, governments and non-governmental organisations (NGOs) from all over the world assisted the school.

In this regard there were problems as well as achievements. There are examples of wasted goods and lost opportunities. For instance, containers of donated goods were sometimes left at Dar es Salaam docks for long periods, with the effect that valuable equipment was damaged through long exposure to the elements. Negligence and laxity sometimes resulted in a thriving trade in stolen goods, and suspects were not always vigorously pursued even when they were known. These and other blunders resulted in delays in construction work. Problems were compounded by the constant shortage of skilled personnel, resulting in the overloading of the few people with the necessary competencies. Sometimes key people were so overworked that they required hospitalisation or rest breaks to recuperate in a more tranquil environment.

Scandinavian and other assistance

Of Western countries, it was the Scandinavian states that supported SOMAFCO most generously and consistently, and provided the funding backbone to educational and other activities at Mazimbu and Dakawa. Without this support, Mohammed Tikly says, 'we wouldn't have succeeded.' There was a surge of popular support for the ANC and SOMAFCO in these countries. Large amounts of cash and material came either directly from the official Nordic aid organisations – Sida, the Norwegian Agency for Development Cooperation (Norad), the Danish International Development Agency (Danida) and the Finnish International Development Agency (Finnida), or through the infrastructure that they provided for the distribution of aid raised by Scandinavian NGOs. This was the case, for instance, in 1985 and 1988, when much of the proceeds of Operation Day's Work – the annual collection of funds by Nordic schoolchildren through a day's voluntary labour – was donated to Mazimbu and Dakawa. About one million dollars was raised on each occasion. The Swedish historian, Tor Sellström, argues that Swedish and Nordic aid to southern African liberation movements was 'more diverse and significant' than that from the Eastern Bloc. Though the Scandinavian countries did not provide military aid, by consistently supporting other aspects of the liberation struggle, resources were freed for the military activities of the various liberation movements. In the case of the ANC, Mazimbu and Dakawa were major beneficiaries of Scandinavian assistance.

Sweden was the largest contributor of the Scandinavian countries to the ANC, with Norway also of great importance. However, because Norwegian policy, unlike that of Sweden, was to give official assistance only to the ANC in exile, and not to opposition organisations in South Africa itself, the Norwegians tended to be particularly prominent at SOMAFCO and Dakawa. Though the Swedes made important contributions at Mazimbu and Dakawa, their main efforts were elsewhere.

Scandianavian assistance was not only copious but intelligently planned. The ANC received large amounts of uncoordinated aid from numerous sources, thus, for instance, being obliged to run a great variety of vehicles with incompatible spares and maintenance systems. Consistent Scandinavian assistance provided welcome continuity in this sometimes-incoherent context, enabling the movement to plan ahead with the certainty that support would be forthcoming.

In the Nordic countries, the deployment of Lindiwe Mabuza as the ANC's Chief Representative in Stockholm opened many doors. Through her efforts the ANC became widely known in Sweden and throughout Scandinavia. Assistance was co-ordinated through Sida, which planned and administered the country's bilateral agreements with the liberation movements of southern

Africa. Sweden's Prime Minister, Olaf Palme, was particularly keen on fostering relations with the ANC. On opening the Swedish People's Parliament Against Apartheid on 21 February 1986, he recommitted his country to support of the ANC in the years until the apartheid regime was overcome. This was one of his last engagements. A week later, he was assassinated. Some have linked this to the activities of South African government agents.

Sida supported various initiatives at SOMAFCO. The Mazimbu farm was one of the most important Swedish-supported projects. Though the farm had its problems – many stemming from tensions between its social and commercial aspirations – it was, as a 1991 Swedish report said, 'in several aspects … the most modern farm in Tanzania'. Pre-school and primary school teachers, auxiliary nurses and office-machine technicians were sent to Sweden for training, an initiative that to some extent turned sour when a number of the trainees applied for political asylum. Sida also supported work at Dakawa, notably the arts centre.

Swedish private organisations also raised large sums, such as the nearly \$500 000 raised by the Swedish Students' Union for the laboratory block, to which Sida also contributed. The Swedish section of Save the Children sent funds, as did student groups, the Teachers' Association, and the youth wings of various political parties – not only those on the left. The Africa Groups Recruitment Organisation recruited Swedish volunteers for SOMAFCO.

Norad, often in collaboration with the NGO, Norplan, made a major contribution to physical planning and infrastructural development at Mazimbu and Dakawa. They supported electrification, water reticulation, sewage and road construction, and Norplan collaborated closely with the ANC in conceptualising and planning the development of Dakawa. In terms of particular projects, the Norwegians, for example, supported the piping of sweet water to Dakawa from a nearby river, essential to make the settlement habitable. They funded most of the agricultural machinery on the farms. Norwegian People's Aid administered supplies of food from the Norwegian government, and financed the tarring of roads and the construction of a sewage system.

The Danish government did not support liberation movements such as the ANC directly, but did so indirectly by supporting unofficial solidarity organisations. Thus Denmark played a significant role in planning and construction programmes, and was an important source of technical assistance through its volunteer agency. Lars Nordbo was the first of many Danish technical experts to work at Mazimbu and Dakawa. After serving at Mazimbu for several years, like many other volunteers she continued to organise support after returning home. Danish NGOs such as Danchurchaid also played an important role, for instance by supplying large quantities of building and household equipment.

17. Donor funding enabled SOMAFCO to build on a generous scale: erecting the roof over the main square

There were various Finnish initiatives also. Non-governmental, and, from 1987, official Finnish support went to the excellent library at Mazimbu. The International Solidarity Foundation (ISF) of Finland played an important part in building and equipping the Vuyisile Mini Furniture Factory. Two experts, T Lantamatti and Leo Sonderquist, were sent to evaluate needs and train workers. The ISF also agreed to assist with on-the-job training at Mazimbu and abroad, to buy and install new machinery and to assist with improving product quality and design. In 1986 the organisation supplied a dust-extraction system and new machinery. The Finns even supplied small items like glue, nails, screws and various hand tools, and sent regular supplies of timber, which had previously been bought at Sao Hill in Iringa. The ANC spent very little on the factory.

In 1988 the ISF commissioned an analysis of the furniture factory. The purpose was to develop ways of changing the factory into an independent and profitable market-oriented enterprise, a move resulting from the positive response to the high quality and excellent design of the few items already put on sale. By this time the factory produced 1 000 items per month, and employed 5 ANC members, 39 Tanzanians, and 1 Norwegian and 2 Finnish experts. The ISF continued to be the main donor, and there was an effort to convince more ANC members to work in the factory. The Vuyisile Mini

18. From left, Spencer Hodgson, architect, and Danish volunteers, Ingeborg Flensted-Nielsen, architectural technician, and Lisa Hansen, architect. The other person has not been identified

Furniture Factory survived for a time after the departure of the ANC, with Leo Sonderquist returning to Tanzania to run the operation as a commercial enterprise.

While direct Dutch governmental assistance was minimal until the late 1980s, official funds were indirectly funneled to SOMAFCO through state support of the Dutch volunteer organisation. Many Dutch experts were assigned to Mazimbu and Dakawa, and Willem van Harderwijk, a civil engineer whose wife Fieke taught at the nursery school, was the longest serving volunteer at Mazimbu. Dutch NGOs gave considerable assistance, as with the building and equipping of the Dutch Solidarity Hospital at Mazimbu.

Support from the Eastern Bloc was crucial to the ANC in general. Since these were virtually the only countries prepared to finance the armed struggle and give military training, the ANC was happy to receive humanitarian aid from well-disposed Western countries, especially to SOMAFCO, thus enabling the communist countries to concentrate on military assistance. However, a steady stream of science and mathematics teachers, especially from the GDR, was sent to the school, as well as considerable assistance in kind, such as tinned food, timber and educational materials.

Western governments on the whole, with the exception of the Scandinavian countries, were suspicious of the ANC. They only began to offer support to its development efforts, notably SOMAFCO, towards the late 1980s, when the balance of world power was starting to shift and it began to seem possible that support for South African liberation need not imply a weakening of the front against the Eastern Bloc. Italy is an example; for some years the Italian NGO, the Centre for Information and Education for Development (CIES), tried, with little success, to get the Italian government to assist SOMAFCO. However, towards the end of the decade, CIES succeeded in goading Italy to reformulate its law on co-operation and assistance. Soon, direct financial assistance was granted for the construction of Residential Block Five at SOMAFCO. On 27 July 1990, the ANC and CIES signed an agreement on 'education and training for the transition from exile to repatriation and for the construction of a post apartheid society'. This was meant to prepare for reintegration into South African society, with the long-term objective of upgrading and reforming the education system, and the creation of job opportunities. It was also intended to look at the feasibility of adapting and continuing the SOMAFCO project in the context of the South Africa to which the exiles were about to return.

There were numerous other official and unofficial supporting organisations. Late in the school's existence, the Indian government gave considerable help in kind. Nigeria assigned a large contingent of teachers. Cuba sent doctors and nurses. NGOs in countries like Japan, Austria, Ireland, Australia and France contributed generously. To illustrate, the following are some particular projects supported by non-official organisations in different parts of the world: Australian People for Health, Education and Development Abroad sponsored students for a librarianship course in Dar es Salaam in 1986 and 1987; an Italian agency, Movimento Liberazione eSviluppo, supported dairy production; World Universities Service, the Commonwealth Secretariat, the African American Institute, the Solidarity Committees of the GDR and of the Soviet Union, and many other organisations provided scholarships. Other bodies, from the African Groups of Sweden Recruitment Organisation to the Inner London Education Authority, recruited teachers for SOMAFCO.

A crucial source of support was sponsorship of individual students, as mentioned above. For example, the Otto Beneke Stiftung (OBS) of the then West Germany played an important role. From 1981 the OBS sponsored students at the school who performed well, in 1984, for example, supporting 120 from Forms 1 to 5. In return SOMAFCO staff informed the OBS, with reasons, of any students whose scholarships were withdrawn. The OBS only paid when all its requirements were satisfied. Such procedures ensured that funding was not committed to activities other than those relevant to those particular students.

SOMAFCO could not have existed without outside donor assistance. People all over the world wanted to be involved with this attempt to build a model of education for post-apartheid South Africa, and the ANC was able to mobilise this goodwill effectively and transform it into the resources to build and develop its school.

SOMAFCO and UN agencies

The ANC's contacts with UN agencies in relation to SOMAFCO date to 1977 when the idea of a school was still in its infancy. The UNDP provided funds, and other agencies, particularly Unesco, worked directly with the ANC. The UNDP brief was outlined in a guideline document:

> The purpose of UNDP assistance to African National Liberation Movements … recognised by the Organization of African Unity … is to prepare the members … for full and responsible participation in the social, cultural, economic and political life of their respective countries of origin when independence is achieved, or conditions are otherwise right in those countries. Since National Liberation Movement members have as a rule tended to reside in countries of asylum, UNDP assistance has the purpose also of assisting them to develop adequate infrastructures aimed at enabling them to attain a reasonable level and standard of living, productivity, civic responsibility and self-reliance in those countries.

Assistance was mainly for skills and manpower development through education at all levels. Also stressed was vocational and technical training intended to empower people for eventual administrative, technical and managerial responsibilities when they returned to their home countries. This seemed to be a long-term aim as far as the South Africans were concerned, and the immediate goal was training that would help them survive in the foreign environment in which they found themselves. On that level UNDP assistance included the development of capacity for self-reliance, particularly in agriculture, and in areas like carpentry, masonry, mechanical repair and maintenance, health and other community services.

Such support helped create an environment where the school could flourish. In the specifically educational field, the UNDP committed itself to strengthening infrastructure at primary and secondary levels. The main justification for this was that the language of instruction for South Africans at these levels was different from that commonly used at Tanzanian schools. In addition, it would have been inappropriate to send children to Tanzanian schools already overburdened with providing for the country's own citizens.

Probably to forestall accusations of preferential treatment, the UNDP added that assistance would only be provided to enable liberation schools to achieve levels and standards of education comparable to those of host countries. However, this is not what happened at SOMAFCO. The Mazimbu complex, with excellent infrastructure, stood in stark contrast to the Tanzanian community surrounding it. Interviews indicate that SOMAFCO students regarded themselves as educationally better off than their Tanzanian counterparts, and the UNDP provided facilities to the ANC much superior to those of local schools. However, they did insist that scholarships for liberation organisations would be granted only for school attendance in African countries. Secondary school pupils were never sent out of the continent on UNDP money.

The UNDP evaluated its projects midway and when they came to an end. Continued assistance depended on the findings and recommendations of a joint investigation by UNDP and the ANC. In a typical evaluation in September 1983, the UNDP praised the ANC, which, they said:

> has been very successful in attracting assistance from bilateral donors and national associations in Europe. With this assistance it has been able to establish well-planned and well-managed settlements in Tanzania and Zambia, with such social infrastructure as medical services, full-fledged educational systems catering for pre-school, primary and secondary school children, and offering education classes, vocational training and production services, and farm production units.

There were similar comments in a 1985 evaluation. This was accompanied by Mazimbu's self-evaluation report, drafted by the director of the complex, which summarised what had been achieved and the role played by outside aid. He acknowledged that through sustained and growing aid, the ANC had been able to develop viable schools where systematic instruction was provided in accordance with ANC educational policy, forming people dedicated to a future non-racist, democratic South Africa. Progress had been made in curriculum and staff development.

However, there were many inadequately served areas. The evaluation stated that more attention would need to be paid to in-service training in various sectors with the help of Unesco and the International Labor Organization (ILO). Vocational subjects should be strengthened in the secondary school. Adult education, the recruitment and training of more teachers, career guidance, more books, better transport, support for the hospital and more storage facilities were mentioned. Thus, while acknowledging the progress made at SOMAFCO, UNDP also pointed to problems that required attention. For instance, by calling for ways of improving the low achievement rate in the sciences, it was implicitly acknowledged that there were problems in this area. The emphasis on in-service courses signified that many teachers were not properly qualified to teach at the school: many graduate teachers were subject specialists but not trained teachers. Increased competence was expected to result in better rapport with students and improved academic results.

These were the wide parameters within which the UN agencies operated. They provided the rationale for a series of projects in support of SOMAFCO and other programmes at Mazimbu. In 1977, with the school still an idea rather than a reality, Unesco undertook to pay for scholarships for South African youth recently exiled in the wake of the 1976 uprisings. At this point what would become the school was merely a staging post, with some unstructured teaching for students waiting to be sent to other countries to continue with their education. Plans for the complex had not yet been fully formulated, and the pressing issue was finding schools for the young people. Those arriving were mostly taken to Nigeria and Sierra Leone, and for tertiary education, to Cuba.

This project terminated at the end of 1978. However, parallel with the growth of the school, a series of further projects was put in place that steadily expanded the areas covered by UN-agency funding and extended the boundaries of what constituted fundable educational support. Fellowships, better stipends, training for staff, travel, holidays for teachers and students, study tours, educational equipment of all sorts, books, kitchen utensils, and many other items were covered. The disbursement of funds was by the appropriate UN agency: the Food and Agriculture Organization (FAO) supported the farm, for instance, and Unesco supported more directly educational needs.

An important project within the school was the erection of a library. The ANC submitted the first project proposal in September 1981, initially estimating that the building would cost $100 000. In an October 1982 document, the *Mazimbu Library Project*, the ANC interpreted the massacre of 1976 'when thousands of young African school children – protesting against the introduction of Afrikaans as a medium of instruction in schools – were brutally attacked by the police of the apartheid regime', as stemming from educational deprivation. An adequate library, it was stressed, must be an integral part of the education facility, providing resources denied by Bantu Education. They foresaw the library eventually including a reference section, reading rooms, and a music room, and stressed that reference books, encyclopaedias, subscriptions to international journals and newspapers, and books related to the general curriculum of the school were urgently needed. Eventually, Finnish aid assisted greatly with the stocking, staffing and running of the library.

By the late 1980s Unesco and UNDP were involved in additional programmes. There was a project to train ex-MK cadres in various fields, and one to support pupils who had not yet been relocated to Mazimbu in schools in various frontline states. There was a project to support the EOC in Dakawa, which was intended, amongst other functions, to receive students destined for

19. Primary school children on donated bicycles

eventual admission to SOMAFCO, and another to support the training of 20 primary and 20 secondary teachers for SOMAFCO at Tanzanian teacher training colleges. Recognising that these teachers were not going to live permanently in Tanzania, special tutors were to be appointed to handle aspects of training specific to the South Africans. Unesco also organised seminars in collaboration with the ANC on themes relevant to education in exile.

Staffing was a constant problem at SOMAFCO, and the ANC approached Unesco for assistance. Unesco, looking for teachers who could deal with children separated from their families, with varied and disrupted backgrounds, in turn requested help from the Tanzanian government. The Tanzanians drew on the pool of school inspectors, reasoning, in the words of Raphael Mwinuka, one of the officials involved, that 'those inspectors are experienced in teaching and that is why they are promoted to be inspectors, so let them go and teach these young people from different backgrounds who have been away from their classrooms for quite a long time'.

As well as requiring progress reports from the school, Unesco sent inspectors to evaluate, among other things, the use made of resources provided to SOMAFCO. The relationship remained close: assistance flowed steadily, so that, for instance, in January 1989 SOMAFCO acknowledged receiving a school bus and a land cruiser, ten primary and ten secondary school teachers, two adult educators, musical instruments, school equipment and spare parts.

The ILO, another UN agency, also assisted. The organisation's 67th session, in June 1981, condemned apartheid and laid the basis for co-operation with South African liberation movements. It resolved that the ILO should increase its assistance in the field of vocational training. The ANC quickly took advantage of this, and sought and received training programmes at various levels for office staff, including those at SOMAFCO.

The ILO was also heavily involved in the VTC in Dakawa. Though South Africa was an industrialised country requiring a sophisticated workforce, apartheid created an artificial restriction on the growth of skills amongst the majority of the people. Thus the ILO sought, in a small way, to establish a core group of skilled people who could contribute to the process of change. Funds also flowed to Dakawa from the UNHCR.

Scholarships

Mazimbu quickly developed into a many-sided educational and quasi-educational complex. It also became the hub of a worldwide educational network, with SOMAFCO students going on to study in many countries, and with Mazimbu becoming the centre for organising and administering the studies even of members of the movement who had not themselves attended the school. This activity did not contribute directly to the funding of SOMAFCO, and scholarships were not a school responsibility. However, it did help make Mazimbu a major educational centre and, by providing a way forward for school-leavers, indirectly contributed to the strength of the institution. Opportunities for further educational development were to be secured from donor countries where ANC personnel, including SOMAFCO graduates, would pursue their studies. The acquisition, distribution and administration of scholarships was an important, and often sensitive and controversial activity.

The question of systematising the previously ad hoc scholarship programme arose as early as 1979. The ANC Education Department invited submissions on the role and composition of a proposed Scholarship Committee. SOMAFCO staff proposed that the committee be based in Mazimbu, and that it be representative of the various interested parties. Merit, which meant political commitment as well as scholastic ability, would govern awards. Wintshi Njobe, the principal of SOMAFCO at the time – no doubt aware of the sensitivity of the issue – recommended that only the proposed committee should be authorised to allocate scholarships. He felt this would help avoid accusations of bias.

On 16 June 1980 the ANC National Working Committee approved the recommendations of the third Neduc meeting on the composition of the committee. There were to be 12 members, with SOMAFCO heavily represented, and the secretariat was to be based at SOMAFCO. It would have access to students' records; the right to attend staff meetings when students' progress was under discussion, the right to attend disciplinary meetings so as to be fully aware of any problems and direct access to individual students.

In February 1982 the committee was dissolved and reconstituted, in part responding to complaints that it was not impartial. After considering applications, the National Scholarship Committee (NSC), as it was now called, would draw up a list of awards and submit it to the Department of Education for approval by the secretary general. Links with education ministries of host countries were to be developed to improve monitoring and guidance of students. The NSC was also responsible for dealing with the inevitable queries and complaints related to scholarships and placements.

Scholarship application procedures were clarified. Crucially, wherever candidates happened to be in the world, they were now expected to await their scholarships at SOMAFCO. This was intended to facilitate political orientation, career guidance, processing of scholarships and travel arrangements. SOMAFCO was considered a good environment for political grounding and the inculcation of commitment, thereby minimising defections in host countries. Such defections were encouraged by the perception among students that scholarships were awarded to the children of leaders who were not in SOMAFCO, but were rather attending prestigious schools elsewhere.

In response to such criticisms and to the growing volume of business, the NSC began to show greater consistency. Safeguards were built into the system to ensure that candidates were truly eligible for their proposed courses of study. This would be in the long-term interest of the students because mistakes would delay progress. Heads of department at SOMAFCO would be accountable for their recommendations, and if a student failed or deserted, the head of department who had made the recommendation would be questioned.

Given the sensitive nature of the NSC's work, operating principles that would guarantee the integrity of office bearers were needed. Those associated with the NSC were on no account to discuss scholarships outside the committee or to offer them to individuals. There were to be strict lines of communication, whether the candidate was from SOMAFCO or elsewhere. The NSC would make all decisions and no correspondence would be sent out on behalf of the NSC without the approval of the chairperson. Relevant members of the NSC met every fortnight to consider applications and attend to correspondence and other matters. Quarterly reports were prepared and distributed. In short, the NSC was becoming a more permanent structure with a secretariat of chairperson, secretary, assistant secretary and education officer that met almost daily.

Linked to the academic quality of the entrants, selection criteria changed gradually over the years. From 1983, countries that had traditionally provided scholarships began to demand higher entry qualifications and the presentation of school certificates. This was probably the result of some students claiming to have passed their secondary qualification, but failing to bring proof, having left South Africa abruptly under police pressure. On arrival in these sympathetic countries, some proved to be far below the standard necessary to succeed in a tertiary institution. This obliged the NSC to apply stricter criteria in vetting applicants, which resulted in fewer meeting entry requirements. Absence of certificates, poor grades, age, poor health and the time elapsed since a candidate had last studied all contributed to the decline in the number of ANC students in some countries. However, in some cases the NSC was able to conduct assessment tests for applicants without school certificates. As a report noted in 1983/1984, 'we prefer that this practice be formalised for all candidates without certificates. Applicants for mature entry must be known to be competent and able to cope with advanced study.'

The NSC also set out deadlines for the submission of applications. However, these had to be implemented making allowance for the uncertain movements and residence of candidates from outside Mazimbu. In reality, the schedule was impossible to keep because of poor communication, and many missions and departments simply ignored it.

One of the most important NSC functions was to monitor students on scholarships. This was done through sending standard forms to mission offices, education committees and student unions. Progress reports were usually submitted at the end of the first term for students who had just arrived and at the end of the academic year for all students. Officials also visited countries with large concentrations of students to attend to issues on the spot.

As the world situation in the late 1980s tilted in favour of the struggle for South African liberation, the NSC positioned itself to deal with the influx of scholarship offers from parts of the world that had previously ignored the ANC. Some of these countries, including India, China, France, and the United States, pressed hard for students to take up their scholarships, some even catering for those who were not formally qualified. Offers claiming to be especially designed for the needs of the ANC and its potential students were received. This helped broaden the base from which future ANC personnel could be drawn.

In utilising these new opportunities, the NSC conferred with the ANC's Department of Manpower Development, which was responsible for placing students on completion of their studies, and therefore recommended which areas should receive priority. African countries in particular were offering more scholarship opportunities. These were welcome since monitoring progress was relatively easy and cost effective within the region. It was felt that placement of students in Western countries had to be undertaken with care, especially when official programmes of countries that had previously been hostile to the ANC, rather than supportive NGOs, were involved. Two criteria needed consideration: academic quality; and the political maturity of students. The ANC looked for the best institutions, avoiding the many that were keen to confer qualifications but were not considered capable of nurturing development. It was felt that in the United States in particular, there were many institutions with doubtful credentials. Disappointment in the political reliability of students continued, with some students returning with hostile attitudes towards progressive ideas. Thus only students considered to be politically dependable were to be sent to these countries, and ANC missions were to pay particular attention to their political formation whilst they were abroad. The political climate in the West, it was felt, was unlike that in the socialist countries where there were readily available opportunities for the development of appropriate attitudes.

The debate as to which side of the ideological divide was best for students was influenced by the fact that the ANC received solid support from Eastern Bloc countries. Questions of ideological orientation are significant, but an even more basic reality was that the ANC was not only involved in a struggle for the liberation of South Africa, but also for survival in foreign countries that were not obliged to help the organisation. Naturally, the ANC welcomed assistance where it could find it.

The NSC, with the Department of Manpower Development, developed guidelines as to how qualified students would be used by the movement. To prevent confusion, they were all to report to the NSC in East Africa, which in turn would report their presence to the secretary of education who would notify all relevant departments of their availability. Those students who could be readily utilised would be referred to the Department of Manpower Development for deployment, preferably in one of the frontline states. Another advantage of requiring qualified students to report in Tanzania was that, with the construction of Dakawa from 1982, most students could be temporarily occupied there while waiting for postings.

To ensure that returned students were usefully employed, the NSC recommended that surveys be carried out at intervals to determine the usefulness of their deployment, and that regular discussions be held with the Department of Education and other relevant bodies. Given the bureaucratic constraints within the ANC – with a thinly stretched administrative structure operating in several countries under difficult conditions – many of these recommendations were never implemented. This can also be gleaned from the many reports handed in during Neduc meetings that were never acted upon.

The work of the NSC, however, developed greatly over the years. Between 1983 and 1986, for example, 347 students were sent out on scholarships, and more than 150 returned with qualifications in the same period, with degrees in fields including medicine, engineering, communications, architecture, finance, agriculture and chemistry. The overwhelming majority had been to Eastern Bloc countries. For example, of the 209 students abroad in 1986, 66 were in Cuba, 65 in the GDR, 43 in Bulgaria, 11 in the Soviet Union and others elsewhere in Eastern Europe. These figures are for civilians, and do not include MK members on military courses.

The ever-increasing numbers of students meant that those withdrawn or expelled also increased for reasons including misconduct, academic weakness and ill health. After 1986, students withdrawn for medical or academic reasons were no longer to be sent to the Rehabilitation Centre at Dakawa. Instead, they were to be redeployed and, after a period of observation, reconsidered for study on the recommendation of the medical team or head of department. It was stated that, 'Some academically week [*sic*] students are encouraged to enroll at SOMAFCO's secondary or adult education divisions or to undertake private study.' These further chances for those who had failed, been expelled for misconduct or who had otherwise dropped out, caused unhappiness amongst students, some of whom had waited unsuccessfully for scholarships for several years.

The reason for the majority of withdrawals from scholarships were misconduct such as non-attendance at lectures, disregard of regulations, dissent, and desertion. For example, from September 1983 to July 1986, 40 students were expelled or withdrawn, 30 of these for misconduct. There were many discussions about this, and continuous attempts to avoid the problem by better selection processes and improved monitoring. Whether this really helped is another matter. It is clear that some students still carried with them all the traits of South African life, good and bad, including the often individualistic and assertive township culture that could clash with the regimented lifestyle of the Eastern Bloc countries to which they were sent.

With the difficulties facing the socialist states in the late 1980s, the NSC had to devise means of looking after students in these countries. It was agreed that they needed financial and material assistance. These uncertainties caused those seeking scholarships to be wary of accepting placements in the Eastern Bloc. Though the NSC felt it had to conduct research into this reluctance, the reasons were no doubt a natural resistance to studying in societies in crisis where large segments of the population were mobilising against unpopular governments. It was fortunate that at the same time, the South African government, under a similar avalanche of condemnation for its apartheid policies, decided to release political prisoners and lift the ban on political organisations, paving the way for the return of exiles.

CHAPTER 13

The end of SOMAFCO

For years SOMAFCO lived in a cocoon of exile, like much of the ANC. Exiles recreate the motherland from memory, needing constantly to reaffirm the existence and importance of an ideal that can easily be lost in the receding past, or buried under the weight of day-to-day existence. As the motherland fades into the past, intractable realities also recede, and to change the nature of society fundamentally may come to seem more feasible than it is. In 1990, with the lifting of the ban on the liberation movements, the release of Mandela and the moves towards a negotiated political settlement, the ANC was confronted by the realities of a society deeply divided by race and class, and experienced a jarring awakening to the limitations as well as the possibilities of political power. As barriers to communication of all kinds began to crumble, SOMAFCO also began to experience the impact of the tumultuous events of the time.

Why South Africa changed as it did in 1990 is a vexed question, and the precise mixture of external and internal pressure that brought about the political events of this period are difficult, and perhaps impossible, to untangle. It is debatable whether, fundamentally, apartheid collapsed because of its own contradictions and weaknesses, or was brought to its knees by domestic and exile opposition combined with economic and political pressures from abroad. These pressures, in a world no longer dominated by the Cold War, were able to play more freely on a state now unable to portray itself as the regional guardian of Western security. Such factors, and many others, contributed to the end of the apartheid state.

The events of the time had immediate and drastic effects on SOMAFCO. The demise of the Eastern Bloc ended aid to the school from that source, even marooning some of its ex-students in countries like Bulgaria and East Germany which, like South Africa, were undergoing profound political change and many-sided social and economic crises. On the other hand, Western powers such as the United States, once reluctant to fund an organisation seen as aligned to the communist world, now began to develop a more favourable attitude. This change was no doubt an aspect of the larger attempt to gain political and economic advantage in the fluid South African situation while moulding developments in ways perceived as broadly in line with capitalist liberal democracy. These changes in the world at large interwove intricately with the domestic situation in South Africa, and in turn affected SOMAFCO.

The changes in South Africa were not only far reaching, but, as far as those at SOMAFCO were concerned, also unexpected at that time. Even Dr Alpheus Mangezi, a significant figure in the ANC, an exile since the early 1960s and in charge of Mazimbu and Dakawa since 1989, expected – up to the point when the ban on the liberation movements was removed and negotiations began – a long haul towards a freedom that would be achieved through armed struggle. While the possibility of returning to South Africa increased, the planning of SOMAFCO's assumed future in Tanzania continued. The upgrading of health services, for example, continued to the end of the South African presence at Mazimbu, with a growing focus on the prevention and treatment of sexually transmitted diseases, amongst them HIV/AIDS.

The immediate reaction of the school authorities to the unbanning of the ANC and the other liberation movements was wary, and there was an attempt to damp down expectations of a rapid return to South Africa. The first hint of a forthcoming return came when Walter Sisulu visited the school. However, with Mandela's two-day visit to the complex in 1990, and his deliriously received announcement: 'Comrades: get yourselves prepared – you are going home!', it became clear that the days of the school were numbered. The exiles really were soon to return to their motherland.

Yet the country to which the students and teachers were to return seemed close to anarchy, with no sector more anarchic than black education. For years, sometimes exaggerated and romanticised rumours of an ANC school had circulated in South African townships. Now, as people actually began to return from exile, and movement within southern Africa began to be somewhat easier, it seemed to some young people that SOMAFCO was the answer to their educational problems. Ironically, just when SOMAFCO was undergoing major dislocation with the departure of many teachers, students and administrators, a new flood of young people began to arrive, many of them with deep-seated educational problems and psychological scars created by a disintegrating and demoralised educational system. It is not surprising, as Mangezi puts it, that such young people would often 'externalise their problems by creating problems'. Demands were thus made of SOMAFCO that it would have been difficult for it to have met even at the height of its activity in the 1980s.

It has been seen that one of the most difficult problems facing SOMAFCO – suffering as it was from a haemorrhage of teachers and administrators as they left for South Africa – was that of recently arrived students from KwaZulu and Natal. They generally came in groups, often having lost their parents in the communal violence, with the youngest, Mangezi remembers, a girl of eight. Many of those already at SOMAFCO were so shocked at the behaviour of some of the new arrivals that they referred to them as 'infiltrators'. Possibly some of them were, but most were in fact desperate and sometimes brutalised youth in flight from the chaos of this particular region rather than actual government agents.

There were other indications of how incompletely South African reality might fit with visions generated in exile. It has been seen that while religious observation was not forbidden or frowned upon at SOMAFCO, it had not been encouraged. However, with the collapse of the Soviet Union and its client states, and with communication between South Africa and Tanzania becoming easier after 1990, the religious elements that had been so important in domestic opposition to apartheid, and the religiosity of many South Africans, became impossible to ignore. The discourses that could result from the mixture of revolutionary rhetoric and Christian commitment could be unexpected. Vuyani Mlati remembers the visit from South Africa of the Reverend Arnold Stofile:

> I don't recall any religious activities ever taking place at SOMAFCO. Even during the funerals these were limited if they ever took place. I can tell you that it was some strange experience when the Reverend Arnold Stofile gave some form of a sermon. I am saying 'some form' because his was a mixture of politics and religion topped with a talk about a new Systematic Theology and the role the church in South Africa was playing in the struggle for freedom.

In 1990, a writer in *Dakawa News and Views* urged spiritual revival, announcing: 'VOX POPULI VOX DEI: THE WORD OF THE PEOPLE IS THE WORD OF GOD!'. Soon after, B Dumile called for 'Spiritual Revival in the year of United Action for a Democratic South Africa'. The comforts of religion could take paradoxical forms.

Mandela's announcement of the return to South Africa was received rapturously. But it was a disturbing as well as a joyful moment. SOMAFCO surrounded its inhabitants with a world that circumstances made it nearly impossible to leave, and, with its strong emphasis on a unifying ideology and its *umphando* mentality, generated tendencies towards conformity and dependence. Thus, when Winnie Mandela visited SOMAFCO in October 1991 to explain that there was to be a temporary halt in repatriation because of violence at home, students were upset. In fact, at Dakawa, stones were thrown at her and she had to be protected by Tanzanian police. South Africa, the students claimed, was their home and it was where they were prepared to die. At the same time, it is clear that this fervent wish to go home was compatible with extreme anxiety about returning to a country which many had left as youngsters years previously, and with which many had effectively lost contact outside the realms of political rhetoric. Wilfred Mgina, a local leader in Dark City, gives a sympathetic Tanzanian's reactions:

> *Kiva hiyo baada ya wote kukusayinke akawaambisa nimekuja kuwapatia visa kwa hiyo kila mmoja ahakikishe kuwa amerudi Africa ya Kusini knanzia mwezi huu. Kwa hiyo wengine walikuwa wanalia kwa uchungu, wengine wanafurahi, wengine wanaona kwenda kwao ndio matatizo, lakini hali ilikuwa ndio hiyo.*
>
> [The evening after everyone had gathered the man told them that he had come to give them visas and that they were supposed to start leaving for South Africa that month, some started crying, others were happy, others did not like the idea of going home. But that's how the situation was.]

Even the most sophisticated and well-educated exiles were caught in this turmoil. Alpheus Mangezi, a crucial figure in organising the return of the exiles, recounts his personal reactions. Away from the hubbub, he lay in his room and thought about himself. He had left South Africa in 1960 and it was now 1990. He had lived and worked in Britain, Nigeria, Mozambique and Denmark. He had a Danish wife. He was from a rural area of the then northern Transvaal that had been battered by forced removals. His parents were dead and his family had scattered. He could live and work at any time in Denmark. 'If I were to land in Johannesburg,' he asked himself, 'where would I go?' How would he and his family survive in a country that had in many ways become strange to him, and where he knew nobody?

Problems of this sort were even starker for those less educated and qualified. Mangezi was struck, for instance, by the uncertainty and distress of one young man who came to his office. He stood in front of the director struggling to articulate his anguish, which seemed to run counter to what he may have taken to be the conventional attitude of joy at his forthcoming return. Breaking down in tears, he eventually blurted out that people from his home area had told him that his family, with whom he had had no contact for 15 years, were no longer living there. There had been no response to his letters, and he was increasingly convinced that his informants had been unwilling to reveal the disintegration or even death of his family. Such stress even pushed some individuals to breaking point, as with the man who held people hostage at knifepoint, demanding an aircraft to fly him back to South Africa immediately. He was eventually disarmed and referred for psychiatric treatment.

Others had not managed to acquire any sort of certificate or qualification while in exile, and thus there was a frantic demand from many of those remaining for whatever short courses could be mounted to enable them to acquire saleable skills and certificates of proficiency. There was, for instance, a sudden clamour for a short course in journalism that had previously had relatively few takers.

The paradox was that such heavy demands were made of the school just when the exodus to South Africa was disrupting its work. At this time, the school in general was not functioning well, and classes were no longer running smoothly. The senior students were preoccupied with going home. The Children's Centre was also beginning to empty as parents removed their infants for repatriation. Some key staff were leaving, disrupting the administration of the campus. There was widespread vandalism, and there were cases of rape and assault. At times even basic needs such as adequate food were not satisfied.

The future of children whose fathers were South African and mothers Tanzanian (there were few if any cases where the gender roles were reversed) proved particularly difficult to handle. Some couples had no problem in going to South Africa with their children. Some Tanzanian women feared going to a country in turmoil, preferring to stay behind with their children while their husbands returned to South Africa. In other instances parents split their families between the two partners. Some men felt they could not return with their Tanzanian families because they had left other wives and children back in South Africa. At worst, the contempt that some South Africans felt for Tanzanians was evident even in such intimate relationships. 'You expect me,' one comrade rhetorically asked Mangezi about his Tanzanian partner, 'to take this *taka-taka* [piece of tattered cloth] back to South Africa?' Today there are Tanzanian women in the Morogoro area, especially those who once lived with South African men in relationships that had not been formalised, who continue to care for children fathered by now departed South African men. This is one of the human tragedies of warfare and exile. On the other hand, there were those amongst the would-be returnees who were not exiles, who had not even one South African parent, and who wanted to use the opportunity to escape poverty and migrate to relatively prosperous South Africa.

There are extraordinary stories of enterprise and resilience. For instance, one of Margaret Joseph's three children (her South African husband Oscar Mali died during their time together at Mazimbu) set out on her own initiative in search of her father's relatives, knowing little more about them than that they lived in Cape Town. She successfully completed the journey, and found her relatives.

Stealing also escalated in these last days of SOMAFCO, as is clear from the account of Alex Francis, the Tanzanian official in charge of liaison with the South Africans. The motivation for this seems to have been similar to that for the rush for certificates: the cadres were about to return home and wanted to accumulate some resources for themselves. They took with them whatever they could, and sold locally what could not be carried away. SOMAFCO came to an end in a final frenzy of 'frying'.

20. Part of the graveyard at SOMAFCO with the memorial in the background on the left

The mood was high, perhaps almost hysterically so, amongst the students and others as they returned to their country of birth. However, a tragic accident took place on the road to Dar es Salaam on 6 February 1992 when a minibus taking students to the airport was involved in a head on collision with a truck. Of the 17 students in the vehicle, 14 were killed, casting a shadow over the whole process. Nevertheless, repatriation went ahead, with students leaving about a hundred at a time. There were individual tragedies, such as the collapse at the airport during repatriation in 1992, and subsequent death of Slim Zindela, the Vice-Principal of the secondary school and stalwart of the teaching force. Finally, on 12 September 1992, SOMAFCO was officially closed when Oliver Tambo handed over the complex to the Tanzanian authorities. They inherited infrastructure worth, in monetary terms, somewhere between US$300 and 600 million.

The Tanzanian authorities have put the Mazimbu and Dakawa complexes to various uses. At Mazimbu, the secondary school, with its classrooms and residences, has become a campus for the Sokoine University of Agriculture. The primary school, Children's Centre and hospital continue under Tanzanian auspices. The farm languishes, a decaying hulk in a sea of Tanzanian peasant agriculture. The ex-solidarity worker from Finland, Leo Sonderquist, and Shadrack Sithole, the Zapu member who spent much of his life working with the ANC, finally failed in their struggle to extract the Vuyisile Mini Furniture Factory from government bureaucracy and revive it as a private concern. The graveyard is well maintained with the help of a subvention from the South African High Commission in Dar es Salaam. Lacking the resources that were available to the ANC, the complex as a whole is undoubtedly shabbier than it used to be. However, most of the facilities are utilised, and Solomon Mahlangu's final words still remain in large letters on the wall at the entrance to the complex, retained and when necessary retouched by the Tanzanian authorities.

Dakawa is in a different situation. Unlike Mazimbu, which is close to the regional capital Morogoro, Dakawa is isolated from any important centre of population and communications. Some of the complex is being used successfully for educational purposes, but the farm has collapsed, and the leatherwork and clothing factories, while they continue, are not flourishing. Buildings, such as a social centre that was being erected when the ANC was still in occupation, remain uncompleted and are unused. There is an air of dilapidation about the complex. The very isolation that in its way served the ANC well has now left Dakawa largely functionless. It is reminiscent of one of the many mission stations scattered over Africa that were once flourishing religious, educational and health centres, but are now stagnating backwaters.

The students, teachers and administrators of SOMAFCO, and the many South Africans and others who were part of life at Mazimbu and Dakawa, are scattered all over South Africa and other parts of the world. There has been no systematic study tracing the subsequent careers of SOMAFCO students; this would be a difficult, but interesting and important study. It would indicate, amongst other things, the extent to which the school prepared its students for fulfilling and successful lives in a South Africa perhaps very different from that envisaged by the school's founders. This is just one of the studies of SOMAFCO and its impact that remain to be carried out. Another is that of adult education at Mazimbu and Dakawa, not covered in this book.

The archives and other artefacts that are now deposited at the library of the University of Fort Hare are an outstanding legacy of the school. Archival sources are seldom as readily or rapidly available to historians and others as those of SOMAFCO. Anyone present will remember the scene in Freedom Square, Fort Hare, on 21 September 1992. A lorry from the port of Durban deposited a large container in the square. A knot of university dignitaries and others gathered around while a workman broke the seal with a crowbar. The doors swung open, there was a scatter of applause, and there was a pile of apparently unorganised papers and objects, with a typewriter balanced on top. The container seemed to exhale the breath of another time and place. These were the records of SOMAFCO, raw from Mazimbu.

It is worth reflecting on this event. In 1992 the ANC had emerged from decades of bitter political and military struggle with a ruthless enemy, the outcome of which was yet to be determined. In the course of this conflict, the camps of the ANC, particularly those in Angola, had become the scene of intra-ANC dissension that resulted, at its most violent, in mutiny and executions. The ANC was, nonetheless, willing to send the SOMAFCO archives direct from Tanzania to Fort Hare, to have them catalogued, and to open them to scholarly investigation with no period of embargo. This suggests a robust determination to examine the recent past, and to confront even possibly controversial aspects of the movement's history. These papers form the backbone of this book.

CHAPTER 14

SOMAFCO in retrospect

SOMAFCO was a remarkable achievement in spite of the tensions and ambiguities that went with its status as both a school and a symbol of the liberation struggle. After many debates and disagreements, and with generous contributions from official and non-governmental international agencies, in the late 1970s the work at SOMAFCO rapidly took on a life of its own. The institution became a flagship, and the ANC began to hold important events and meetings at SOMAFCO, not all directly connected with education. The leaders of the movement, particularly Oliver Tambo, a consistent supporter of the school, visited the campus regularly. A scholarship programme was set up for students who wanted to pursue tertiary studies overseas. Many who took up this opportunity would later come back to make their contribution to the school. There were also those for whom the discipline or some other aspect of the school was unendurable. In some cases, these students were expelled. For the great majority who remained, SOMAFCO gave opportunities and experiences completely different from those provided by township life and education in South Africa in the 1980s.

The diversity of students meant that teachers had to assume many different roles. They were counsellors, guidance instructors and surrogate parents. They took the lead in sports and manual activities, organised political debates and acted as role models. This was not easy, and some complained to the Education Department that they were 'overworked to the point of collapse'. This was not so much because they had exceptional teaching loads, but because of unremitting and exhausting involvement with the institution. Students came to teachers' houses with their problems, and often stayed for lengthy periods. Even after hours there was dormitory duty to be done. The institution pervaded every aspect of teachers' lives, and the circumstances of exile, where students could not return home, meant that there were not even the holiday breaks that are normal in a conventional boarding school. Similar pressures faced administrators and other workers at the necessarily enclosed and intense worlds of Mazimbu and Dakawa.

The school, initially conceived as necessary at secondary level only, expanded into a large campus offering many types of education. With the completion of the new Children's Centre in Mazimbu in 1984, the ANC had a first-rate children's centre equipped to the highest standards, staffed by a core of dedicated and well trained teachers. Although faced with problems like staff shortages, and working in the aftermath of the horrific experiences that some of the pupils had experienced, there is no doubt that the Centre was a remarkable institution that brought laughter and hope to the teachers and to the children.

Similarly, the fact that there were South African children of primary school age in and around Mazimbu could not be ignored. Terry Bell began his bold experiment in 'democratic schooling' in establishing the primary school. There was official opposition to this approach in terms of school organisation and teaching environment, though content was not so fundamentally contested. However, Terry and Barbara Bell were completely identified with a democratic, almost libertarian approach to education, and they found the atmosphere at Mazimbu too antipathetic to their approach to remain. Subsequently, under the leadership of Dennis September, the primary school, while retaining aspects of its progressive curriculum, implemented a more conventional organisational and pedagogic model. The school grew considerably in size, and experienced overcrowding and staff shortages, in spite of the presence of teachers from countries like the GDR and Sweden. Perhaps the greatest deprivation suffered by many primary-age children, however, was not in the classroom and playground, but rather in the lack of a family environment and parental care.

SOMAFCO as experienced by its students seems in many ways very different to, and far in advance of, the schools of the time in South Africa, especially those of the under-resourced and pedagogically conservative 'black' education systems – whether that of the Department of Education and Training in black areas of 'white' South Africa, or the various departments of education in the homelands. However, in other ways, such as in the abiding problem of teenage pregnancy and the generally formal teaching methods, it mirrored South African conditions. Though courses such as history of the struggle and development of societies were outside the experience of even the most liberal independent schools in South Africa in the 1980s, it is possible to interpret SOMAFCO as a good conventional boarding high school.

Students' social lives revolved around the dormitories and the dining-halls. They took part in sport and other recreational activities. They organised dances and plays. Sometimes the older students got into trouble, drinking, smoking dagga and stealing. They slipped out of the campus and entertained themselves in Morogoro or in neighbouring villages such as Dark City.

The difference from conventional boarding schools, however, was that SOMAFCO was obliged to act not only as a school but also as a complete environment. The students were in exile, and had no homes to go to. For instance, in most schools young women who become pregnant will be expected or instructed to leave the institution. However, at SOMAFCO young single mothers and the fathers of their children continued to be the responsibility of the school, which took decisions in areas that would normally have been left to parents, families, and the young people themselves. The decisions in this and other fields may not always have been the right ones. However, the situation that made it necessary for the school to act like this was forced upon it by the abnormal circumstances in which it operated.

The people of Mazimbu were from diverse backgrounds. The ANC had the opportunity not only to start a school, but to create a kind of social laboratory where different views could be given a hearing, and where it was able to put its policies into practice. Students were introduced to ideas and ways of learning that they could not possibly have experienced in the society that they had left, and were exposed to the varied lifestyles and cultures of their cosmopolitan teachers. With many differences of emphasis on the political left, the level of discussion was vigorous; the strongly-held opinions gathered from interviewees during research for this book attest to this. In many ways the actual development of SOMAFCO went well beyond the model of a dedicated and narrowly focussed revolutionary institution advocated by some of its early proponents. In the midst of a struggle that called for unity in the face of a ruthless enemy, it managed to remain intellectually diverse.

Questions of social organisation and authority often had a sharp practical edge when they arose in the process of building a real community such as SOMAFCO. Gender issues, played out in the WS, are an example. Women played an important role at most levels in the ANC, and this was true at Mazimbu also; yet there was a tendency for the WS to be given, or to take to itself, the predominant role of guardian of the rights of children, concentrating on those at primary school level and below. There was and is no easy answer to this dilemma. The care of young children is crucial, yet easily becomes an area within which women are limited, rather than a general human responsibility shared by both sexes. The role of the WS as a pressure group tended to lead the ANC women into clashes with the administrating directorate when it came to the boundaries of their responsibilities. Perhaps, however, quarrelling over such boundaries was in the long run less significant in terms of real power and authority than would have been a more robust involvement by the women's movement in matters of overall policy and practice.

An irony of SOMAFCO is that while most of the surrounding Tanzanians existed in extreme poverty, and while their schools lacked resources of all kinds, the exiled South Africans lived in comparative comfort and benefited from the assistance of international donors. Certainly, SOMAFCO's material situation was far better than that of Tanzanian schools. However, it also inherited many of the deep-seated problems of the South African educational system, arguably a more intractable challenge than the presence or absence of physical resources.

The schools and training facilities at Mazimbu and its younger educational and developmental partner, Dakawa, were intended to educate young South Africans and provide skills that would support the exiles and prepare them for life in a liberated South Africa. But the indirect and unanticipated consequences were often as important as actual intentions. The mingling of communities produced unforeseen and creative adaptations that went far beyond formal agendas. The people of the Morogoro area and those of the ANC settlements had each inherited the combination of attitudes, skills, languages and a myriad other attributes that make up any community. Mixed, they created new ways of living that were exciting, unpredictable, sometimes uncomfortable, occasionally downright criminal, never statically traditional, but always unselfconsciously exploring what it might mean to live across boundaries and certainties.

SOMAFCO's legacy

Suggestions that SOMAFCO might be transferred as a functioning school to South Africa after 1990 were not pursued, though Yeoville Community School, in Johannesburg, was set up to serve the needs of young returned exiles. Art development at the Dakawa Development Centre, supported by Sida, was transferred to Grahamstown, in the Eastern Cape, but this project led a precarious life, closing down once, and then reopening.

What then was the legacy of SOMAFCO? Did the experience of the school in Tanzania influence the liberation movement when facing the reality of power in a free South Africa, and specifically when attempting to reform the educational system? In 1996, in a rare public reference by a political leader, Minister of Public Works, Jeff Radebe said of SOMAFCO during a speech in Tanzania, that 'many of its students and teachers today play significant roles in many sectors of our society'. This is true. He could be challenged when he added that 'the basic elements of our programme at SOMAFCO are now law'. It is in fact difficult to identify particular ways in which the school has contributed to the formation of educational policy, and key educational policy documents do not refer to it. The wider literature on contemporary South African education is also largely silent on SOMAFCO. However, a number of ex-teachers and others from SOMAFCO are in important positions in educational administration. Through them the spirit of the institution may have percolated into the contemporary system.

SOMAFCO implicitly and explicitly challenged an educational system battered by decades of racial and class division, and by policies – Bantu Education above all – intended to foster these divisions. This is a historical, and not a policy study, and we will leave it to the reader to draw from the story whatever policy implications he or she may perceive. However, in current moves to align South African education with trends in other parts of the world, especially the Western world, it would be regrettable if the experience of South Africans and their supporters from many countries in the extraordinary educational experiment in Tanzania was to be overlooked. Those who were young in townships in the 1980s now speak of their awareness at the time of a liberation school in Tanzania, romanticised and inexact though their vision of it may have been. The often-difficult reality was invisible from Soweto or Mdantsane, but SOMAFCO had a symbolic importance that spoke of different possibilities and of the ability to challenge a loathed system in ways that affirmed education rather than totally rejecting it.

We hope that this book has indicated some of the many questions raised by the experience of SOMAFCO. They were raised with particular intensity in the atmosphere of a school in exile, menaced by attack and subversion, and dedicated to the ANC's programme of liberation. What curriculum was appropriate for a school dedicated to political liberation? What should policy be towards language in education in a multi-lingual community? How should adult students be treated in a school where a classificatory childhood was assumed? How should sexual relations and parenthood amongst students be handled? What should be the relationship between practical work and academic study? How should discipline and authority be handled in a school dedicated to liberation? These are only a few of the questions raised by the SOMAFCO experience.

Though educational reform is often seen as a panacea through which it is possible apparently to influence the shape and development of society, it is in fact a difficult and slow process, painful to implement and unpredictable in its effects, nationally and at the level of individual institutions. Therefore, it may not be constructive to approach SOMAFCO as an educational menu from which this or that piece of wisdom can be extracted to be put to use in solving current educational problems. The context and scale were different to those of today's South Africa. It is more helpful to see the school within its context, and to discuss it in terms of what was possible in its time and place, remembering that for people then there could be no clear realisation of what was to come, and that their future, our present, was as obscure to them as our future is to ourselves. This approach may help us to understand the school more fully, and, where it was contradictory or illogical as aspects of it may now seem, to sympathise with this through our attempt at historical comprehension. Reflection on SOMAFCO may then yield insights into how South Africans confronted the extraordinary difficulties of education for liberation in the context of exile, and generate realism and humility in face of our own challenges. A voice from within SOMAFCO, that of Patrick Mtshaulana, sums up the challenges, achievements and limitations of this unique school:

> The curriculum at SOMAFCO was an attempt to transform education in South Africa. But it is possible that … [it] … did not succeed, not because the curriculum itself was wrong, but because what we were trying to do was … impossible … to try to transform an education for a people who were not there … [W]e did not really know what was going on in South Africa, in the educational field. We … were not sufficiently in contact with the progressives in the country who were trying to change Bantu Education … taking into account the practical and complete realities of South Africa, its people, and their background … all our ideas to transform were based on what we knew when we left, and yet things were changing in South Africa. … The task was difficult, because you can't change … a culture of the people without the people, in a vacuum. And yet, I don't think that the attempts we made were that futile, because we did produce students who today are … making some contribution. But the attempt to make a new education system, I don't know if there we succeeded. But I hope that those of us who were involved, and those of us who are involved in education today, learned a lot of lessons.

Notes

This book is a popular history that we hope will be widely read by those interested in South African education, politics and history, and by concerned and involved citizens in South Africa and elsewhere. Therefore we have kept endnotes to a minimum. However, we acknowledge our obligations to our discipline of history, and we hope that these 'silent' endnotes, the description of sources, and the more detailed footnotes in our academic articles and theses, will be sufficient guidance to our sources and methodology.

In these notes, archival sources have been given in as brief a form as possible. When we were working on the SOMAFCO papers in the ANC archives at the University of Fort Hare, the papers were only partly sorted, and indeed there have been changes in classification subsequently. This process is not yet complete. References are to the papers as classified when we referred to them.

The first figure before each note refers to the page, and the second to the line on that page. Each note refers to the section of text that ends at the line mentioned. Oral sources have been noted where the interviewee is not indicated by name in the text; where they are so indicated, readers should refer for details to the list of oral informants. Secondary sources have been given in short author and title form: further details are in the sources.

Chapter 1. Education and the struggle for freedom

This chapter is based on a range of historical work on South Africa, particularly on South African education. Especially valuable are Kallaway (ed) *Apartheid and Education*; Kallaway (ed) *The History of Education under Apartheid*; Hyslop, *The Classroom Struggle*, and Nkomo (ed) *Pedagogy of Domination.*

7, 1 Hyslop, *The Classroom Struggle*, pp.10–20.

9, 10 Meli, *A History of the ANC*, p.186.

9, 15 Ndlovu, *The Soweto Uprisings*, p.45.

Chapter 2. Origins and early years of SOMAFCO

13, 2 *Sechaba*, June 1979, p.11. See also http://www.anc.org.za/ancdocs/history/people/mahlangu_s.html

13, 24 *Sechaba*, June 1979, p.1.

14, 22 Meeting with SOMAFCO Advisory Group, 26 April 2001.

14, 38 Nare, 'Education and War', in Bhebe & Ranger (eds.), *Society in Zimbabwe's Liberation War*; Nordkvelle, 'Teachers, Culture and Politics'; Isaacman, *Mozambique*; Eva Helene Østbye, 'The Namibian Liberation Struggle' in Eriksen (ed), *Norway and National Liberation.*

15, 10 SOM/7/Official opening, 21 to 23 Aug. 1985.

15, 41 SOM/14/ 'Education for Liberation: Overcoming Apartheid at Solomon Mahlangu Freedom College', *Student Journal*, 1983, p.1.

16, 16 Int. Wilfred Mgina.

17, 31 SOM/15/ Strategy for the Implementation of the Proposals of the ANC (SA) School, 23 Dec. 1977.

17, 38 SOM/75, Role of SOMAFCO: Discussion Paper, May 1979.

18, 11 SOM/Neduc I, 3 Oct. 1978; SOM/20, An Assessment of the Organisation, Work and Political Direction of the ANC Education Department: London Education Committee, Oct. 1979.

18, 17 Int. Terry and Barbara Bell.

18, 26 SOM/Neduc I, 3 Oct. 1978.

18, 42 SOM/20, London Education Committee, Neduc II Supplement, Sept. 1979.

19, 18 Int. Makho Njobe.

19, 26 SOM/234/Correspondence, 1978–1980.

19, 37 SOM/160/Progress Report, School Building Project, May 1981.

20, 11 SOM/18/Supplies, August 1981.

21, 8 SOM/7/Progress Report, 1983.

22, 14 SOM/PMD (Project Management Department)/5/30/UNDP Project Documents, Assistance to Self-help Community Development Projects, n.d.

22, 27 SOM/PMD/5/30/UNDP, Project Documents, June 1980.

22, 38 SOM/PMD/1/4/Manager's Office, Terms of Reference of Projects Department, n.d.

23, 24 SOM/TFD (Tanzanian Farm Department)/1/7, Agricultural Department, Production Training, n.d.

24, 19 SOM/PMD/5/27/UNHCR, General: Project Submission, n.d.; SOM/PMD/8/51/Sida, Correspondence Re Mazimbu Dairy Project, n.d.

25, 2 SOM/HD (Health Department)/2/7/Directorate – Health Matters, Report of the East African Team, Kurasini, 10 May 1981.

25, 19 SOM/HD/7/24, Minutes of the Special Health Council Meeting held in Lusaka, 25 to 25 Jan. 1982.

25, 31 SOM/HD/2/4/Circulars, Consultative Committee Meeting between the Working Committee and Health Department 30 Nov. to 2 Dec. 1982.

25, 40 SOM/HD/2/7/Directorate – Health Matters, 1982, Letter to Secretary of Health, 23 Feb. 1982; ibid., Memorandum by Terry Bell, 16 March 1982.

26, 19 SOM/HD/2/7/Directorate – Health Matters, 1982, Regina Nzo to Secretary of Health, 28 April 1982; SOM/HD/2/7/Minutes, Regional Health Team, Mazimbu, 12 Sept. 1982; SOM/5/15/Minutes, Commission into Health Team, 16 March 1982.

26, 28 SOM/HD/6, Medical Notes, n.d.

26, 37 SOM/HD/7/25/Miscellaneous, 1 May 1984.

27, 5 SOM/HD/7/Papers, Health Care in Exile Community – Report on Health Planning in the ANC; Chapter 3 – Health supply in the Tanzanian Region, JM Hippe & AW Persen, the Norwegian Trade Union Research Centre, n.d.

27, 10 SOM/WD (Works Department)/5, Production Units, Various Sections, 1983–1986.

27, 23 SOM/PMD/6/33, letter Oswald Dennis to UNDP Co-ordinator, 27 Jan. 1982.

28, 3 Int. Leo Sonderquist.

Chapter 3. Teachers, administrators and students

Most of this chapter is based on interviews with the people mentioned.

29, 33 SOM/5/Central Administration, Neduc III Minutes, p.10, 1980.

31, 2 Ibid.

32, 16 Jürgens, *The Many Houses of Exile.*

38, 3 Mayibuye/ANC/4, Department of Education, Reports, 1978–1981, 26 March 1980.

Chapter 4. The Charlotte Maxeke Children's Centre

41, 15 SOM/DCCD (Daycare Centre Division)/1, Residential Children's Centre; int. Bessie Netsianda.

41, 20 SOM/DCCD/1, Why an ANC crèche?

42, 2 SOM/DCCD/1, document on Residential Children's Centre, July, 1979.

42, 7 Ibid.

42, 15 Ints. Jane Dumasi, Farida Mussagy.

42, 32 Int. Dudu Makhoba.

42, 36 Int. Jane Dumasi.

42, 39 Ints. Bessie Netsianda, Dudu Makhoba.

43, 10 SOM/DCCD/1, untitled document.

43, 14 Int. Farida Mussagy.

43, 33 Int. Jane Dumasi.
44, 2 Int. Farida Mussagy.
44, 8 Int. Bessie Netsianda.
44, 11 DAK/29/225, ANC Development: Education Sectors – Reports, Report of the ANC (SA) Development Centre Educational Sectors for the 3rd Education Council Meeting of the ANC (SA) held on 28 Aug. to 2 Sept. 1986, 18 Aug. 1986.
45, 22 Ints. Farida Mussagy, Bessie Netsianda.
45, 32 Int. Jane Dumasi.
46, 2 Int. Bessie Netsianda.
46, 7 SOM/DCCD/1, Childrens' films.
46, 12 SOM/NSD (Nursery School Division)/1, Marius Schoon to Farida Mussagy, 21 April 1987.
46, 28 Int. Bessie Netsianda.
46, 36 SOM/DCCD/2, Pre-school Children Mazimbu, Dakawa.
47, 1 SOM/NSD/2, J Mfene's marks on first year term, Dec. 1983.
47, 6 SOM/NSD/2, Nursery School Report, Nov. 1985.
47, 13 Ibid.
47, 33 SOM/DCCD/ 2, Letter M Schoon to GDR ambassador, Dar es Salaam, 24 April 1987.
47, 37 Int. Farida Mussagy.
48, 3 SOM/DCCD/2, Letter pre-primary school to school director, 29 March 1983.
48, 8 Int. Nkosana Sithole.
48, 11 SOM/DCCD/1, Letter Acting Principal G Mabena to Catering Officer Doris Mabena, 23 Sept. 1987.
48, 12 SOM/DCCD, 2, Letter Kenneth to Manamela, 30 Aug. 1989.
48, 17 Int. Farida Mussagy.
48, 22 SOM/DCCD/1, Needs of the Daycare Centre, 1986.
48, 24 Int. Farida Mussagy.
48, 29 ANC/DCCD/1, Letter J Dumasi to Freda and Monica, 16 Aug. 1986.
49, 16 Int. Jane Dumasi.
50, 8 SOM/NSD/2, Letter Farida Mussagy to Director, Mazimbu Complex, 10 April 1985.

Chapter 5. The primary school

51, 6 SOM/PSD (Primary School Division)/1, English Methodology in the Primary School, 1981.
51, 21 Int. Terry and Barbara Bell; Terry Bell Papers, Methodology in the Primary School, Dec. 1981.

51, 32 Int. Terry and Barbara Bell; SOM/PSD/4, English Methodology in the Primary School, n.d.
52, 9 Terry Bell Papers, Methodology in the Primary School, Dec. 1981.
53, 26 Terry Bell Papers, SOMAFCO Primary School Division, End of Year Report: prepared by Terry and Barbara Bell, Aug. 1981.
54, 19 Int. Terry and Barbara Bell.
55, 7 Terry Bell Papers, Methodology in the Primary School, Dec. 1981.
55, 12 Terry Bell Papers, Report of the Primary School, Dec. 1981.
56, 8 Terry Bell Papers, Methodology in the Primary School, Dec. 1981.
56, 13 Int. Terry and Barbara Bell.
56, 17 Terry Bell Papers, Primary School Report prepared by the Bells, Aug. 1981.
56, 29 Int. Terry and Barbara Bell.
56, 36 Terry Bell Papers, Letter Terry Bell to Oliver Tambo, 1 May 1982.
57, 8 Int. Terry and Barbara Bell.
57, 19 Mayibuye/ANC/2/6, Primary School Report, 1984.
57, 29 Meeting with SOMAFCO Advisory Group, 26 April 2001.
57, 40 SOM/PSD/6, Grade 7: Political Education Test.
58, 10 SOM/PSD/1, Children's Magazine: Children of the Township Speak Out.
58, 19 Mayibuye/ANC/2/6, Primary School Report, 1984.
59, 2 Mayibuye/Wolfie Kodesh Papers/MCH/86/2; Meeting with SOMAFCO Advisory Group, 26 April 2001.
59, 38 Mayibuye/ANC/2/2, Primary School Report, 1984, p.1.
59, 41 Int. Thami Mali.
60, 31 Mayibuye/ANC/2/2, Primary School Report, pp.11–12, 1984.
61, 2 SOM/PSD/9, Letter Babu September to Vusi, 9 April 1987.
61, 5 Bernstein, *The Rift*, p.105.
61, 10 Int. Nkosana Sithole.
61, 12 SOM/PSD/3, Letter Babu September to Mohammed Tikly, 24 Oct. 1983.
61, 14 Ints. Marius Schoon, Sherry Maclean.
61, 16 Int. Sherry Maclean.

Chapter 6. The secondary school

63, 12 Meeting with SOMAFCO Advisory Group, 26 April 2001.
63, 24 SOM/SSD (Secondary School Division)/55: Existing School Code of Conduct.
63, 34 SOM/SSD/55, Smoking and Regulations 14 April 1986; SOM/SSD/167: Letter J Jacobse to School Principal, 6 May 1984.
64, 1 SOM/SSD/180, Pre Form 1 Meeting, Minutes, 19 Jan. 1989.
64, 20 SOM/SSD/113, Lesson Plan, 2 July 1990.

64, 25 SOM/SSD/167: Letter J Jacobse to School Principal, 6 May 1984.
64, 30 Meeting with SOMAFCO Advisory Group, 26 April 2001.
64, 37 SOM/SSD/55, ANC Staff Handbook, n.d.
65, 1 SOM/SSD/113, Lesson Observation Form, 9 May 1990.
65, 4 SOM/SSD/13, Letter Ernest Khaile to the Vice Principal, 10 March 1983.
65, 9 SOM/SSD/180, Minutes of Pre Form 1 Meeting, 6 Oct. 1986.
65, 12 SOM/SSD/13, The case of two students who smoked dagga, 1982.
65, 23 SOM/SSD/180, Minutes of Form 5 Class meeting, 22 Sept. 1986.
65, 25 SOM/SSD/180, Memorandum by M. Tikly, 1986.
65, 31 SOM/SSD/180, Form 3y Minutes, 10 Nov. 1986.
66, 4 SOM/SSD/55, End of the year awards, 31 July 1982.
66, 7 SOM/SSD/55, Letter from a teacher to the Emulation Committee recommending Mosipa, n.d.
66, 10 SOM/SSD/55, Letter of recommendation from a teacher, n.d.
66, 17 Meeting with SOMAFCO Advisory Group, 26 April 2001.
66, 22 SOM/SSD/180, Minutes of English Department, n.d.
66, 25 SOM/SSD/167, Letter Principal to the Heads of Department, 30 March 1984.
66, 40 SOM/SSD/13, Letter from OT Mahlasela to TK Maseko, 12 Sept. 1984.
67, 2 SOM/SSD/180, Minutes of class meeting, Form 5, 22 Sept. 1986.
67, 16 Int. Sindiso Mfenyana.
68, 3 SOM/Uncatalogued document, Neduc VI meeting held at Mazimbu, 28 Aug. to 3 Sept. 1986.
68, 10 Meeting with SOMAFCO Advisory Group, 26 April 2001.
68, 22 SOM/SSD/13, Letter from a student to the School Principal, 19 July 1983.
68, 38 Int. Vuyani Mlati.
69, 20 SOM/SSD/31, African National Congress Administrator's Report to Neduc VII, 12 to 19 Dec. 1988.
69, 34 Int. Diana Cumberledge.
70, 25 Int. Barney Mogane.
71, 7 Ints. Diana Cumberledge, André Proctor, Richard Jürgens; Mayibuye/ANC/2/2, Primary School Report, 1984, p.12.
73, 21 Int. Mzwandile Kibi.
73, 29 Meeting with SOMAFCO Advisory Group, 26 April 2001.
76, 8 Books from SOMAFCO library now in ANC archives.
77, 24 Mayibuye/ANC/54/Department of Education (1986–1989)/1, June–Dec. 1986, 'Some thoughts about SOMAFCO–Dakawa', Jack Simons.
77, 30 Terry Bell Papers, Letter of termination of services, 23 March 1982.

Chapter 7. Curriculum and pedagogy at SOMAFCO

81, 21 SOM/Education Department/1/Minutes, Neduc I, p.10, October 1978.

81, 31 SOM/5/Education Department/Minutes, Neduc III, Minutes, Aug. 1980.

81, 38 Int. Raphael Mwinuka.

82, 13 SOM/11/Neduc IV, Mazimbu, 18 to 21 Aug. 1981.

82, 34 SOM/1/CA (Central Administration)/Neduc I, Minutes, p.9.

83, 3 SOM/3/Progress Reports, 1983.

83, 30 SOM/6A/Curriculum Development Report, August 1983.

84, 10 Int. Farida Mussagy.

84, 14 Ints. Sasa Zikalala, Vuyani Mlati, Tladi Ditshego.

85, 6 SOM/CA/Neduc III, Minutes, 14 to 18 Aug. 1980, pp.14–15.

85, 22 SOM/CA/5, Neduc III, Minutes, pp.14–18, August 1980; int. Sindiso Mfenyana.

86, 20 Int. Wintshi Njobe; Ellis & Sechaba, *Comrades Against Apartheid.* p.135.

86, 31 Int. John Pampallis.

87, 38 SOM/SSD/ Foundation for Education with Production – uncatalogued documents.

88, 11 SOM/ SSD/ Foundation for Education with Production – uncatalogued documents; int. John Pampallis; G Hyden, *Beyond Ujamaa in Tanzania*, p.224.

88, 16 Maaba, 'The Archives', pp.424, 435.

89, 11 SOM/5/Neduc II, April 1979; Mayibuye/ANC/54, Secondary School, 1979–81.

92, 19 Mayibuye/ANC/Unesco, ANC Educational Institution in Tanzania, 1990.

93, 16 SOM/SSD/55, Student Code of Conduct; int. Vuyani Mlati; int. Wintshi Njobe.

93, 33 Int. Vuyani Mlati.

94, 15 SOM/SSD/1, ZYC meeting, 1988; int. Nana Masusu.

94, 18 Int. Lungi Mankazana.

94, 34 SOM/SSD/1, Speech by S Mabizela during the ANC Youth Seminar at SOMAFCO, 17 Nov. 1984; SOM/SSD, 159, Speech by OR Tambo at the opening of the Second National Youth Conference, SOMAFCO, 14 Aug. 1987.

94, 39 SOM/SSD/159, *Student Journal*, Jan. to March 1986, pp.15–16.

95, 14 SOM/SSD/1, The World Festival of Youth and Students, 8 July 1989.

95, 16 SOM/SSD/1, Letter Pioneer Secretary to School Principal, 4 May 1989.

95, 24 SOM/SSD/1, Speech by the SOMAFCO representative during the celebration of Tanzania's Day of Independence, June 1982.
95, 36 SOM/SSD/1, Zonal Youth Committee meeting, n.d.
95, 38 SOM/SSD/1, ZYC meeting, 1988.
96, 3 SOM/SOM/SSD/1, Report of the ZYC Commission on the ANC External Youth; int. Wintshi Njobe.
96, 13 SOM/SSD/159, various issues of *Student Journal.*
98, 13 Soul et al., (eds.), *If You Want to Know Me*, pp.7, 21, 61.

Chapter 8. The social life of students

101, 11 SOM/SSD/1, Code of Conduct and Regulations for the Matrons and Sub-matrons of the Boarding of the Lilian Ngoyi Daycare Centre, n.d.
101, 13 Int. Bessie Netsianda.
101, 17 Int. Nkosana Sithole.
101, 21 Int. Marius Schoon.
102, 1 Int. Nkosana Sithole.
102, 2 SOM/PSD/3, Letter from Babu September to M Tikly, 24 Oct. 1983.
102, 9 Int. Nkosana Sithole.
102, 17 Int. Mosoabuli Maamoe.
102, 23 SOM/SSD/13, The background and the final decisions on the case of two students who were quarrelling, 18 March 1985.
102, 24 Int. Mosoabuli Maamoe.
102, 33 Int. Vuyani Mlati.
102, 41 SOM/SSD/1, Letter E Manamela to P Vulindlela, 12 Sept. 1989.
103, 6 SOM/SSD/1, Letter from John and Xoliswa Bolton, 27 Jan. 1989 (name altered).
103, 12 Int. Sasa Zikalala.
103, 21 SOM/SSD/2, Letter Sibongile Dlamini to Jane Dumasi, n.d.
103, 29 Int. Lungi Mankazana.
103, 33 SOM/SSD/13, Case reported on 2 Jan. 1983 (names altered).
103, 38 SOM/SSD/13, Case reported on 22 May 1985.
104, 3 Int. Vuyani Mlati.
104, 14 SOM/SSD/13, Boarding Report, 30 Dec. 1984.
105, 2 Int. Vuyani Mlati.
105, 17 SOM/SSD/60, Report on the tour of the drama group, Dec. 1983.
106, 4 Int. Lungi Mankazana.
106, 11 Int. Sasa Zikalala.
106, 26 Int. Siphiwe Xaba.
106, 31 Meeting with SOMAFCO Advisory Group, 26 April 2001.

106, 40 Int. Nana Masusu.
107, 4 Int. Mercedes Seete.
107, 7 Ints. Daniel Rafube and Gerald Dube.
107, 10 Meeting with SOMAFCO Advisory Group, 26 April 2001.
107, 17 Int. Tladi Ditsego.
107, 26 Int. Dr Siphokazi Sokupha.
107, 35 Int. Huddleston Pompi.
107, 40 Int. George Mwali.
108, 28 Int. Vuyani Mlati.
108, 31 SOM/SSD/13, Case reported on the 22 May, 1986.
109, 2 SOM/SSD/13, Case reported on 2 Jan. 1983.
109, 24 Int. Miriam Mashego.
110, 3 SOM/SSD/13, Case Reported on 3 April, 1984.
110, 7 Int. Wintshi Njobe.
110, 11 SOM/SSD/234, Letter Mendi Msimang to J Pampallis, 23 Sept. 1980.
110, 18 SOM/SSD/13, Record of the case reported in 1981.
110, 22 Int. Wintshi Njobe.
111, 23 SOM/HD/8, ANC Seminar: Psychological Effects on Life in Exile, n.d.
111, 37 Ibid.

Chapter 9. South Africans and Tanzanians

114, 29 Int. Anna Abdallah.
115, 41 Int. Alex Francis.
116, 13 Int. Emily Dennis.
116, 17 Int. John Pampallis.
116, 34 Int. Mohammed Tikly.
116, 37 Int. Tladi Ditsego.
117, 1 Int. Manala Manzini.
118, 3 Int. Siphiwe Xaba.
118, 35 DAK/58/552, Third Dakawa Seminar, Minutes, 24 to 26 April 1989.
119, 29 SOM/TFD/1/7, H Tudor-Evans, Food Processing: Possibilities for Production/Training Unit at SOMAFCO in Central Tanzania, Oct. 1983.
120, 3 SOM/TFD/5/1, Correspondence, 23 March 1985.
120, 15 SOM/TFD/7/1, Correspondence, 27 July 1985.
120, 18 SOM/TFD/5/1, Letter HJ Hansen to T Maseko, Chief Administrator, n.d.
120, 28 Ibid.; SOM/TFD/5/1, Correspondence, 6 Sept. 1985.

121, 36 SOM/PMD/5/30, UNDP Project documents, n.d.; ANC/SOM/HD/7/Papers: Health Care in Exile Community – Report on Health Planning in the ANC, Chapter 3 – Health Supply in the Tanzanian Region, JM Hippe & AW Persen, The Norwegian Trade Union Research Centre, n.d.

122, 12 SOM/DCCD/9, undated letter to the Chief Administrator of Mazimbu from Phambo.

123, 3 SOM/SSD/159, Student Journal, March 1986.

123, 6 Int. Lajavu Khasimbazi.

123, 18 SOM/SSD/60, Report on the trip to Dar es Salaam, n.d.

124, 2 SOM/HD/9, Letter Joe Nhlanhla to S Mabizela 31 May 1982.

124, 32 Mayibuye/ANC/18/12, Letter from the Women's Section in Mazimbu to Head of the Women's Section in Lusaka, G Shope, 17 July 1984.

125, 16 DAK (Dakawa)/54/500, Lillian Ngoyi Residence meetings, n.d. [but 1985], Gladstone Zenzo, Commissar (Residential).

125, 25 SOM/HD/7, Health Care in the Exile Community – Report on Health Planning in the ANC, n.d.

127, 1 Int. Vuyani Mlati.

127, 3 Int. Lungi Mankazana.

127, 9 Int. Vuyani Mlati.

127, 14 Int. Lungi Mankazana.

127, 18 SOM/SSD/13, Report from the College Disciplinary Committee, 1981.

127, 23 SOM/SSD/13, Report on Two Students, 1985.

127, 26 Int. Mary Thuse.

129, 11 Ellis and Sechaba, *Comrades Against Apartheid*, p.140.

129, 37 Int. Lungi Mankazana.

130, 8 Int. EM Siyo.

130, 22 Int. Helen Radebe.

130, 34 Int. Lajavu Khasimbazi.

131, 4 See, for instance, Paul Chintowa, 'Human Rights – Tanzania: Abandoned Children Cry for Help', Inter Press Service, http://www.oneworld.org/ips2/feb98/tanzania_children.html

131, 17 Ints. Wilfred Mgina and Saidi Nassoro.

131, 19 Int. Lajavu Khasimbazi.

131, 37 Ints. Joe Kabetso and Emily Dennis.

Chapter 10. Women at SOMAFCO

135, 16 SOM/WS (Women's Section)/4/99/Women's Struggle – Miscellaneous, German Mission, n.d.

135, 24 SOM/WS/4/1, Secretariat Minutes, 3 Sept. 1971.

136, 20 SOM/WS/8/40, Women's Section – East Africa, Correspondence, Structures as agreed in Aug. 1984, amended 17 March 1985.

137, 2 SOM/WS/4/1, Secretariat Minutes, 3 Sept. 1971; Horn, 'Post-Apartheid South Africa', p.37.

137, 15 Mayibuye/10/5/ANC Women's Section, Secretariat, Morogoro Provisional Headquarters, n.d.

137, 29 SOM/WS/4/2, Correspondence and Statements, Zambia/Tanzania, 1978–1981.

138, 6 SOM/WS/4/1, Secretariat Minutes, ANC Morogoro Technical Committee, n.d.

138, 30 SOM/WS/1/3, Joint Meeting, Administration, WS, Sector Heads, 12 Feb. 1985.

139, 19 Mayibuye/ANC/50/3/Women's Section, 1980–1983, Report on East Africa Women's Section, SOMAFCO Hall, 20 June 1983.

140, 21 S. Hassim, 'Gender, Social Location and Feminist Politics' p.65; S Meintjes, 'The Women's Struggle', p.57.

140, 40 SOM/CA/, Neduc III, Minutes, 1980; SOM/WS/Minutes, Staff recommendations on Pregnancies and Abortions to the National Education Council, Aug. 1983.

141, 14 SOM/WS/Memorandum, 5 May 1986; SOM/Boarding Section/Memorandum, 29 April 1986; Int. Pule Motsabe.

141, 38 SOM/WS/Minutes, 1 July 1983.

142, 14 SOM/WS/Minutes, 'Staff recommendations on pregnancies and abortions to the National Education Council, n.d.

Chapter 11. Dakawa Development Centre

143, 19 Int. Spenser and Claudia Hodgson.

143, 23 DAK/16/87, Seminars, 1982 and 1984: Seminar on the Development of Dakawa, held from 28 July to 1 Aug. 1982.

143, 31 Ints. Simon Mohale, Spenser and Claudia Hodgson, Kilian Masipa.

144, 10 DAK/19/113, Norway: Workshop on Dakawa, 27 and 28 April 1989.

144, 25 DAK/49/345, Liaison Meetings Mazimbu/Dakawa, Miscellaneous: Report of Commission to look into the Activities of the Administration and the Central Membership in Dakawa, May 1982.

144, 41 DAK/16/87, Seminars, 1982 and 1984: Seminar on the Development of Dakawa, 28 July to 1 Aug. 1982.

145, 9 DAK/16/91, Seminars, 1982 and 1984: Second Seminar on Dakawa Development Centre, 17 to 19 Nov. 1984 [*recte* 1983]; DAK/12/56, 1984 Development Plan: 1984 Development Plan (Norplan), Vols. 1–3.

145, 20 Mayibuye/ANC/55/3, Department of Education (1989–1991): Revised 1984 Development Plan for Dakawa, Final Draft Report, Aug. 1990; DAK/34/265, Census: Dakawa Census, 11 April 1990; ints. Spenser and Claudia Hodgson, Emily Dennis.

145, 36 DAK/49/453, Correspondence, Dakawa–Lusaka: Report on Personnel Survey Mazimbu/Dakawa, Hintsa Tshume, Lusaka, Aug. 1984.

146, 10 Int. Mary Thuse (Ngozi); DAK/18/110, General: Papers and Documents: The History, Social Problems and Future Prospects: African National Congress of South Africa Dakawa Development Settlement. Paper by MW Njobe to ANC in-house seminar, Lusaka, 27 to 30 July 1988.

146, 21 Ints. Andrew Mohammed, Wintshi Njobe.

146, 38 DAK/9/41, Miscellaneous: ANC Development Centre – Dakawa: Monthly Report, J Morake, 4 Nov. 1985.

147, 6 DAK/13/63, VTC Background Documents: Dakawa Development Centre, Appendix 9, [1983].

147, 17 DAK/29/225, ANC Development: Education Sectors – Reports: Report of the ANC Development Centre Educational Sectors for the 3rd Education Council Meeting held 28 Aug. to 2 Sept. 1986, 18 Aug. 1986; int. Andrew Mohammed.

147, 20 DAK/18/110, Dakawa Development Centre: Guidelines for the Dakawa Development Centre, n.d.

147, 35 DAK/7/32, Reports, 1989: Jan van der Laan, Report on an Irrigation Mission to the Horticulture Project, Dakawa, Nov. 1989.

148, 2 DAK/43/290, Administration, Monthly Meetings: Zonal Annual Report, Development Centre [1989].

148, 3 DAK/16/91, Reports, Agricultural Development, 1987: Second Seminar on Dakawa Development Centre, 17 to 19 Nov. 1984 [*recte* 1983].

148, 4 DAK/18/110, General: Papers and Documents: The History, Social Problems and Future Prospects: African National Congress Dakawa Development Settlement, paper by MW Njobe to ANC in-house seminar, Lusaka, 27 to 30 July 1988.

148, 8 DAK/13/63, VTC Background Documents: Dakawa Development Centre, Appendix 9; DAK/9/41, Miscellaneous: Report on Seminar re. Agricultural Development at Dakawa; Mayibuye/ANC/55/3, Department of Education (1989–1991): Revised 1984 Development Plan for Dakawa, Vols. 1 and 2, Aug. 1990.

148, 10 DAK/29/228, Documents of Dakawa Seminar: The Dakawa Seminar, TT Nkobi.

148, 19 DAK/47/292, Minutes: Departments to Administration: Report of Daycare Centre, April 1990.

148, 22 Int. Spenser and Claudia Hodgson; DAK/53/490, DCD Own Evaluation: Report on Visit to Kilosa 11 Dec. 1984, M. Tikly.

149, 13 DAK/18/110, General: Papers and Documents: The History, Social Problems and Future Prospects: African National Congress Dakawa Development Settlement, paper by MW Njobe to ANC in-house seminar, Lusaka, 27 to 30 July 1988; DAK/53/496, Miscellaneous: Dakawa Zonal Political Committee Report to the RPC, 10 Dec. 1988.

149, 22 DAK/431/291, Minutes Dakawa-Mazimbu: Development Centre, Dakawa, Minutes: Administration Meeting held 11 April 1988.

149, 29 DAK/40/282, Vocational Training Subjects, 1979–1980.

149, 33 DAK/13/64, Management (Miscellaneous): Draft Terms of Reference, Dakawa Vocational Training Centre – Education Scheme, 13 Nov. 1986.

149, 41 DAK/23/163, Miscellaneous: Ministry of Labour, Culture and Social Welfare, Evaluation of ANC Vocational Training Centre, MH Manyanga, Director, National Vocational Training Directorate, Dar es Salaam.

150, 7 Int. Simon Mohale.

150, 10 Mayibuye/ANC/55/2, Department of Education (1989–1991), B Watson, M de Groot, M Cummins: Report of Education Task Force of NCCR: Investigation of Current Provision of Education and Educational Needs at Projects Established for Exiled South Africans in Mazimbu and Dakawa, 30 April to 2 May 1991.

150, 18 DAK/47/304, Miscellaneous Documents: Dakawa Garment Factory.

150, 20 DAK/43/290, Administration, Monthly Meetings: Zonal Annual Report, Development Centre Dakawa [1989].

150, 22 DAK/57/548, Reports: Report of the Situation at Dakawa ANC Leather Factory, Marja Huttunen, Instructor.

150, 31 DAK/10/52, Regional Reports: Sello Tau (Political Commissar) to Regional Commissar, Mazimbu, 19 May 1982.

150, 39 DAK/16/91, Seminars, 1982 and 1984: Second Seminar on Dakawa Development Centre, 17 to 19 Nov. 1984 [*recte* 1983].

151, 15 DAK/52/490, CDC: Own Evaluation: Henry Makgothi to Alfred Nzo, 3 May 1995.

151, 22 DAK/17/100, Monthly Reports, 1986–87: Commissar's Report, 30 Oct. 1986, Soks Sokupha.

151, 33 DAK/16/91, Report, Agricultural Development, 1987: Report: Situation in Dakawa, 18 Nov. 1986, Soks Sokupha, Zonal Commissar, Jackie Morake, Acting Co-ordinator.

151, 36 DAK/17/100, Monthly Reports, 1986–1987: The ANC Development Centre, Dakawa: Monthly Report to the Directorate (1 to 30 Nov. 1986), Jackie Morake (Administration Co-ordinator).

152, 6 DAK/58/552, Third Dakawa Seminar: Minutes: Dakawa Zonal Youth Section Report for the Third Dakawa Seminar.

152, 13 DAK/58/552, Third Dakawa Seminar: Minutes: Construction Report, Third Dakawa Seminar, 24 to 26 April 1989, O Dennis.

152, 18 DAK/58/552, Third Dakawa Seminar: Minutes: The Future of Dakawa, Reg September.

152, 22 DAK/58/552, Miscellaneous: Third Dakawa Seminar. Final Paper. Projects. Commission III. Commission on Administration Structures. April 1989.

152, 34 DAK/43/290, Administration, Monthly Meetings: Zonal Annual Report, Development Centre Dakawa [1989].

153, 18 DAK/18/110, General: Papers and Documents: The History, Social Problems and Future Prospects: African National Congress Dakawa Development Settlement, paper by MW Njobe to ANC in-house seminar, Lusaka, 27 to 30 July 1988.

153, 24 DAK/47/292: Health Team Report – Jan. 1990; DAK/34/252, Students from Abroad – Studies: The Report of the Commission of Enquiry on the Dakawa Health Service, Mazimbu, 5 July 1990.

153, 30 Mayibuye/ANC/55/2, Department of Education (1989–1991), B Watson, M de Groot, M Cummins: Report of Education Task Force of NCCR: Investigation of Current Provision of Education and Educational Needs at Projects Established for Exiled South Africans in Mazimbu and Dakawa, 30 April to 2 May 1991.

153, 39 DAK/39/280, Miscellaneous Correspondence, Minutes and Meetings: South African Extension Unit Monthly Report, 29 Nov. 1986; DAK/7/32, Reports, 1989: Monthly Report Adult Education, 28 Feb. 1989; DAK/47/292, Dakawa-Mazimbu Minutes: Adult Education Division, Monthly Report for April 1990, 8 May 1990; int. Elizabeth Ligate.

154, 3 DAK/23/158, Sipho Thabethe to Eddie Fundo, 10 April 1986, Dakawa.

154, 5 DAK/33/249, Library, files from early 1990s.

154, 15 DAK16/91, Seminars, Dakawa, 1982 and 1984: Second Seminar on Dakawa Development Centre, 17 to 19 Nov. 1984 [*recte* 1983]; DAK/29/225, ANC Development Education Sectors – Reports: Report of the ANC (SA) Development Centre Educational Sectors for the 3rd Education Council Meeting of ANC (SA) held 28 Aug. to 2 Sept. 1986.

154, 37 DAK/53/496, Miscellaneous Matters: Paper presented by Department of Arts and Culture to Third Dakawa Seminar, 24 to 26 April 1989; facsimile message Anne Giertz to Dakawa Art and Craft Community Centre, Marieborg, Sweden, 13 April 1998.

155, 10 DAK/28/216, Various Programmes and Projects Reports: Textile Printing Workshop Report, 21 Feb. 1988, [Jackson Dira].

Chapter 12. Funding SOMAFCO

157, 20 Int. Mohammed Tikly; SOM/1/1/ Neduc I, 3 Oct. 1978.

158, 17 Int. LP Kaihula; int. Brig. Hashim Mbita.

158, 27 Int. Leo Sonderquist.

158, 40 SOM/18/Supplies, Aug. 1981.

159, 1 Information on Scandinavian assistance drawn from Eriksen (ed), *Norway and National Liberation*; Sellström, *Sweden and National Liberation in Southern Africa,* Vol. 2; Soiri and Peltola, *Finland and National Liberation.*

160, 4 Int. Mohammed Tikly; SOM/54/215,5/SIDA-ANC Co-operation, 1982–1987.

160, 31 DAK/16/91, Second Seminar on Dakawa Development Centre, 17 to 19 Nov. 1984 [*recte* 1983]; DAK/12/56, 1984 Development Plan (Norplan), Vols. 1–3.

161, 12 Int. Leo Sonderquist; SOM/PMD/2/9, Mazimbu – Carpentry, Project Analysis on Vuyisile Mini Furniture Factory, Mazimbu, n.d.

162, 3 SOM/PMD/2/9, Mazimbu – Carpentry, Project Analysis on Vuyisile Mini Furniture Factory, Mazimbu, n.d.

162, 10 SOM/HD/7/25, Miscellaneous, 1 May 1984.

163, 16 SOM/Education Department, CIES-ANC Co-operation Framework, 1982–1992.

163, 30 SOM/Education Department/174/846, Sponsoring NGOs, n.d.

163, 39 SOM/SSD/Otto Benneke Stiftung, n.d.

164, 30 SOM/SSD/UNDP-Unesco, Reports, ad hoc Meeting re UNDP/Unesco projects, 2 March 1981; SOM/SSD/UNDP – Reports, Report of Joint Mid-Term Evaluation Mission (UNDP), 6 to 24 Sept. 1983.

165, 9 Int. Daniel Rafube and Gerald Dube.

166, 2 SOM/UNDP, Reports: Report of Joint Mid-term Evaluation Mission (UNDP), 6 to 24 Sept. 1983; SOM/SSD/UNDP – Mid Term Evaluation, 11 to 13 Sept. 1985, Report Summary; ANC/SOM/SSD/UNDP Evaluation Mission, 11 to 13 Sept. 1985, Self-Evaluation Report.

166, 13 Ints. Sindiso Mfenyana, Ntombi Carneson.

166, 22 SOM/UNDP/Unesco, Reports, n.d.
166, 36 SOM/78/344/ UNDP/Unesco, SOMAFCO Project.
167, 6 SOM/SSD/Neduc VII, Dec. 1988; Int. Raphael Mwinuka.
167, 21 SOM/1/9/Unesco-UNDP, Progress Report, Jan.–June 1989.
168, 3 SOM/Education Department/NGOs, ILO, June–Dec. 1983.
168, 9 SOM/SSD/Education Department/ILO – VTC (1983 & 1984); ANC/SOM/ Education Department, Assistance to ANC Development Centre, Dakawa, Tanzania, 1985.
168, 34 SOM/NSC (National Scholarships Committee)/1/1/ Reports, Proposal, 1979.
169, 2 SOM/NSC/5/3/Minutes, Composition, June 1980.
169, 10 SOM/CA/Neduc IV, Recommendations, 1983.
169, 19 Ints. Sindiso Mfenyana, Tladi Ditshego.
169, 38 SOM/NSC/9/1/Minutes, n.d.
170, 26 SOM/NSC/17/3/Reports, 1983–1984.
170, 35 SOM/Neduc VI, 1986.
171, 15 SOM/NSC/15/1/Reports, 1982–1983.
171, 32 SOM/NSC/19/3
171, 41 SOM/NSC/20/1/Report to Neduc, 1986.
172, 9 Int. Mohammed Tikly; SOM/NSC Report, Neduc VI, 1986.
172, 21 SOM/CA/Reports, Neduc VI, 1986; ints. Huddleston Pompi, Steven Nhlebeya.
172, 31 Ellis and Sechaba, *Comrades against Apartheid*, p.140.
172, 42 SOM/NSC/107/309, Recommendations.

Chapter 13. The end of SOMAFCO

174, 19 Int. Alpheus Mangezi.
175, 26 DAK/5/23, *Dakawa News and Views*, 23 Nov. and 7 Dec. 1990.
175, 36 Int. Alpheus Mangezi.
178, 6 Int. Alex Francis; *Daily News* report.
178, 10 Meeting with SOMAFCO Advisory Group, 26 April 2001.
178, 13 Commemorative Brochure, uncatalogued.

References and sources

Books, chapters and articles

Bernstein H (1994) *The Rift: The Exile Experience of South Africans*, London: Jonathan Cape.

Bhebe N & Ranger T (eds) (1995) *Society in Zimbabwe's Liberation War*, London: James Currey.

Brickhill J & Brooks A (1980) *Whirlwind Before the Storm: The Origins and Development of the Uprising in Soweto and the Rest of South Africa from June to December 1976*, London: International Defence and Aid Fund.

Brittain V & Minty AS (eds) (1988) *Children of Resistance: Statements from the Harare Conference on Children, Repression and the Law in Apartheid South Africa*, London: Kliptown Books.

Christie P (1991) *The Right to Learn: The Struggle for Education in South Africa*, Second edition, Braamfontein: Ravan Press.

Colligan P (1981) *Soweto Remembered: Conversations with Freedom Fighters*, Atlanta: World View.

Davis SM (1988) *Apartheid's Rebels: Inside South Africa's Hidden War*, Craighall: AD Donker.

Ellis S (1991) The ANC in Exile, *African Affairs*, 90: 439–447.

Ellis S (1994) Mbokodo: Security in ANC Camps, 1961–1990, *African Affairs*, 93: 279–298.

Ellis S & Sechaba T (1992) *Comrades Against Apartheid: The ANC and the South African Communist Party in Exile*, London: James Currey.

Eriksen TL (ed) (2000) *Norway and National Liberation in Southern Africa*, Uppsala: Nordiska Afrikainstitutet.

Frederikse J (1990) *The Unbreakable Thread: Non-Racialism in South Africa*, Johannesburg: Ravan Press.

Freire P (1972) *Pedagogy of the Oppressed*, Harmondsworth: Penguin.

Hartshorne K (1992) *Crisis and Challenge: Black Education 1910–1990*, Cape Town: Oxford University Press.

Hassim S (1991) Gender, Social Location and Feminist Politics in South Africa, *Transformation*, 15: 65–88.

Heldal IA (ed) (1996) *From Cape to Cape Against Apartheid: Norwegian Support for Democracy in South Africa*, Bellville: Mayibuye Books in association with Norsk Folkhjelp.

Hirson B (1979) *Year of Fire, Year of Ash. The Soweto Revolt: Roots of a Revolution?* London: Zed Press.

Hlatshwayo SA (2000) *Education and Independence: Education in South Africa, 1658–1988*, Westport, Conn.: Greenwood Press.

Holland H (1989) *The Struggle: A History of the African National Congress*, London: Grafton.

Horn P (1991): Post-Apartheid South Africa: What About Women's Emancipation? *Transformation*, 15: 25–39.

Horrell M (1968) *Bantu Education to 1968*, Johannesburg: SAIRR.

Hyden G (1980) *Beyond Ujamaa in Tanzania: Underdevelopment and an Uncaptured Peasantry*, London: Heinemann.

Hyslop J (1999) *The Classroom Struggle: Policy and Resistance in South Africa 1940–1990*, Pietermaritzburg: University of Natal Press.

Isaacman A & Isaacman B (1983) *Mozambique: from Colonialism to Revolution, 1900-1982*, Boulder, Colorado: Westview Press.

Jansen J (1991) *Knowledge and Power in South Africa: Critical Perspectives Across Disciplines*, Johannesburg: Skotaville.

Johns S & Davis R. Hunt (eds) (1991) *Mandela, Tambo and the African National Congress: the Struggle Against Apartheid, 1948–1990: a Documentary Survey*, Oxford: Oxford University Press.

Jürgens R (2000) *The Many Houses of Exile*, Weltevredenpark: Covos Day.

Kallaway P (ed) (1984) *Apartheid and Education: The Education of Black South Africans*, Johannesburg: Ravan Press.

Kallaway P (ed) (2002) *The History of Education Under Apartheid 1948–1994: The Doors of Learning and Culture Shall be Opened*, Cape Town: Pearson Education South Africa.

Kane-Berman J (1978) *Soweto: Black Revolt, White Reaction*, Johannesburg: Ravan Press.

Karis TG & Gerhart GM (eds) (1997) *From Protest to Challenge: A Documentary History of African Politics in South Africa, 1882–1990*, Vol. 5, *Nadir and Resurgence, 1964–1979*, Pretoria: UNISA Press.

Lodge T (1983) *Black Politics in South Africa Since 1945*, Harlow: Longman.

Lodge T & Nasson B (1991) *All, Here and Now! Black Politics in South Africa in the 1980s*, Cape Town: Ford Foundation and David Philip.

Maaba BB (2001) The Archives of the Pan Africanist Congress and the Black Consciousness-orientated Movements, *History in Africa*, 28: 417–438.

McFadden P (1990) Youth Transform Education: Observations at the Solomon Mahlangu Freedom College. In Nkomo (ed), *Pedagogy of Domination,* Trenton, New Jersey: Africa World Press.

McKinley D (1997) *The ANC and the Liberation Struggle: A Critical Political Biography,* London: Pluto Press.

Meintjes S (1996) The Women's Struggle for Equality During South Africa's Transition to Democracy, *Transformation,* 30: 47–63.

Meli F (1988) *A History of the ANC: South Africa Belongs to Us,* Harare: Zimbabwe Publishing House.

Morrow S (1998) Dakawa Development Centre: An African National Congress Settlement in Tanzania, 1982–1992, *African Affairs,* 97: 497–521.

Morrow S (1998) *The African National Congress Dakawa Development Centre in Tanzania, 1982–1992,* Grahamstown: Dakawa Art and Craft Community Centre.

Morrow S, Maaba B & Pulumani L (2002) Education in Exile: The African National Congress's Solomon Mahlangu Freedom College (SOMAFCO) and Dakawa Development Centre in Tanzania: 1978 to 1992. In Kallaway P (ed) *The History of Education Under Apartheid 1948–1994*: 155–173, Cape Town: Pearson Education South Africa

Morrow S, Maaba B & Pulumani L (2002) Revolutionary Schooling? The Solomon Mahlangu Freedom College, the African National Congress Liberation School in Tanzania, 1978 to 1992, *World Studies in Education,* 3: 23–37.

Mzamane MV (1996) *The Children of the Diaspora and Other Stories of Exile,* Johannesburg: Vivlia.

Nare PM (1995) Education and War. In Bhebe & Ranger (eds) *Society in Zimbabwe's Liberation War*: 130–138, London: James Currey.

Ndlovu S (1998) *The Soweto Uprisings: Counter-memories of June 1976,* Randburg: Ravan Press.

Nkomo M (ed) (1990) *Pedagogy of Domination: Toward a Democratic Education in South Africa,* Trenton, New Jersey: Africa World Press.

Nordkvelle Y (1995) Teachers, culture and politics: The struggle for a curriculum for the free Namibia. A case-study of the Namibia Secondary Technical School, *Journal of Education Policy,* 10: 361–371.

Nyerere J (1968) Education for Self Reliance. In Nyerere J, *Freedom and Socialism,* 267–290. Dar es Salaam: Oxford University Press.

Pampallis J (1991) *Foundations of the New South Africa,* London: Zed Books.

Schleicher H-G & Schleicher I (1998) *Special Flights: The GDR and Liberation Movements in Southern Africa,* Harare: SAPES Books.

Sellström T (1999) *Liberation in Southern Africa: Regional and Swedish Voices. Interviews from Angola, Mozambique, Namibia, South Africa, Zimbabwe, The Frontline and Sweden,* Uppsala: Nordiska Afrikainstitutet.

Sellström T (1999) *Sweden and National Liberation in Southern Africa. Vol. 1: Formation of a Popular Opinion (1950–1970),* Uppsala: Nordiska Afrikainstitutet, 1999.

Sellström T (2002) *Sweden and National Liberation in Southern Africa. Vol. 2: Solidarity and Assistance 1970–1994,* Uppsala: Nordiska Afrikainstitutet.

Shubin V (1999) *ANC: A View from Moscow,* Bellville, Mayibuye Books.

Soiri I & Peltola P (1999) *Finland and National Liberation in Southern Africa,* Uppsala: Nordiska Afrikainstitutet.

Soul YK, Morrow S, Forman S et al. (eds) (1999) *If You Want to Know Me – Voices from SOMAFCO: Student Works from the Solomon Mahlangu Freedom College, Mazimbu, Tanzania,* Alice: Lovedale press.

Stapleton T & Maamoe I (1998) An Overview of the African National Congress Archives at the University of Fort Hare, *History in Africa,* 25: 413–422.

Tambo A (ed) (1987) *Preparing for Power: Oliver Tambo Speaks,* London: Heinemann.

Thomas S (1996) *The Diplomacy of Liberation: The Foreign Relations of the African National Congress Since 1960,* New York: IB Tauris.

Unterhalter E & Wolpe H (eds) (1991) *Apartheid Education and Popular Struggles,* Johannesburg: Ravan Press.

Unterhalter E, Wolpe H & Botha T (eds) (1992) *Education in a Future South Africa: Policy Issues for Transformation,* Johannesburg: Ravan Press.

Van Rensburg P (1974) *Report from Swaneng Hill: Education and Employment in an African Country,* Stockholm: Dag Hammerskjold Foundation.

Theses and unpublished papers

Govender R (1997) *The Rhetoric and Reality of Curriculum Development at the Solomon Mahlangu Freedom College, 1978–1984,* University of the Western Cape, M.Phil.

Maaba LB (1999) *The Students of Solomon Mahlangu Freedom College: 1978–1992,* University of Fort Hare, M.A.

Massey D (2001) *"Who would not have been aware?": The History of Fort Hare and its Student Activists, 1933–1973,* University of Fort Hare, M.A.

Pulumani L (2001) *African National Congress Education in Exile in Tanzania, 1978–1992: Dilemmas and Ambiguities,* University of Fort Hare, M.A.

Serote P (1992) 'Solomon Mahlangu Freedom College: A Unique South African Experience in Tanzania' Paper delivered at the conference of the Southern African Comparative and History of Education Society, Broederstroom, 29 October.

Some websites

http://www.ufh.ac.za/collections/an
This site, still being built, gives details of the SOMAFCO and other ANC papers at the University of Fort Hare. Accessed 13 February 2004.

http://www.anc.org.za/ancdocs/history/people/mahlangu_s.html
Material on Solomon Mahlangu, executed 1979. Accessed 13 February 2004.

http://www.mayibuye.org
Robben Island/Mayibuye site. Archives contain various SOMAFCO-related material. Accessed 13 February 2004.

http://www.revolutionary-history.co.uk/supplem/Hirson/Quadro.html
Article 'Inside Quadro' by Paul Trewhela that alleges various abuses at ANC bases, including Mazimbu and Dakawa. Accessed 13 February 2004.

http://www.doj.gov.za/trc/trccom.htm
ANC submission to the Truth and Reconciliation Commission on the question of alleged atrocities at ANC bases, including Dakawa and Mazimbu. Accessed 13 February 2004.

http://www.oneworld.org/ips2/feb98/tanzania_children.html
An example of media attention to the question of children left in Tanzania after the return of their ANC fathers to South Africa. Article by Kenyan journalist Paul Chintowa. Accessed 13 February 2004.

Archival sources

ANC archives, library, University of Fort Hare

These archives form the main documentary source of this study. Material has been sorted into boxes and files, and handwritten finding aids are available in the Fort Hare Library. These await typing: when this task is completed, they will be placed on the Fort Hare Library website (see above). Much material has been rearranged since the research on which this book is based was completed. For example, the printed catalogue to the secondary school papers is no longer an accurate guide to these papers; researchers should for the moment consult the handwritten guide that replaces it. Figures below indicate numbers of boxes.

Departments

Arts and Culture	4
Boarding	4
Catering	2
Computers	2
Department of Information and Publicity	2
Department of Manpower Development	17

Director	93
Farm	1
Health	11
Housing	16
Library	14
National Scholarships Committee	110
Project Management	27
Resources Department	7
Transport	2
Works Committee	5
Education divisions	
Adult education	20
Daycare centre	2
Nursery school	2
Primary school	9
Secondary school	177
Political organisations	
Department of Political Education	6
Regional Political Committee	8
Regional Youth Committee	2
Women's Section	5
Youth Section	2
Zonal Political Committee	6
Zonal Youth Committee	1
Dakawa	
Dakawa Development Centre	52

Robben Island/Mayibuye Centre Archives, Cape Town

ANC papers Boxes 2, 10, 45, 50, 54, 57, 60

Hilda Bernstein Oral Interviews Collection (transcriptions)

Wolfie Kodesh Oral Interviews Collection (some transcribed)

Terry and Barbara Bell Papers, privately held, Cape Town

Letter Terry Bell/SOMAFCO administration, 23 March 1982

Letter Terry Bell/Oliver Tambo, 1 May 1982

Letter Karen/Terry Bell, 24 March 1983

'Methodology in the Primary School', December 1981

'SOMAFCO Primary Division: End of Year Report', Terry and Barbara Bell, August 1981

'Report of the Primary School', December 1981

Daily News *archives, Dar es Salaam, Tanzania*

Files of press cuttings from the *Daily News.*

Oral sources

Interviews were carried out by Seán Morrow, Brown Maaba and Loyiso Pulumani, individually and in various combinations. Most were in English, though some were partly in other South African languages. Some interviews with people around Mazimbu were carried out in Swahili with the assistance of an interpreter.

Abdallah, Anna, Dar es Salaam, Tanzania, 10 May 1997.

Abrahams, Bea, Cape Town, 13 March 1998.

Bell, Terry and Barbara, Cape Town, 10 March 1997.

Carneson, John, Nelspruit, 2 September 1997.

Carneson, Ntombi, Nelspruit, 2 September 1997.

Coedoe, Palmiro, Peninsula Technikon, Cape Town, 10 June 1997.

Cumberledge, Diana, Johannesburg, 30 August 1997.

Dennis, Emily, ANC Headquarters, Johannesburg, 23 June 1997.

Ditshego, Tladi, Auckland Park, Johannesburg, 29 August 1997.

Dumasi, Jane, ANC Headquarters, Johannesburg, 19 June 1997.

Francis, Alex, Dar es Salaam, Tanzania, 6 May 1997.

Fritz, Portia, East London, 7 June 1997.

Fungo, FA (Dr), Mazimbu, Tanzania, 15 May 1997.

Hodgson, Rica, Berea, Johannesburg, 29 November 1997.

Hodgson, Spenser and Claudia, Pretoria, 31 August 1997.

Jambwali, Mohamed, Mazimbu, Tanzania, 13 May 1997.

Joseph, Margaret, Mazimbu, Tanzania, 13 May 1997.

Jürgens, Richard, Johannesburg, 1 September 1997.

Kabetso, Joe, Alexandra, Johannesburg, 8 February 1997.

Kaihula, LP, Dar es Salaam, Tanzania, 9 May 1997.

Khasimbazi, Lajavu Shabani, Dark City, Mazimbu, Tanzania, 13 May 1997.

Khumalo, Vusi, Grahamstown, 30 March 1998.

Kibi, Mzwandile, Department of Education, Pretoria, 6 April 1998.

Legobya, Nozipho, Yeoville, Johannesburg, 23 June 1997.

Ligate, Elizabeth, Dar es Salaam, Tanzania, 7 May 1997.

Lujabe-Rankoe, Thandi, Dar es Salaam, Tanzania, 16 May 1997.

Maamoe, Mosoabuli, University of Fort Hare, Alice, 11 October 1996.

Maclean, Sherry, Yeoville, Johannesburg, 2 September 1997.

Madenge, Edith, Dar es Salaam, Tanzania, 6 May 1997.

Mahlangu, Jabu, Arcadia, Pretoria, 7 April 1998.

Makhoba, D, ANC Headquarters, Johannesburg, 20 June 1997.

Majola, Oscar, Peninsula Technikon, Cape Town, 6 June 1997.

Makgopa, Mida, Yeoville, Johannesburg, 23 June 1997.

Makgoti, Henry, Parliament, Cape Town, 6 June 1997.

Makhoba, Dudu, ANC Headquarters, Johannesburg, 20 June 1997.

Mali, Thami, Selby, Johannesburg, 4 February 1998.

Mangezi, Alpheus, Midrand, 3 September 1997 and Randburg, 29 November 1997.

Mankazana, Lungi, University of Fort Hare, Alice, 13 October 1996.

Manzini, Manala, Kempton Park, Johannesburg, 31 May 1997.

Maphisa, Jabulile, Johannesburg, 22 December 1997.

Mashego, Maureen, Yeoville, Johannesburg, 17 April 1998.

Masipa, Kilian, Pretoria, 7 April 1998.

Masondo, Andrew (General), Pretoria, 28 September 2001.

Masusu, Nana, Dar es Salaam, Tanzania, 9 May 1997. Also telephone conversation, 16 June 1998.

Mathe, Monica, Mazimbu, Tanzania, 13 May 1997.

Mbigwa, Grace, Mazimbu, Tanzania, 12 May 1997.

Mbita, Hashim (Brigadier), Dar es Salaam, Tanzania, 6 June 1997.

Mfenyana, Sindiso, Parliament, Cape Town, 10 June 1997.

Mgina, Wilfred, Mazimbu, Tanzania, 13 May 1997.

Mgotshana, Enoch and Anne, and Maureen Morodi, Johannesburg, 30 November 1997.

Mkya, Marco (Dr), Mazimbu, Tanzania, 12 May 1997.

Mlati, Vuyani, University of Fort Hare, Alice, 12 October 1996.

Mogane, Barney, Braamfontein, Johannesburg, 17 April 1998.

Mohale, Simon, Soweto, Johannesburg, 2 September 1997.

Mohammed, Andrew, Johannesburg, 1 December 1997.

Motsabe, Pule, Cape Town, 7 June 1997.

Mtshaulana, Patrick, Johannesburg, 9 April 1998.

Mukwalo, Joe, Johannesburg, 30 November 1997.

Mussagy, Farida, ANC Headquarters, Johannesburg, 27 June 1997.

Mwali, George, Soweto, Johannesburg, 18 June 1997.

Mwinuka, Raphael J, Dar es Salaam, Tanzania, 10 May 1997.

Naidoo, Shanti, ANC Headquarters, Johannesburg, 1 September 1997.

Nassoro, Saidi, Mazimbu, Tanzania, 13 May 1997.

Netsianda, Bessie, Johannesburg, 24 June 1997.

Ngakane, Don, Johannesburg, 22 December 1997.

Ngxala, Phumeza, Yeoville, Johannesburg, 8 February 1998.

Nhlebeya, Steven, Peninsula Technikon, Cape Town, 7 June 1997.

Njobe, Makho, Parliament, Cape Town, 10 June 1997.

Njobe, Wintshi (Dr), Bisho, 29 August 1996.

Otto, Isdory, Mazimbu, Tanzania, 13 May 1997.

Pampallis, John, Emmarentia, Johannesburg, 29 August 1997.

Pampallis, Karin, Emmarentia, Johannesburg, 29 August 1997.

Pompi, Huddleston, Peninsula Technikon, Cape Town, 6 June 1997.

Proctor, André, Cape Town, 9 June 1997.

Radebe, Helen, ANC Headquarters, Johannesburg, 19 June 1997.

Rafube, Daniel, and Gerald Dube, Peninsula Technikon, Cape Town, 11 June 1997.

Sadiki, Othur, Mazimbu, Tanzania, 13 May 1997.

Schavemaker, Wilma, ANC Headquarters, Johannesburg, 25 June 1997.

Schoon, Marius, Yeoville, Johannesburg, 30 November 1997.

Seete, Mercedes, ANC Headquarters, Johannesburg, 25 June 1997.

Serote, Phetu, Athlone, Cape Town, 11 March 1998.

Seseseko, Boyoyo 'Boss', Auckland Park, Johannesburg, 24 April 1998.

Sithole, Nkosana, Mazimbu, Tanzania, 13 May 1997.

Sithole, Shadrack, and Allan Mun'gong'o, Mazimbu, Tanzania, 13 May 1997.

Siyo, EM, Soweto, Johannesburg, 27 June 1997.

Smith, Bentry, Fish Hoek, Cape Town, 10 June 1997.

Sokupha, Nomagqabi, Cape Town, 10 June 1997.

Sokupha, Siphokazi (Dr), East London, 2 June 1997.

Sonderquist, Leo, Mazimbu, Tanzania, 12 July 1997.

Teme, Mothers, Johannesburg, 20 June 1997.

Thunga, TR, Mazimbu, Tanzania, 12 May 1997.

Thuse, Mary, ANC Headquarters, Johannesburg, 20 June 1997.

Thwala, George, Pretoria, 3 February 1998.

Tikly, Mohammed, Pretoria, 31 August 1997.

Tweedie, Dominic, Braamfontein, Johannesburg, 29 August 1997.

Xaba, Siphiwe, Dar es Salaam, Tanzania, 6 May 1997.

Zikalala, Sasa, Soweto, 17 May 1997.

Zikalala, Snuki, SABC, Johannesburg, 14 October 1996.

Index

Page references in italics indicate figures and photographs